Accolades for Charles Harrington Elster's
There's a Word for It

"Elster aims to entertain, and he succeeds. He also excites curiosity about the language."

—Diane White, *Boston Globe*

"If you've ever had a yen to out-Buckley William F. Buckley Jr., here's a brilliant chance to do so . . . Page after page, Elster amuses, entertains. . . . And when it's all read and done, the reader will have gained a few lessons on life by observing the asides and comments that accompany the generally boisterous text."

—Mae Woods Bell, *Rocky Mountain Telegraph*

"If the words in *Reader's Digest*'s 'It Pays to Enrich Your Word Power' aren't providing the challenge that your vocabulary-hungry mind needs, try *There a Word for It* . . . Elster has collected . . . worthy words about all kinds of people and topics."

—Judyth Rigler, *San Antonio Express-News*

"This book will be in demand by all word mavens and language lovers. . . . Elster plumbs the oceanic depths of the English language. . . . His collector's collection of obscure and wonderfully exact words concentrates in turn on extraordinary words relating to health and medicine, love and sex, people, religion, politics, academia, and uncommon words for everyday things. . . . The style of the essays is conversational, though it resembles a fevered all-night conversation with an amazingly learned and wildly obsessed friend."

—*Library Journal*

THERE'S A WORD FOR IT

Revised & Updated

A Grandiloquent Guide to Life

❖

CHARLES HARRINGTON ELSTER

POCKET BOOKS

New York   London   Toronto   Sydney

POCKET BOOKS, a division of Simon & Schuster, Inc.
1230 Avenue of the Americas, New York, NY 10020

ISBN-13: 978-1-4165-1086-4
ISBN-10:   1-4165-1086-9

First Pocket Books trade paperback printing of this revised edition July 2005

10 9 8 7 6 5 4 3 2 1

POCKET and colophon are registered trademarks of
Simon & Schuster, Inc.

Manufactured in the United States of America

For information regarding special discounts for bulk purchases,
please contact Simon & Schuster Special Sales at 1-800-456-6798 or
business@simonandschuster.com

For Carmen Veronica,
with storge

CONTENTS

7

ACKNOWLEDGMENTS

My deepest thanks go to Doggerelope, the muse of loquacity and light verse, without whom this book would not be implausible. Thanks also to Dr. Wallace Johnson, for actually buying a copy of my last book and showing sincere interest in this one; Norman W. Storer, for permission to use two of his delightful limericks; Ralph Emerson and Michael Bay, for helpful suggestions; Patricia Karnes and June Cooper of the San Diego Public Library, for their indulgence; Jeff McQuain, for a providential recommendation; my eximious agent, Deborah Schneider; my editor, Jane Rosenman, for her patience, enthusiasm, and remarkable level of tolerance for explateration; my wife, Myrna Zambrano, for keeping the faith; and my parents, Nancy and Reinhardt Elster, for creating a dwaling logomaniac.

Pronunciation Key

Vowel Sounds

A, a—*flat, back, pass, exact*
AH, ah—*spa, father, odd, not*
AHR, ahr—*car, jar, alarm*
AIR, air—*hair, stare, bear*
AY, ay—*hay, wait, came, state*
AW, aw—*raw, all, walk*
E, e—*yes, let, step*
EE, ee—*see, beat, key*
EER, eer—*pier, beer, fear*
I, i—*in, hit, sip*
Y, y and EYE, eye—*by, nice, pie, right, aisle*
    Note: Y is used in combination with other letters to form
    a syllable: SLYT-lee (*slightly*). EYE is used when this
    sound by itself forms a syllable: EYE-land (*island*).
OH, oh—*go, sew, coat*
OO, oo—*do, ooze, rule*
OR, or—*for, door, born, war*
OOR, oor—*poor, tour, lure*
OW, ow—*cow, out, tower, doubt*
OY, oy—*oil, loin, boy, ahoy*
UH, uh—*up, dull, some, color;* also *ago, allow*
UR, ur—*turn, stir, were, learn*
UU, uu—*pull, full, good, took, would*

Obscure, Unstressed, Lightened, or Variable Vowel Sounds

a̲—*ago, final, woman, librarian*
e̲—*item, taken, shipment, difference*
i̲—*edible, policy, charity, nation*
o̲—*connect, polite, gallop, carrot*
u̲—*focus, circus, lettuce, raucous*

Consonant Sounds

B, b—*boy, cab, bubble*
CH, ch—*chip, catcher, peach*
D, d—*dog, add, sudden*
F, f—*fat, effort, staff*
G, g—*get, bigger, bogus, tag*
H, h—*hit, hope, behind*
HW, hw—*wheat, whale, whet, awhile*
J, j—*jug, juice, tragic, age*
K, k—*king, cup, take, actor, pack*
L, l—*leg, also, bell*
'l—*ladle, cattle, turtle, apple*
M, m̐—*my, humble, emblem*
'm—*spasm, prism, chasm, sarcasm*
N, n—*no, knee, end, winner*
'n—*hidden, cotton, open, satin, reason*
NG, ng—*sing, anger, tank*
P, p—*pen, pepper, pop*
R, r—*red, arrive, car*
S, s—*sit, ask, pass*
SH, sh—*she, rush, nation, conscious*
T, t—*top, bitter, list*
TH, th—*thin, thirst, nothing, bath*
T̲H̲, t̲h̲—*there, this, brother, bathe*
V, v—*very, even, live*
W, w—*will, wait, power*

Y, y—*yes, you, layer*

(Y), (y)—indicates that some speakers employ the Y sound of *you* and others do not: N(Y)OO, *new;* D(Y)OO-tee, *duty;* uh-ST(Y)OOT, *astute.*

Z, z—*zoo, daze, please*

ZH, zh—*vision, measure, azure,* or French *je*

FOREIGN SOUNDS

KH, kh—German *ach,* Scottish *loch,* Hebrew *l'chaim:* a guttural sound, like that of clearing the throat.

(N), (n)—French *vin, bon, blanc, garçon:* a nasalized sound— the N is stopped in the nose.

STRESS/ACCENT

- Syllables are separated by a hyphen [-].
- Syllables printed in CAPITAL letters are stressed.
- Syllables printed in small (lowercase) letters are not stressed.
- Words of one syllable are printed in CAPITALS.
- Words of more than two syllables that have primary and secondary stress are transcribed in the following manner: The syllable with secondary stress is printed in CAPITALS, and the syllable with primary stress is printed in **BOLDFACED CAPITALS:** ED-i-fi-**KAY**-shin (*edification*).

INTRODUCTION

If you're looking for a sane, sedate, even-tempered treatise on improving your command of the English language, I advise you to look elsewhere immediately, for what you're about to read (if you dare) is a work of the utmost intellectual incontinence written by a man who is plumb crazy, stark raving mad, and out of his grandiloquent gourd about words.

In a word, I am a **logomaniac** (LAHG-uh-**MAY**-nee-ak), a person obsessed with words (from the Greek *logos*, word, and *mania*).

Bring up the subject of language and I'll talk your ear off. Hand me a dictionary and I'm lost in its pages for a week. Ask me to find an obscure word and I won't sleep until I track it down. If there were a twelve-step program for wordaholics, you'd never catch me at a meeting sipping coffee and swapping gloomy stories about **lethologica** (LEE-thuh-**LAHJ**-i-kuh), the inability to recall the precise word for something, or **loganamnosis** (LAHG-an-um-**NOH**-sis), an obsession with trying to recall a forgotten word. I am an unrepentant, irremediable word nerd and proud of it, for language is the most pleasant obsession I know.

Chances are *There's a Word for It* piqued your interest because you're a bit of a nut about words too, perhaps even a closet **verbivore,** a person who devours words. If so, then I guarantee you will relish feasting on the many rare and succulent morsels dished up here. On the other hand, you don't have to be a major league lexical loon like me to enjoy and profit from this book.

Your mission, should you choose to accept it, is not impossible. Simply click your ruby reading slippers three times, whisper "Where there's a will, there's a word," and take off with me into the wild blue verbal yonder for an out-of-this-world tour of the twilight zone of language, where seldom is heard a discouraging word, and the skies are not cloudy with mixed mass-cultural metaphors.

As your grandiloquent guide on this excursion into the linguistic stratosphere, my docent duties are twofold: first, to feed you a steady diet of unusual and unusually useful words, ones that may be esoteric but that bear directly on your life; and second, to amuse, entertain, and occasionally exasperate you with jokes, puns, pop quizzes, anecdotes, artful digressions, egregious alliteration, spurious quotations, and a dazzling display of hilarious light verse.

If you prefer to ingest your word lore unsalted and fat free, the menu here will probably elevate your blood pressure and clog your brain; however, if you like your words served up with a wily wink, a toothsome smile, and a savory splash of panache, then I think you'll find this concoction quite palatable.

In writing this grandiloquent book I have plumbed the unparalleled vastness of the ocean of English and lived to tell the tale. As a result, I can assure you that there are some astonishing lexical creatures lurking in those depths. For example, did you know that there's a word to express each of the following definitions?

1. the state of having sore or bleary eyes
2. the groove in the middle of your upper lip
3. the metal sheath on the end of an umbrella
4. the act of puttering around aimlessly
5. sex without passion or desire
6. lovemaking in a parked car
7. food that you spit out, such as seeds and pits
8. the fear of undressing in front of someone
9. the wild look that accompanies delirium
10. someone in love with his or her own opinions

If you have latent logomaniacal tendencies, you may know one or two of the words associated with those definitions. But if you were completely dumbstruck by that list, don't worry.

Those ten wonderful words, along with hundreds of other exceptional specimens, await you in the pages of this book.

(*Warning:* If you're feeling woozy because you *have* to know *every one* of those ten words *right now* or you may collapse, just take a deep breath, check the answers I've provided at the end of this introduction, and come back when you're feeling better.)

Many of the words in this book may seem unreal, if not downright bizarre. I've selected them, however, not because they are strange but because what they denote has a strange way of crawling out of the woodwork and into our everyday lives, often leaving us at a loss for words. Allow me to string together (in the present tense, for the heck of it) a few examples from personal experience to illustrate the point.

At a meeting of the San Diego Public Library's Board of Library Commissioners (I'm a member of the board), the city librarian woefully discourses on the stressed-out state of his overworked, underpaid staff. One employee, he laments, got to the point where she was pulling out tufts of her hair and making her scalp bleed. Never one to pass up an opportunity for **lexiphanicism** (LEKS-i-FAN-i-siz'm, showing off with words), I shamelessly interject that the word for that hair-tearing compulsion is **trichotillomania** (TRIK-oh-TIL-uh-MAY-nee-uh). It's one of numerous mental and physical disorders you'll find diagnosed in chapter 1, "Dr. Elster's Verbal Health Center."

Later, in the supermarket checkout line, I notice that *Reader's Digest* has an article on coping with a relationship in which one partner wants to have sex more often than the other. Aha! I think, cackling logomaniacally. How many of the *Digest*'s readers know that the word for that sexually unequal state is **imparlibidinous** (im-PAHR-li-BID-i-nus)? I doubt you'll come across that one in the *Digest*'s word-power quizzes, but you'll find it right here in chapter 3, "Erotographomania," along with scores of other unabashed locutions about love and sex.

At home, I turn on the TV and watch one of those primetime newsmagazines. They're doing a story on people with phobias. One poor fellow confesses his paralyzing fear of riding on subways. Aha again! cries the verbivoracious beast in my brain. Does the man, or even his therapist, know that the name for that dreadful condition is **bathysiderodromophobia** (BATH-ee-SID-ur-oh-DROH-muh-FOH-bee-uh)? You'll come face to face with that redoubtable term in chapter 6, "Frightful Words," which features what I believe is the largest collection of phobias ever assembled in print.

When that fearsome segment is over, I turn off the TV and pick up *"F" Is for Fugitive* by mystery novelist Sue Grafton, seeking some relief from all these unbearably precise, polysyllabic words. But sure enough, on page 47 Grafton's protagonist, Kinsey Millhone, wonders if there's a word for it: "I had a friend who ate pencil shavings. There's a name for that now, for kids who eat inorganic oddities like gravel and clay. In my day, it just seemed like a fun thing to do and no one ever gave it a passing thought as far as I knew."

Had Kinsey not abandoned the chase so quickly (the scene takes place in a library, for Pete's sake!), or had her creator had the passing thought of giving me a call, Kinsey and her many fans could have experienced the thrill of disinterring the words **geophagy** (jee-AHF-uh-jee), the act of eating dirt, clay, or other earthy substances, and **pica** (PY-kuh), a craving for unnatural or indigestible food such as chalk, ashes, coal, paint chips, or pencil shavings. You'll be nibbling on those and other exquisitely edible terms in chapter 2, "Food for Thought."

The question remains: Why write a book about words that hardly anyone uses or understands? No matter what I say, certain callous critics will conclude that I did it because I am an insufferable pedant who wants you to cultivate your powers of obfuscation and assert a pseudointellectual superiority over your peers. My answer to that charge: I may be insufferable, but I am not contemptible. My sole and sincere desire, gentle reader, is to broaden your lexical horizons and give you an inimpeachable excuse to join me in going completely gaga over words.

Most of us—especially those **criticasters** (third-rate, mean-spirited, contemptible critics)—slog ineloquently through the morass of life, padding the drab discourse of our days with **circumlocutions** (roundabout modes of expression) and **battology** (tiresome repetition and idle talk). Every so often we stumble upon something for which we're sure there must be a word but we don't know what it is. At such times our dime-a-dozen word store is useless. We need the extraordinary term that expresses the seemingly inexpressible, but we just can't come up with it.

There's a Word for It is a remedy for that tongue-tied state. It will help you plug gaping holes in your vocabulary and apply vibrant color to the blank spots in your picture of the world. If you've ever been tantalized by a desire to know whether there is in fact a word for it (whatever your peculiar, pesky "it" may be), I am sure you will find satisfaction in these pages. Along the way I suspect you will also discover many elusive words that have been slithering around on the tip of your tongue. (Time to spit those critters out, don't you think?)

In short, I wrote this book to help you attain some measure of verbal mastery over the multifarious phenomena of experience. That mastery, and the mental acuity that accompanies it, is what I mean to imply in my subtitle, *A Grandiloquent Guide to Life.*

Although dictionaries often list *pompous* and *bombastic* as synonyms of *grandiloquent,* no such pejorative sense is intended here. Throughout this book, I have used *grandiloquent* and *grandiloquence* to suggest diction (a choice of words) that is both eloquent and precise, elevated in tone but rigorously exact in sense. As the ancient Greek philosopher Lexiphagoras of Aphasia opined in this aphoristic verse,

> Of language it may be averred
> That precision is always preferred.
> Thus to blur is to err,
> And from that we infer
> It's absurd not to use the right word.

In compiling this eclectic collection I tried to eschew words for which there exists a simple, more familiar synonym.

Why say "She's a *zetetic* journalist" when you mean "She's an investigative reporter"? Is anything gained by using *discalced* for *barefoot*, *algid* for *cold*, *habile* for *able*, or *mephitic* for *smelly?* Nifty words, but their utility is limited. Again, my aim is edification and entertainment, not pretentious obfuscation.

Except for a handful of my own neologisms, which are duly noted, I guarantee that every last oddball word you will find in these pages is real and documented in at least one dictionary or reference book. (I just can't remember which one at the moment.)

Some of my word stock is obsolete, of course, but who cares? Just because a word is no longer used doesn't mean it's no longer useful. As Ambrose Bierce remarks in his *Devil's Dictionary*, *obsolete* means "no longer used by the timid." According to Bierce (and I wholeheartedly agree with him), "If it is a good word and has no exact modern equivalent equally good, it is good enough for the good writer."

Chief among the sources I relied on in writing this book are the ten-volume *Century Dictionary* (1914); the second edition of the venerable *Oxford English Dictionary* (1991); *Webster's New International Dictionary*, second edition (1934), possibly the finest word hoard ever assembled in one volume; the *Random House Dictionary of the English Language*, second edition, unabridged (1987); and the *American Heritage Dictionary of the English Language*, third edition (1992). (Throughout the book I often refer to the first four of these tomes as the *Century*, the *OED*, *Webster 2*, and *Random House II*.) If you still have an itch to expand your grandiloquent vocabulary when you've finished this escapade in exalted expression, I urge you to consult the selected bibliography, where you will find other invaluable references on unusual English words.

As the subtitle suggests, I've designed this book as a series of lighthearted lessons on life—and specifically on how to live "the grandiloquent life." My leisurely lexical tour takes you through the physical, mental, spiritual, material, and immaterial realms of language, covering most of the major human affairs and preoccupations. It's a flexible, loosely structured format, suitable for perusal, browsing, or reference. So delve in wherever you please to learn and enjoy.

There's a Word for It is an open-hearted invitation to become a moonstruck wayfarer in the **multivious** world of words. (*Multivious*, pronounced muhl-TIV-ee-us, means having many paths or roads.) Imbibe its contents as an antidote for **omnistrain**, the stress of trying to cope with everything at once (otherwise known as everyday life). Swallow some of its words daily as an Rx for **nullibiety** (NUHL-i-BY-i-tee), the state of being nowhere.

When all is read and done, I think you'll conclude that what you've ingested is **proficuous** (proh-FIK-yoo-us), advantageous, profitable, and useful—rather than **frustraneous** (fruh-STRAY-nee-us), vain, unprofitable, and useless. I also hope you will have found much to make you **checkle** (laugh heartily).

1. *lippitude* (chapter 1)
2. *philtrum* (chapter 1)
3. *ferrule* (chapter 11)
4. *horbgorbling* (chapter 10)
5. *acokoinonia* (chapter 3)
6. *amomaxia* (chapter 3)
7. *chankings* (chapter 2)
8. *dishabillophobia* (chapter 6)
9. *periblepsis* (chapter 1)
10. *philodox* (chapter 5)

CHAPTER ONE

❖

DR. ELSTER'S
VERBAL HEALTH CENTER

THE GRANDILOQUENT GUARANTEE

Welcome to Dr. Elster's Verbal Health Center, where we always pick your brains before poking, piercing, and probing your body. At the Verbal Health Center, we guarantee we'll thoroughly test your **longanimity.** And if we can't cure your **nullibiety,** or if you experience **mentimutation,** we'll be happy to refund your **dysphoria,** no questions asked.

Longanimity (LAWNG-guh-**NIM**-i̱-tee) is the ability to suffer patiently (or, from our clinical perspective, the ability of a patient to suffer). It is endurance in the face of hardship, tolerance of mental or physical pain. As you learned in the introduction, *nullibiety* (NUHL-i̱-**BY**-i̱-tee)—also called *nullibicity* (NUHL-i̱-**BIS**-i̱-tee)—is the state of being nowhere. *Mentimutation* (MEN-ti-myoo-**TAY**-shi̱n) is a change of mind or the act of changing one's mind. And *dysphoria* (dis-**FOR**-ee-uh), the opposite of *euphoria,* means an unwell feeling, a generally unwholesome state.

Thus, in plain, ungrandiloquent English, we assure you that after trying your patience and testing your ability to suffer, if we can't determine where you are (or "where your head is at") and you decide you're not happy with our verbal therapy, then you're free to schlep yourself and your malaise somewhere else.

One further proviso: If you're the kind of person who wonders whether there's a word that means "a ticklish sensation in the ears caused by grotesque hairs sprouting from the aural cavity," then you've come to the wrong clinic. (Go to a real doctor, quick!) However, if you've always experienced a peculiar, uncomfortable sensation when handling peaches, cotton, silk, or anything else with a fuzzy surface, then Dr. Elster's Verbal Health Center can help you, because you have **haptodysphoria** (HAP-toh-dis-**FOR**-ee-uh).

See, don't you feel better already knowing the word for that weird feeling? I promise that if you stick around for the full treatment, I'll give you a glorious injection of grandiloquent **omniana** (AHM-nee-**AY**-nuh, bits and pieces of information about almost everything), which will either make you **abderian** (ab-DEER-ee-in, given to incessant or idiotic laughter) or knock you **agroof,** flat on your face.

So, dear reader, if you are willing to be patient, I am more than willing to play doctor. Just let me gather my ancient verbalistic remedies and dig my **caduceus** (kuh-D(Y)OO-see-us) out of my desk, and we'll begin the examination.

Ah, but wait a minute. I bet you're wondering, "What's a *caduceus?*" That's a good question, and one you might want to pose to any doctor who seems a bit too eager to play cut-and-stitch with your vitals or pump you full of drugs with bizarre names like *warfarin* (an anticoagulant used in rat poison) or *paradichlorobenzene* (an ingredient in mothballs also used as an agricultural insecticide).

The *caduceus* is "that snakie wand," as the poet Edmund Spenser put it, that serves as the insignia of the U.S. Army Medical Corps. Surely you've seen it: the rod or staff entwined by two snakes, with a pair of spread wings at the top. (Technically, the symbol of the medical profession and emblem of the American Medical Association is the staff of the Greek god of medicine, Asclepius, or Aesculapius in Latin; it has only one snake and no wings. But since the sixteenth century, says the third edition of *The Columbia Encyclopedia,* the caduceus "has largely replaced the one-snake symbol of Asclepius as a symbol of medicine.")

In classical mythology, the caduceus was the wand borne by Hermes, or Mercury, the messenger of the gods—whose familiar winged shoes, by the way, are called **talaria** (tuh-LAIR-ee-uh). According to the *Century Dictionary*, "the rod represents power; the serpents represent wisdom; and the two wings, diligence and activity."

With all the power, wisdom, diligence, and activity that this good grandiloquent doctor can muster, I shall now prescribe a few efficacious words for your verbal health, first for the state of your mind and then for the condition of your body.

THE PSYCHOLOGICAL EVALUATION

How have you been feeling lately? Is your life in good shape, or are things all **aflunters,** in a state of disorder? Is your head screwed on tight, or have you been sort of **nebulochaotic** (NEB-yuh-loh-kay-**AHT**-ik), hazy and confused? Perhaps a thorough sweeping of the attic is in order.

What's your mood? Happy? Sad? Maybe a little of both? The old word **merry-go-sorry** means feeling a mixture of joy and sorrow, and the new word **joviomelancholy** (JOH-vee-oh-**MEL**-un-kahl-ee, my coinage) means wearing a jovial face to mask the gloom within.

If it's not your heart but your mind that's at war, pulled in opposite directions or vacillating between extremes, then you are **diophysitic** (DY-oh-fi-ZIT-ik), possessed of two distinct, conflicting natures, like Dr. Jekyll and Mr. Hyde.

Speaking of natures, how would you characterize yours? Inner-directed? Outer-directed? Perhaps outer space–directed? *Egocentric* is the familiar word for the inner-directed, self-absorbed person whose center of reference is himself. Nothing new there, I admit. But do you know the opposite word, the one that describes someone who is wholly focused on others and whose life revolves around them? That person is **alterocentric** (AL-tuh-roh-**SEN**-trik). Though most of us possess some mixture of the egocentric and alterocentric, a few folks have more quixotic natures that transcend these pedestrian, sublunary orientations and embrace the extraterrestrial. Such people, often called "space cadets" by the ungrandiloquent, are better fixed in the verbal cosmos by the word **selenocentric** (suh-LEE-nuh-SEN-trik), revolving around or centered on the moon.

Earth to reader—can you still hear me? This is your nebulochaotic, abderian doctor speaking. Are you feeling high and dry, hung out to dry, or left out on a limb? If so, then your forlorn state is best described as **neaped** (rhymes with *beeped*), a word used of boats that have been caught by high tide and run aground or washed ashore. If your situation is so dire that you are convinced your whole life is neaped, then you are in the clutches of the wonderfully weird word **wanweird** (WAHN-weerd), a Scottish term meaning "unhappy fate." Feeling neaped and victimized by wanweird can lead to a wicked case of **lypothymia** (LY-puh-THY-mee-uh), a woeful word that *Webster 2* disconsolately defines as "profound melancholy; great mental prostration."

Does comprehending the profoundly grandiloquent desolation of *lypothymia* give you a **glisk?** Unlike the **curglaff,** the shock felt when plunging into cold water, or the **frisson** (free-SAW(N), with a nasalized *n*), a shudder of excitement or quivering thrill that courses through the body, the glisk is a subtle sensation: a slight touch of pleasure or twinge of pain that penetrates the soul and passes quickly away. (Just writing the definition of that beautiful word gives me a glisk!)

But enough of these cheap thrills. Let's talk about stress. Do you feel overworked, underpaid, unloved, or unappreciated? To remedy that condition you need to know the word **anxiolytic** (ANG-zee-uh-LIT-ik), which means serving to reduce anxiety. *Anxiolytic* came into the language in the early 1960s, about the same time that American society had a major nervous breakdown. Since then our mounting anxiety over how to cope with the adverse effects of stress has made anxiolytic drugs and therapies the rage in medicine.

For example, according to a report in *The New York Times Magazine* (May 22, 1994), "anxiolytic music, which has no melody, rhythm, or lyrics but does have waves of vaguely orchestral sound," is now being tested in various hospital operating rooms for its potential relaxing effect on patients undergoing surgery. Of course, the oldest anxiolytic remedy—booze, straight up or with an anxious twist—remains the drug of choice for millions of stressed-out folks. (I'm still waiting for them to invent "I Can't Believe It's Not Vodka.")

Given the myriad pressures of modern life, it would be too much to expect *anxiolytic* to do its soothing work all alone. Our anxious English language contains (at least) three other grandiloquent stress-reducing words: **phrontifugic,** which by derivation means "helping one to escape one's thoughts or cares"; **dolorifuge** (duh-LOR-i-fyooj), something that cures or alleviates grief; and **nepenthe** (nuh-PEN-thee), a drug or magical potion that makes you forget your sorrows or misfortune:

> *Nepenthe* is a drink of sovereign grace,
> Devised by the gods, for to assuage
> Heart's grief, and bitter gall away to chase.
> —EDMUND SPENSER,
> *The Faerie Queene*

> Quaff, oh, quaff this kind *nepenthe,*
> and forget this lost Lenore!
> —EDGAR ALLAN POE,
> "The Raven"

One favorite pastime of the especially anxious is **onychophagy** (AHN-i-KAHF-uh-jee), the habit of biting one's fingernails (from the Greek *onyx, onychos,* a nail or claw, and *phagein,* to eat). If you manifest your stress by nibbling on your nails, you are an **onychophagist** (AHN-i-KAHF-uh-jist).

Do you often feel as if you got up on the wrong side of the bed? Perhaps it would help to know that there's a specific word for that condition: **matutolypea** (muh-T(Y)OO-tuh-LIP-ee-uh), formed from the Latin *matutinus,* early in the morning, and the Greek *lype,* grief. Now, even if you continue to get up on the wrong side of the bed, at least you won't get even more grumpy and depressed because you have to use that hackneyed phrase to describe your mood. Instead you can sport a joviomelancholy grin and announce with merry-go-sorry grandiloquence, "I'm sorry I smashed your Ming dynasty vase in a fit of pique. I'm afraid I'm having a bad bout of *matutolypea* today."

Are you active? Do you exercise? Are you early to bed and early to rise? If so, then I have no words for you—except perhaps some insulting specimens from chapter 4 (where you will learn how to use grandiloquently insolent words like *zob*, which means a worthless person, a nobody). On the other hand, if you are a slothful, unrepentant zob like me, then surely you suffer from **dysania** (dis-AY-nee-uh), the state of having a rough time waking up and dragging yourself out of bed in the morning.

If your dysania becomes so pronounced that you're practically catatonic, then you may have **abulia** (uh-B(Y)OO-lee-uh), also known as *dysbulia*. These conditions spell big trouble, because they mean a complete loss of willpower or the ability to act. Such immobility may also be a symptom of a severe disorder known as **cerebropathy** (SER-uh-BRAHP-uh-thee). According to the *Century Dictionary*, this is "a hypochondriacal condition, approaching insanity, which sometimes supervenes in persons whose brains have been overtaxed." Talk about megastress!

When you're conversing with someone, do you find yourself looking at your feet, or all around, or anywhere but in your interlocutor's eyes? If so, then you have **opsablepsia** (AHP-suh-BLEP-see-uh), the inability to meet another's gaze. Persistent obsablepsia may be a sign that you need to inspect your emotional baggage for a cumbersome bundle of guilt or self-doubt.

Do you ever experience fits of **glumsiness?** This useful neologism, coined by poet and translator Jane Hirschfield, cleverly combines *glum* and *clumsy* to mean awkwardness brought on or exacerbated by a sour mood. *Glumsiness* may refer either to physical maladroitness, a propensity to mishandle or break things when you are depressed, or to a lack of verbal grace, saying hurtful things to others when you feel sullen and morose.

How's your level of concentration? Do you have trouble maintaining your mental focus, or are you usually just the opposite—so intensely focused that you block out everything around you? When you are unable to concentrate, you have **aprosexia** (AP-roh-**SEK**-see-uh); when your attention is fixated and excessive, you have **hyperprosexia** (**HY**-pur-proh-**SEK**-see-uh); and when your attention is intensely fixated on sex, you have **supersexiprosexia**, a joculism I couldn't resist tossing in so you could finish reading this paragraph with a satisfied smile.

As long as we're on the subject of scrutiny, two other abnormal forms of attention deserve a quick look. If you suffer from the delusion that things are more beautiful than they actually are, the word for your condition is **kalopsia** (kuh-**LAHP**-see-uh). When you see something repugnant and can't refrain from staring at it, or when you do something repugnant such as pick your ears or nose and feel compelled to examine the offending finger, then you are in the repulsive grip of a disorder called **cacospectamania** (**KAK**-oh-**SPEK**-tuh-**MAY**-nee-uh), a word I've coined from the Greek *kakos*, bad; the Latin *spectare*, to look at carefully, observe; and -*mania*, compulsion.

Classic cases of kalopsia include the starry-eyed lover who can see no flaw in the object of affection and the person who looks at life through rose-colored glasses. Classic symptoms of cacospectamania include a morbid fascination with TV reports of gory murders or highway fatalities; watching impassively as a cockroach scurries across the floor and disappears under your refrigerator; and an irresistible urge, when conversing with a person, to focus on some unsightly feature such as a pimple, protruding nose hairs, dirty fingernails, or a salient wart.

Since we're discussing disgusting things, do you have a **cacoëthes** (**KAK**-oh-**EE**-theez)? Flawed creatures that we are, most of us have at least one. A *cacoëthes*, from the Greek *kakos*, bad, and *ethos*, habit, is a bad habit, incurable itch, insatiable urge or desire.

I can remember how I learned this word with a clarity that can come only from having lived a linguistically dissolute life. Years ago, back in my stuttering salad days, I was watching one of the PBS *Firing Line* programs hosted by that most ornery master of the grandiloquent gibe, William F. Buckley, Jr.

A learned professor was discoursing on some subject, knowledgeably but rather dully; from Buckley's body language you could see that he had, to put it mildly, serious reservations about her point of view. When the professor finished speaking, closing with something on the order of "and that is why I object to Mr. Buckley's stand on this issue," Buckley shifted in his seat, gave her that predatory, ophidian squint—like a viper about to bite—and said, "Well, I suppose that's *your* cacoëthes." The professor was nonplussed, the audience was in stitches over the inscrutable put-down, and I was up and running for the nearest dictionary.

If expressing your bad habits in Anglicized Latin gives you a glisk or a frisson, *Webster 2* lists three forms of cacoëthes: **cacoëthes loquendi** (loh-KWEN-dee or loh-KWEN-dy), an insatiable urge to talk; **cacoëthes carpendi** (kahr-PEN-dee or kahr-PEN-dy), a compulsion to criticize or find fault; and **cacoëthes scribendi:** (skri-BEN-dee or skry-BEN-dy), an incurable itch to write—one of many verbal maladies afflicting your humble grandiloquent guide.

Whenever I think of cacoëthes scribendi, I am reminded of what William, Duke of Gloucester, said to Edward Gibbon, author of *The History of the Decline and Fall of the Roman Empire* and other formidable tomes. "Another damned, thick, square book!" cried Gloucester. "Always scribble, scribble, scribble—eh, Mr. Gibbon?" I'm sure the scribbling Gibbon was stung by that remark, but I doubt it cured his cacoëthes.

Speaking of stinging slaps in the face, have you ever been blindsided, literally or figuratively, after you had dropped your guard? The perfect word for that felling blow is **afterclap.** In its original, literal sense, an *afterclap* is an unexpected physical assault, usually one that occurs after you think the fight is over or the danger has passed; the slang synonym is a *sucker-punch*.

The third edition of *The American Heritage Dictionary* ably defines the later, figurative sense of *afterclap* as "an unexpected, often unpleasant sequel to a matter that had been considered closed." The *OED*'s earliest citation for *afterclap* dates from 1420. It's hard to believe that such a rarely used but eminently useful word has been in the language for nearly six hundred years!

Do you ever jump to conclusions about people based on a first impression, or by your first glimpse at their face? If so, and if your judgments tend to be favorable, then you may have **prosopolepsy** (pruh-**SOH**-puh-**LEP**-see), an inclination to accept people based on their personal appearance, by derivation "a taking to the face." (The word may also apply to the act of falling in love at first sight.) If you find yourself unable to remember the faces of people you know or meet, then it may help you save face if you know the name of your disorder: **prosopolethy** (pruh-**SOH**-puh-**LEE**-thee).

Seriously *prosopoleptic* or *prosopolethic* people may also suffer from *oneirataxia* (oh-**NY**-ruh-**TAKS**-see-uh), a disconcerting condition in which one cannot distinguish between reality and fantasy. You may not be oneirataxic, but if you dwell in a strange land where what you dream seems real and what is real seems like a dream, then the word you need to grasp is **hypnopompic** (HIP-noh-**PAHM**-pik), pertaining to the fuzzy, semiconscious state between sleep and wakefulness.

Well, my patient reader, or reader-patient, if you've read this far without growing impatient, or **semisomnous** (SEM-ee-**SAHM**-nus, half-asleep), let's see if the following selection of exceptionally crackpot words won't knock you right off your rocker and around the bend.

amentia: (uh-**MEN**-shee-uh) temporary insanity, sometimes associated with illness; also, a rapturous trance or daze, e.g., being "out of one's mind with joy."

anhedonia: (AN-he-**DOH**-nee-uh) the inability to experience pleasure or happiness.

bibliomania: a mania for reading or buying books.

The three types of book nuts, in ascending intensity, are as follows: the *bibliophile,* who loves books; the *bibliomaniac,* who is crazy about them; and the *biblioholic,* who is consumed by them to the point of self-destruction.

In his amusing and admirably grandiloquent book *Biblioholism: The Literary Addition,* Tom Raabe, a confessed biblioholic, defines the disease as "the habitual longing to purchase, read, store, admire, and consume books in excess." Raabe's well-chosen epigraph is worth reprinting here:

> What wild desires, what restless torments seize,
> The hapless man, who feels the book-disease.
> —JOHN FERRIAR,
> "The Bibliomania"

boanthropy: (boh-AN-thruh-pee) the delusion that one is an ox.

bruxomania: (BRUHKS-uh-MAY-nee-uh) compulsive grinding of the teeth. Habitual grinding of the teeth is called *bruxism.*

cynanthropy: (si-NAN-thruh-pee) the delusion that one is a dog. This is a very rare disorder. It is far more common for a person to actually *be* a dog, and to snarl in denial when others point that out.

drapetomania: (DRAP-uh-toh-MAY-nee-uh) an overwhelming urge to run away (from home, a bad situation, responsibility, etc.).

formication: (FOR-mi-KAY-shin) the sensation that bugs (especially ants) are crawling over one's body.

> Two lovers who went on vacation
> Turned a picnic into a sensation.
>   They began a love-dance
>   And got ants in their pants—
> You have never seen such formication!
> —RICHIE SKRATCH

galeanthropy: (GAL-ee-**AN**-thruh-pee) the delusion that one is a cat.

> One of the finest novels for children ever written, in my opinion, is Paul Gallico's *The Abandoned,* in which a young boy named Peter, struck by a van while running across the street to pet a cat, falls into a coma and experiences galeanthropy. The story's delightful twist is that although Peter is **feliform** (FEE-li̲-form), meaning he has the body of a cat, in his mind he is still a boy. To survive on the mean streets of London, Peter must learn how to think and behave like a real cat.

gigmania: (gig-**MAY**-nee-uh) obsessive preoccupation with achieving or maintaining smug, middle-class respectability.

hebephrenia: (HEE-buh-**FREE**-nee-uh) a pubescent or adolescent psychological disorder characterized by silly behavior, volatile emotions, hallucinations, and mental deterioration. (Gee, and I thought I was just another normal, tortured teen.)

hypermnesia: (HY-purm-**NEE**-zhuh) exceptional memory, the opposite of *amnesia.*

hypobulia: (HY-puh-**BYOO**-lee-uh) trouble making up one's mind; the inability to come to a decision.

iconomania: (eye-KAHN-uh-**MAY**-nee-uh) infatuation with icons, either as objects of worship or as works of art.

lethonomia: (LEE-thuh-**NOH**-mee-uh) the whoosis complex; a tendency to forget or the inability to recall names.

lycanthropy: (ly-KAN-thruh-pee) the werewolf complex: the delusion that one is a wolf, or the belief that people can change themselves into wolves or other wild beasts.

melomania: (MEL-uh-**MAY**-nee-uh) a consuming passion for music.

neoteinia: (NEE-oh-**TY**-nee-uh) a state of prolonged immaturity; postadolescent *hebephrenia* (q.v. above).

nostomania: (NAHS-tuh-**MAY**-nee-uh) overwhelming homesickness.

oikomania: (OY-koh-**MAY**-nee-uh) mental disorder caused by wretched or abusive domestic circumstances.

paramnesia: (PAR-am-**NEE**-zhuh) a disorder in which one claims to remember events that didn't happen. Also known as *pseudomnesia.*

periblepsis: (PER-i-**BLEP**-sis) the wild look that accompanies delirium. *Peribleptic* is the adjective.

    It almost gives me periblepsis to rescue this wild word from oblivion. To the best of my knowledge, *periblepsis* has not seen the light of print for almost a century. Of all the dictionaries and reference books I consulted, only the *Century* (1914) lists it, citing Dunglison's *Dictionary of Medical Science* (1874) as its source.

    That's a heck of a long time to be locked away, don't you think? After so long, wouldn't you be a bit moonstruck, even *peribleptic,* to be wandering again in the teeming world of words? I'd be delirious if you saw fit to give *periblepsis* and *peribleptic* a new lease on life.

phaneromania: (FAN-uh-roh-**MAY**-nee-uh) the compulsive habit of picking at scabs or growths on the skin.

planomania: (PLAN-uh-**MAY**-nee-uh) an urge to roam; the itch one gets when it's "time to move on."

rhytiscopia: (RIT-i-**SKOH**-pee-uh) an obsession with one's facial wrinkles.

    Plastic surgeons and manufacturers of beauty products make big bucks off people with rhytiscopia.

siderodromomania: (SID-uh-roh-DROH-moh-**MAY**-nee-uh) a mania for traveling by train, a disorder unknown in southern California.

tarantism: (TAR-un-tiz'm) a paradoxical state in which one has an overwhelming urge to overcome one's melancholy by dancing.

trichotillomania: (TRIK-oh-TIL-uh-**MAY**-nee-uh) a compulsion to pull out one's hair.

    I outlined a new book about people with trichotillomania— people who compulsively pull out their hair. There are 2 million to 4 million Americans who have trichotillomania. That's a lot of books! (That's a lot of hair, too!)

               —MARK LEYNER, *Et Tu, Babe*

uranomania: (YUUR-uh-noh-MAY-nee-uh) the delusion that one is of heavenly descent (from the Greek *ouranós*, the heavens).

   This malady is epidemic among artists, writers, actors, entertainers, and other glitterati. When it affects professional athletes, it is called *josecansecoism* (HOH-zay-kan-SAY-koh-iz'm) or *andreagassism* (AHN-dray-AG-uh-siz'm). When athletes believe they are of royal descent, the delusion is called *sircharlesbarkleyloungerism*. (All three are my jocular nonce-words.)

zoanthropy: (zoh-AN-thruh-pee) the delusion that one is an animal.

   For the delusion that one is *not* an animal—which many pet owners will tell you is common among cats, and which any woman will tell you is rampant among men—I have taken the liberty of coining the word **anzoanthropy.**

And now it's time for your puerile, planomaniacal physician to abandon your zoanthropic brain, grab his handy-dandy **sphygmomanometer** (the device with the inflatable cuff that measures your blood pressure, pronounced SFIG-moh-muh-NAHM-uh-tur), and proceed with the second part of the verbal examination.

THE PHYSICAL EVALUATION

The soul is not the body,
And the body is not the soul,
Because one goes up to heaven,
And the other down the toilet bowl.
   —GEVALT WHITMAN,
      "Song of My Health"

How well do you know your body? Or perhaps I should put the question this way: How well do you *want* to know your body?

In recent years there has been an effusion of bestsellers on the subject of body language. The self-help shrinks have made a tidy profit telling us everything from how to find our erogenous zones to how to evaluate job candidates by the way they handle their napkins at a business lunch. You may know what it means when a woman crosses her legs or a man touches his hair. You may even have a degree in social or behavioral psychology. But do you know whether you are *sciapodous*, *labrose*, or *macrotous*, or whether you are *matroclinous* or *patroclinous*? Are you *Apollonian* or *cucurbitaceous*? Do you have a *buccula*?

As you probably surmised from that volley of polysyllables, there's a lot of interesting body language that you won't find in those ungrandiloquent bestsellers, or almost any other book besides an unabridged dictionary. Here's what those words mean:

sciapodous: (sy-AP-uh-d<u>u</u>s) having huge feet.
labrose: (LAB-rohs) having large or thick lips.
macrotous: (muh-KROH-t<u>u</u>s) having great big ears.
matroclinous: (MA-truh-**KLY**-n<u>u</u>s) looking more like your mom than your dad; having physical characteristics inherited from the mother.
patroclinous: (PA-truh-**KLY**-n<u>u</u>s) looking more like your dad than your mom; having physical characteristics inherited from the father.
Apollonian: (AP-uh-**LOH**-nee-<u>i</u>n) exhibiting the classic physical beauty of Greek and Roman sculpture.
cucurbitaceous: (kyoo-KUR-b<u>i</u>-**TAY**-sh<u>u</u>s) resembling a cucumber or squash.
buccula: (BUHK-yuu-luh) a double chin.

If you don't mind scrutinizing your physique in the privacy of your own book, allow me to lead you step by step through an exercise in **prosopography** (PRAHS-uh-**PAHG**-ruh-fee), the description of a person's appearance, and an experiment in **anthroposcopy** (AN-thruh-**PAHS**-skuh-pee), which *Random House II* defines as "the art of determining character or personal characteristics from the form or features of the body."

All right, then. Just step behind that screen over there, take off your clothes, slip on this ridiculous, humiliating little rag we doctors like to call a "gown," then sit up here on this skinny examination table and see if you can make yourself comfortable with a swatch of waxed paper stuck to your butt. In the meantime, I'll go get my **plexor** (PLEKS-ur), that rubber-headed hammer doctors use to bang your knee and test your reflexes (also called a *percussor* or *plessor*), and Nurse Ratchet over here will take your vitals—don't worry, she's quite adept at removing them. Then we'll take a grandiloquent tour of your physical terrain.

Let's begin with your face. I'm sure you've examined it in the mirror more than a few thousand times and never once thought of yourself as **prognathous** (PRAHG-nuh-th<u>u</u>s). That's probably just as well. If you're prognathous your jaws project beyond the upper part of your face—in other words, you look something like Arnold Schwarzenegger in *The Terminator* or Popeye the Sailor Man.

How would you describe your nose? If you're **platyopic** (PLAT-ee-**AHP**-ik) or **leptorrhinian** (LEP-tuh-**RIN**-ee-in), you have plenty of company: *platyopic* means having a broad, flat nose; *leptorrhinian* means having a long, narrow one. If you happen to belong to the Salient Schnoz Society, then your respiratory appendage probably is either **accipitrine** (ak-SIP-i-trin), like a hawk's beak, or **proboscidiform** (PROH-buh-**SID**-i-form), like an elephant's trunk. If your nose has a bump in it, it's a **kyphorrhinos** (KY-fuh-**RY**-nohs).

Most people know that the **septum** is the cartilaginous wall between the nostrils, but did you know that the slender bone that forms a large part of the septum is called the **vomer** (VOH-mur)? And those fleshy bulbs on each side of your nose have a name, too: the **alae** (AY-lee), with the singular *ala* (AY-luh).

Okay, put your trigger finger on your **tragus** (TRAY-g<u>u</u>s). Confused? We're about to do a little touchy-feely with your ear.

Your *tragus* is the bump of cartilage between your ear and your temple, that fleshy wedge in front of the opening to your ear (called the *external acoustic meatus*). Put the tip of your index finger on your tragus and let it slip down toward your earlobe. Do you feel a small groove or notch? That's your **intertragic** (IN-tur-**TRAY**-jik) **notch.**

Now insert your finger deeper into your ear, as if you were trying not to hear something harsh. If you wedge it in there nice and snug against your tragus, blocking the external acoustic meatus, your finger should completely fill your **concha** (KAHNG-kuh), the innermost cavity of the external ear.

All right, that's enough earplay; you may remove the offending digit. I'd rather not be held responsible for the consequences if someone walks in, asks you why you're reading with a finger stuck in your ear, and you answer, "I've just been fiddling with my tragus and exploring my concha."

Here's one of my favorite anatomical trivia questions: What's the word for the vertical groove in the middle of your upper lip, just under your nose? ("Final Jeopardy" music, please.) It's your **philtrum** (FIL-trum), from the same Greek root as *philter*, a love potion or charm, a word you will meet again in chapter 3.

Now that we're discussing your mouth, perhaps you should go to a mirror right now, open your maw, say *aaahh*, and look inside. *Way* inside. You see that thing that looks like a fleshy stalactite hanging down in the back of your throat? If your dentist hasn't told you already, that's your **uvula** (YOOV-yuh-luh), from the Latin *uva*, grape. Now open wide and stick out your tongue. Curl it up and look at the underside. Do you see the tendinous membrane that's holding it to the bottom of your mouth? That's your **frenum** (FREE-num).

Now put your slimy tongue away and let's have a smile. Say "cheese." Show some teeth. Whoa, Nelly! You are positively **selachostomous** (SEL-uh-**KAHS**-tuh-mus), shark-mouthed. Just kidding! You're actually a **gubbertush,** a person with buck teeth.

Here's something every dentist wants to know: Have you

been flossing your **embrasures** (em-BRAY-zhurz), the spaces between your fangs? Have you been sticking toothpicks in your **diastemata** (DY-uh-STEE-muh-tuh)? A **diastema** (DY-uh-STEE-muh), the singular, is a pronounced gap between two teeth; **diastematic** (DY-uh-sti-MAT-ik), gap-toothed, is the adjective. There's nothing unusual about being diastematic, but let's hope you don't have a **kag,** for that is either the stump of a broken tooth or a tooth standing alone. (That versatile word, by the way, listed in Joseph Wright's *English Dialect Dictionary,* may also mean the stump of a severed tree branch or "an angular tear or rent in cloth.")

Let's take a look at your hair. If you're **hispid,** you'd better go back to boot camp, for *hispid* means rough with bristles, stiff hairs, or minute spines. If you're like most folks, though, you probably have enough dead protein dangling from your skull to wake up in the morning with a **litch,** a mass of tangled, matted hair, or with some feisty **feesks,** tufts of unruly, disordered hair. Those are two great words you can use the next time you have a "bad hair day"!

Now let's examine the shape of your head. If it's more long than wide, you're **dolichocephalic** (DAHL-i-koh-suh-FAL-ik). If it's broad, you're **brachycephalic** (BRAK-i-suh-FAL-ik). If it's pointy, you're **acrocephalic** (AK-roh-suh-FAL-ik). If you have a head (or face) like a dog, you're **cynocephalous** (SY-nuh-SEF-uh-lus). And if your neck sinks into your shoulders so that your head seems soldered to your torso, then the word for you is **hunksit.** Football players tend to be hunksit, and hunksit celebrities (who are definitely not hunks) include Ed Sullivan, Richard Nixon, Uncle Fester from *The Addams Family,* and Hans and Franz, the Pump-You-Up Brothers from *Saturday Night Live.*

How's your skin? If it's **cretaceous** (kri-TAY-shus), you need some sun: *cretaceous* means chalky, grayish white. If it's **coriaceous** (kor-ee-AY-shus), you've probably had enough sun: *coriaceous* means leatherlike. If it's **shistaceous** (shi-STAY-shus), you'd better check your pulse: *shistaceous* means slate-colored, livid. These skin types pale compared with an epidermis that is **squamous** (SKWAY-mus) or **squamulose**

(SKWAM-yuh-lohs), for *squamous* means covered with scales, like a fish, and *squamulose* means covered with minute scales, like a snake.

What about your shape, your body type? Are you **ecto-morphic**, slight and slender, or **asthenic** (as-THEN-ik), lean and frail? Are you **endomorphic**, short, broad, and powerful; **mesomorphic** (MEZ-uh-), big-boned and muscular; or **pyknic** (like *picnic*), stocky and round?

Whatever you are—whether you're a **leptosome** (LEP-tuh-sohm), a person of asthenic build, or **pyriform** (PIR-i-form), shaped like a pear—with a little luck, a little skin cream, and a lot of cosmetic surgery, you may be able to get rid of some of those irksome **lirks** (wrinkles, creases, or folds in the skin) and achieve the next best thing to nirvana: **agerasia** (AJ-e-RAY-see-uh), the enviable state of looking younger than one's years or of not appearing to age (from a Greek word meaning "eternal youth").

We shall conclude our examination with a pop quiz on a few more unusual and useful bits of body language. Do you know the meanings of these anatomical words?

canthus	olecranon
glabella	peristalsis
hallux	popliteal
lunula	purlicue
malleolus	rasceta
Extra credit word: oxter	

(Answers appear at the end of the chapter.)

AILMENTS, SENSATIONS, AND OTHER CURIOSITIES

Now that you have mastered the rudiments of anatomy from your head to your **minimus** (your little finger or toe), it's time to take a look at some of the many things that can go on or go awry in your miraculous mass of flesh and bone.

Did you know that your humble body is capable of such grandiloquent sensations as **gargalesthesia**, **obdormition**, and *lippitude?* In fact, these are all quite ordinary feelings you can have on any given day.

This morning, for instance, if you awakened with sore or bleary eyes, then Mr. Sandman and Morpheus, the god of dreams, conspired to leave you in a state of *lippitude* (LIP-i-t(y)ood). *Obdormition* (AHB-dor-MISH-un) is the odd, tingling, slightly numb feeling you get when a limb "falls asleep"; it is caused by pressure on a nerve. And when certain especially sensitive nerves are stimulated in a pleasurable way, the resulting sensation is *gargalesthesia* (GAHR-guh-les-THEE-zhuh). Now there's a grandiloquent word you can giggle about, for *gargalesthesia* denotes the feeling caused by tickling.

Not all perceptions are pleasant, of course. For example, have you ever had the distinctly disagreeable experience of getting stuck next to someone who stinks to high heaven? If that should ever happen, you have your pick of three words for the offender's putrid condition: **bromidrosis** (BROH-mi-DROH-sis), **osmidrosis** (AHZ-mi-DROH-sis), and **kakidrosis** (KAK-i-DROH-sis). All denote fetid perspiration—or as they say in the vulgate, "totally awesome B.O."

In the halitosis department, we have two totally awesome words: **saprostomous** (sa-PRAHS-tuh-mus), emanating an offensive odor from the oral cavity; and **ozostomia** (OH-zah-STOH-mee-uh), foul-smelling breath. Have you ever woken up in the morning with breath that could curdle the milk in your coffee or wilt your house plants? That's *matutinal ozostomia*, otherwise known as "morning breath." (*Matutinal*, pronounced muh-T(Y)OO-ti-nul, means pertaining to the morning.)

If your nose picks up an aroma that isn't there, you may have **parosmia** (pa-RAHZ-mee-uh), or **pseudosmia** (soo-DAHZ-mee-uh), a disorder characterized by nasal hallucinations. If you detect a particularly noxious nonexistent emanation, then you have **cacosmia** (ka-KAHZ-mee-uh). And if your olfactory organ has trouble picking up any aroma, whether rank or appealing, you're a victim of **hyposmia** (hy-PAHZ-mee-uh), a deficient sense of smell.

Do you ever suffer from **ombrosalgia** (AHM-bruh-SAL-juh), aches and pains felt when it rains? Have you ever had a

dwam, a sudden fit of illness or feeling of faintness? How about a **galea** (GAY-lee-uh)? That's a headache that hurts your whole head (from the Latin *galea*, helmet).

I'll be the first to admit that a galea is a real headache, that a dwam is nothing to sneeze at, and that ombrosalgia can rain on your parade, but in my insalubrious opinion the *ne plus ultra* of agony is the **terebration** (TER-uh-**BRAY**-shin), a pain that feels as if a drill is boring through some part of your body.

Do any of these disorders ring a bell? If so, you may have **acouasm** (uh-KOO-az'm), a buzzing or ringing in the ears, also called *tinnitus* (ti-NY-tus). If these painful words fall upon deaf ears, you may have **presbycusis** (PREZ-bi-**KYOO**-sis), loss of hearing due to old age, or too much **cerumen** (si-ROO-min), earwax.

If a doctor's **palpation** (probing with the fingers) and **auscultation** (AW-skul-**TAY**-shin, listening through a stethoscope) do not reveal the source of your **dyscrasia** (dis-KRAY-zhee-uh, unwholesome or morbid condition, general malaise), perhaps you can diagnose the problem yourself by perusing the following medicine chest full of disorderly and constitutional words.

acronyx: (AK-ruh-niks) an ingrown fingernail or toenail. See **paronychia** below.
agria: (AG-ree-uh) an acute pustular eruption, such as a cold sore or the pimple commonly called a "whitehead."
ankylosis: (ANG-kuh-**LOH**-sis) stiffness or immobility in a joint.
chalcenterous: (kal-SEN-tur-us) having bowels of brass.
In *Unlocking the English Language,* the late Robert Burchfield, an editor of the *Oxford English Dictionary,* writes that "one minor curiosity of the project was the discovery, against all expectations, that a few members of staff had no stomach for the crudities of sexual and scatalogical vocabulary. I had assumed from the beginning that *Homo lexicographicus* was a chalcenterous species of mankind, that is, a person with bowels of brass."

You've got to be tough if you want to make it in the land of lex. Brazen-boweled word buffs like Burchfield eat grandiloquent gems like *chalcenterous* for breakfast.

coenesthesis: (SEE-nes-**THEE**-sis) awareness of one's body, especially an overall sense of one's general health. In grandiloquent lingo, the pedestrian question "How ya doin'?" becomes "May I inquire as to your coenesthesis?"

dactylion: (dak-**TIL**-ee-ahn) the tip of the middle finger.

In certain extreme cases, even the grandiloquent must forgo speech and resort to obscene gestures. If you truly aspire to grandiloquence, however, in such a situation you will never "give someone the finger." Instead you will "display the dactylion."

decubitus: (di-**KYOO**-bi-tus) one's posture or position in bed.

Ungrandiloquent: "At the party last night, I met this jerk who was a total wolf. He kept making passes at me, so finally I flipped him off and he split."

Grandiloquent: "I met some lupine goop at the party last night who was intensely interested in studying my decubitus. He desisted when I displayed the dactylion."

diathesis: (dy-**ATH**-uh-sis) a constitutional or genetic predisposition to a particular disease or disorder.

dorsodynia: (DOR-soh-**DIN**-ee-uh) pain in the back.

dyschezia: (dis-**KEE**-zee-uh) difficulty and pain in defecating.

dyschromatopsia: (dis-KROH-muh-**TAHP**-see-uh) feeble or impaired perception of color.

dysepulotic: (dis-EP-yuh-**LAH**-tik) not healing quickly or easily.

dysesthesia: (DIS-es-**THEE**-zhuh) impairment of the senses, particularly the sense of touch.

dyskinesia: (DIS-ki-**NEE**-zhuh) difficulty making voluntary movements.

dysmenorrhea: (dis-MEN-uh-**REE**-uh) difficult or painful menstruation.

dyspepsia: (dis-**PEP**-see-uh) indigestion.

"The term is applied with a certain freedom to all forms of gastric derangement," says the *Century*.

dyspnea: (**DISP**-nee-uh) labored breathing.

dysrhythmia: jet lag.

dysuria: (dis-YOOR-ee-uh) difficult and painful urination.

errhine: (ER-in) *adj.*, designed to be inhaled through the nose; pertaining to the nose or nasal discharge; *n.*, nasal discharge.

graphospasm: writer's cramp.

> Aspiring writer,
> make your prose tighter.
> Verbosity
> creates animosity.
> Pleonasm
> causes graphospasm.
> —WARD F. D'WARD

gronk: a dialectal term for the dirt or scuzz that collects between your toes, colloquially known as *cheese* or *toe-jam*.

humdudgeon: an imaginary pain or illness.

iatrogenic: (eye-AT-truh-JEN-ik) pertaining to a medical problem caused by a doctor's diagnosis or treatment.

meteorism: (MEE-tee-ur-iz'm) a serious pathological condition, also called *tympanites* (TIM-puh-NY-teez), in which the abdomen is abnormally distended by gas in the intestines or peritoneal cavity.

For our nonmedical and grandiloquently crass purposes, we could stretch the definition a bit to mean a bloated feeling accompanied by an urge to break wind.

nyctalopia: (NIK-tuh-LOH-pee-uh) night blindness; reduced vision in dim light or darkness. The opposite disorder is called *hemeralopia* (HEM-ur-uh-LOH-pee-uh), day blindness, trouble seeing in bright light.

paronychia: (PAR-uh-NIK-ee-uh) an infected hangnail or cuticle. The colloquial (but now uncommon) terms for this painful condition are *whitlow* and *felon*.

passulation: (PAS-yuh-LAY-shin) the act or process of drying up and turning into a raisin. The verb is **passulate** (PAS-yuh-layt), to turn (a grape) into a raisin.

NURSING HOME BLUES
(to the tune of "Twinkle, Twinkle, Little Star")

Wrinkle, wrinkle, every day,
We shrivel up in every way:
Wizened flesh and brittle bones,
Constant aches and pains and groans.
Wrinkle, wrinkle, every day,
We *passulate*, then pass away.

—PRUNELLA CROON

phthiriasis: (thy-RY-i-sis) infestation with lice. Also called *pediculosis*.

piloerection: (PY-loh-) erection of the hairs on the head or extremities; having your hair "stand on end." Also called *hystriciasis* (HIS-tri-SY-uh-sis).

pilosism: (PY-luh-siz'm) excessive or abnormal hairiness.

The word *hirsutism* (HUR-s(y)oo-tiz'm) means the same thing, but it usually refers to unsightly hairiness in women.

pogoniasis: (POH-goh-NY-uh-sis) beard growth in a woman.

presbyopia: (PREZ-bee-OH-pee-uh) the natural deterioration of vision due to the aging process.

ptosis: (TOH-sis) a drooping of one or both upper eyelids, a common condition in old age.

pygalgia: (py-GAL-juh) a pain in the butt.

Proctalgia (prahk-TAL-juh) is a pain in the anus, and *rectalgia* (rek-TAL-juh) is a pain in the rectum. I doubt you need me to elaborate on how these three words might be employed outside the field of medicine.

saccade: (sa-KAYD or sa-KAHD) rapid movement of the eyes; the jerky motions your eyes make as you look quickly from one thing to another.

Saccade comes from a French word meaning a twitch or jerk and has two other fascinating meanings. *Random House II* notes that its original sense is the act of checking a horse with a strong tug of the reins. *Webster 2* adds that the word is also used in music to refer to "a sudden, strong pressure of the violin bow" that causes two or more strings to sound at once.

scotodinia: (SKAHT-uh-**DIN**-ee-uh or SKOH-tuh-) dizziness accompanied by headache and impaired vision.

stratephrenia: (STRAT-i-**FREE**-nee-uh) neurosis caused by serving in the military.

ustulate: (UHS-chuu-lit) scorched or discolored from heat. This is a good word for someone who is badly sun-burned.

valetudinarian: (VAL-e-T(Y)OO-di-**NAIR**-ee-in) a person obsessed with some ailment or who is in generally poor health.

The *valetudinarian* and the *hypochondriac* are both whiners and complainers who are preoccupied with their health, but the hypochondriac often experiences hum-dudgeons (see entry above), whereas the valetudinarian's symptoms and ailments, though often exaggerated, are real. *Valetudinarian* may also be used as an adjective to mean sickly, frail, in poor health.

zoonosis: (zoh-AHN-uh-sis or ZOH-uh-**NOH**-sis) a disease that can be passed from animals to human beings.

Doctors usually advise pregnant women not to handle cats or kitty litter to avoid a form of zoonosis called *toxo-plasmosis,* a parasitic infection caused by contact with cat feces or by eating inadequately cooked meat.

Answers to the Body Language Pop Quiz

Check your responses (or wild guesses) against the definitions below. Give yourself a point for every one you got right and a half point for those where you came close but no cigar.

canthus: either of the two corners of the eye, where the eyelids meet.

glabella: (gluh-BEL-uh) the flat area of the forehead between the eyebrows.

hallux: the big toe.

lunula: (LOON-yuh-luh) the half-moon or crescent-shaped pale area at the base of the fingernail or toenail. The plural is *lunulae* (LOON-yuh-lee).

malleolus: (muh-LEE-uh-lus) the bony protuberance on each side of the ankle.

olecranon: (oh-LEK-ruh-nahn) the bony tip of the elbow.

> *Ungrandiloquent*: "He doesn't know his ass from his elbow."

> *Grandiloquent*: "He can't tell his glutei [GLOO-tee-eye] from his olecranon."

The so-called funny bone (which is really the ulnar nerve) is situated in the slightly soft area just above the olecranon, where the olecranon meets the lower end of the humerus (the bone in the upper half of your arm) to form the elbow joint.

peristalsis: (PER-i-STAWL-sis) *Mosby's Medical, Nursing, and Allied Health Dictionary* offers this well-written definition: "the coordinated, rhythmic, serial contraction of smooth muscle that forces food through the digestive tract, bile through the bile duct, and urine through the ureters." It is an **autonomic** (AW-tuh-**NAHM**-ik, independent, self-governing) excretory function of the body.

> *Peristalsis* sounds like a word a traffic reporter would use to describe a bottleneck or stop-and-go activity:

> "Things are moving smoothly today on the 805, but if you're heading downtown on 163, watch for some heavy peristalsis at the Enema Street exit. There's an overturned sump pumper blocking two lanes, and it's a real mess."

popliteal: (pahp-li-TEE-ul) pertaining to the soft area behind the knee.

purlicue: the web of flesh between your thumb and forefinger.

rasceta: (ruh-SEE-tuh) the deep, horizontal creases in the skin on the inside of the wrist. Also called *rascettes* (ra-SETS).

Extra credit word

oxter: the underarm or armpit.
      The verb *to oxter* means to walk arm in arm.

Here is Dr. Elster's prescription for your score:

0–5:	Take two aspirin and read a dictionary.
5.5–8.5:	You probably went to medical school. Go back.
9–11:	Get out of my office, you grandiloquent quack!

❖

FOOD FOR THOUGHT

Words Good Enough to Eat and Drink

Welcome to La Maison Prolixe, where we serve only the finest and rarest words for your palatal pleasure.

Allow me to tell you about our specials: We have the manager's favorites, **aristology** (AR-i-STAL-uh-jee), the science of dining, and **abligurition** (uh-BLIG-yuh-RISH-in), excessive or prodigal spending on food and drink. We have the chef's delight, **bromatology** (BROH-muh-TAHL-uh-jee), which sounds like a fizzy drink for an upset stomach but is in fact a discourse on food. We have an irresistible **sialagogue** (sy-AL-uh-gahg), a mouthwatering word meaning anything that promotes salivation. For the verbally voracious we have a thick, juicy cut of **deipnosophy** (dyp-NAHS-uh-fee), artful or learned conversation conducted while dining. And we have my personal favorite, **opsophagy** (ahp-SAHF-uh-jee), the ingestion of delicacies, of which there are plenty in our remarkable menu.

Now, just sit back and relax, and I'll escort you through this lexical feast, as the ancient Romans liked to say, *ab ovo usque ad mala*, from the egg to the apples. But first, would you care for a **preprandial libation,** a before-dinner drink? We serve both cocktails and **mocktails,** nonalcoholic drinks.

A FEW WORDS TO IMBIBE

The vocabulary of drink and drinking is vast and colorful. It has also been the subject of various tracts and volumes dating back at least to 1650, when an anonymous pamphlet appeared in England elucidating the drinking lingo of professors, students, lawyers, judges, civil servants, soldiers, and sailors.

Benjamin Franklin, writing as Silas Dogood, listed 228 terms for drunkenness in his *Drinker's Dictionary* of 1737. Old Ben may have preached abstemious virtue in public, but I'll bet that on those cold winter nights he liked to get wrapped up in warm flannel as much as any Poor Richard—or, as we say today, any Joe Sixpack. Robert L. Chapman remarks in his *Thesaurus of American Slang* (1989) that "*drunk* is one of the most prolific of slang concepts, probably because drunkenness has proffered the most persistent need of euphemism, both clever and defensive." The truth of that statement was proved to the last drop by the relentless word collector Paul Dickson. In his *Word Treasury* (1992), Dickson lists 2,660 terms for inebriation, a feat acknowledged by the folks at Guinness as the world's record for synonyms.

Out on the high seas is where many of the words for feeling half-seas-over were born. Three sheets in the wind, according to Brewer's *Dictionary of Phrase and Fable* (1894), means "unsteady from overdrinking." When the sheet (rope or chain) attached to the corner of a sail is unfastened, "the sail flaps and flutters without restraint." (The word for that, by the way, is **luffing.**) "If all three sails were so loosened," writes Brewer, "the ship would 'reel and stagger like a drunken man.'" If a sailor got too sozzled or sloshed to the gills, he might become an admiral of the narrow seas. That dubious rank, says the *1811 Dictionary of the Vulgar Tongue*, is conferred upon "one who from drunkenness vomits into the lap of the person sitting opposite to him."

While seafarers prefer to get shipwrecked, soaked, or slopped to the gills, landlubbers would rather get blitzed, bombed, clobbered, smashed, stoned, tanked, and totaled. It all goes way back, at least as far as the legendary Saturnalia of the ancients, "a time of licensed disorder and misrule," says Brewer. "With the Romans it was . . . celebrated the 17th, 18th, and 19th of December. During its continuance no public business could be transacted, the law courts were closed, the schools kept holiday, no war could be commenced, and no malefactor punished."

No matter what your profession or preoccupation, if you've ever succumbed to alcoholic **anadipsia** (great or excessive thirst), otherwise known as **dipsomania** (periodic insatiable craving for alcohol), then there's an appropriate drinking word for you—or, as the marketing folks at Budweiser might put it, "For all you do, there's a buzz word for you."

For example, the professor can get muddled, the lawyer obfuscated, the priest baptized, the philosopher illuminated, the farmer plowed, the police officer bullet-proofed, and the jailbird sprung. The laborer who gets off the nail can be hammered, sawed, shellacked, stuccoed, bulldozed, wallpapered, plastered, and put to bed with a shovel. The musician can get all jazzed up, piper-merry, tight as a drum, or high as a fiddler's fist. The salesperson who knows not the way home can get on a bus, get halfway to Concord, or make a trip to Baltimore. The physician who takes Hippocrates' Grand Elixir can get afflicted, fractured, and stitched. And when the politically correct get paralyzed, they prefer to call themselves challenged or impaired.

The **gastronome** (GAS-truh-nohm), the lover of good food and drink, can be oiled, fried, toasted, boiled, basted, juiced, scrambled, stewed, sauced, creamed, corned, mashed, pickled, pie-eyed, or canned. The undertaker who overdoes it can be dead to the world, stiff, bagged, laid out, embalmed, and buried. And an animal lover who eats the dog or swallows a hare can get aped, owled, foxed, skunked, or bitten by a barnmouse, especially if he or she likes to suck the monkey—a vivid phrase that according to the *1811 Dictionary of the Vulgar Tongue* means "to suck or draw wine, or any other liquor, privately out of a cask, by means of a straw, or small tube."

Finally, if you're a literary tippler, sluicing your gob can be more elegantly (and euphemistically) described as being exalted, flustered, jocular, petrified, oscillated, ossified, temulent, torrid, salubrious, saturated, spiflicated, up on Olympus, or in tipium grove (Ben Franklin's elegant variation on "tipsy"). One doesn't have to look far to find famous writers who were also **swillbowls** (prodigious drinkers), but in my opinion the literature of lushdom reached its zenith with the great nineteenth-century bard of the bottle, Seamus McWhisky (who dried out late in life and published a number of dull tracts on virtue under the pseudonym E. Z. Duzzette). Here is an exemplary passage from McWhisky's magnum opus, *Bacchi Plenus:*

> I slipped onto the stool, that most heavenly station,
> A tad **capernoited** after much **popination.**
> 'Twas tea time by then, and I fancied a drop
> Of champagne or cognac—or any **slipslop.**
> Alas, I 'adn't a farthing to buy me some grog,
> So I knew it was time to find a **shot-clog.**
> Beside me there sat a young **bibulous** fellow
> With 'is nose in his **barm,** looking quite mellow.
> I winked at the **publican,** then turned to me mate;
> 'E was deep in his **downdrins,** unaware of 'is fate.
> I patted 'is **seidel** and flashed 'im a smile;
> 'E belched in reply, and 'is breath was right vile.
> Undaunted, I said, "For some **blash,** me old chum,
> I will teach you to drink **supernaculum.**"
> After **xertzing** a **jubbe,** and then three more apace,
> I was sozzled with **stinkibus,** 'e was flat on 'is face.

Here is a glossary to the poem:

Bacchi plenus: (BAK-eye PLEE-nuus) Latin for "full of Bacchus," blazing drunk. Bacchus, also known as Dionysus, was the ancient Greek and Roman god of wine and orgiastic drunkenness.

barm: beer foam (also called *fob*).

bibulous: (BIB-yuh-l<u>u</u>s) fond of drinking, especially excessively.

blash: weak or watered-down liquor or beer (*blashy,* adj.).

capernoited: (KAP-ur-**NOY**-t<u>i</u>d) slightly intoxicated, tipsy. This Scottish dialectal word may also mean irritable, peevish.

downdrins: an afternoon drinking session.

jubbe (rhymes with *rub*): a large vessel for drinking ale or wine.

popination: (PAHP-<u>i</u>-**NAY**-sh<u>u</u>n) a playfully pompous term for barhopping, apparently formed from "pop in" (as for a drink) and the noun suffix *-ation.* The adjective *popinal* (stress on *pop*) means pertaining to bars or restaurants.

publican: a saloon keeper or bar manager.

seidel: (SY-d<u>u</u>l or ZY-d<u>e</u>l) a large beer mug with a hinged cover.

shot-clog: a simpleminded drinking companion that one tolerates only because he or she is willing to buy the drinks.

slipslop: bad liquor (same as **stinkibus**).

stinkibus: bad liquor (same as **slipslop**).

supernaculum: see discussion below.

xertz: (ZURTS) to gulp down, swallow quickly and greedily.

Other unusual terms for rapid ingestion include **lurrep** (used with *up*), to swallow liquor or food avidly; **yaffle** and **gruzzle,** to eat ravenously while making unpleasant noises; and **glunsh,** to devour food in hasty, noisy gulps.

Supernaculum (SOO-pur-**NAK**-yoo-l<u>u</u>m) has an interesting history. The word comes from Latin and means literally to drink upon (*super*) the nail (*naculum*)—in today's lingo, to drink to the last drop. Brand's *Popular Antiquity* (1813) offers this elucidation: "To drink *supernaculum* was an ancient custom, not only in England, but also in several other parts of Europe, of emptying the glass and then pouring the drop or two that remained at the bottom upon the person's nail that drank it, to show that he was no flincher." According to tradition, if the **heeltap**—the bit of liquor left in the glass after drinking—fell off the nail, the drinker was obliged to fill up and drink again.

Supernaculum came to be used in a general sense to mean good liquor, and there is even an adjective, *supernacular,* that I'm surprised Madison Avenue hasn't revived. Can't you imagine a bunch of obese ex-football players, in one of those pricey beer commercials during the Super Bowl, slamming down their mugs and, with the barm streaming from their lips, bellowing, "Dis beer iz supernacular!" With a super slogan like that, how could anyone resist the urge to run to the refrigerator and xertz a can of suds?

On the other hand, if you eschew brew and think that sort of pitch is balderdash (which once meant "adulterated wine"), then you're probably a **vinolent oenophilist** (VIN-uh-lent ee-NAHF-i-list), a wine-drinking lover of wine.

BREAD

Of all the words you will discover in this book, and even, perhaps, of all the words in the belly of that gluttonous and gargantuan beast, the English language, I cannot think of any more mundane, more insipid, or more useless than **paneity** (puh-NEE-i-tee), the state of being bread. God, I love that word.

From the dictionary definition it would seem that *paneity* is applicable only to the bread used in the Christian ritual of communion. Even that use, though, seems not only arcane but somewhat fatuous: Why would anyone have occasion to refer to the condition of being not yet holy bread? Indeed, it's hard to imagine (without laughing or dozing off) how or why anyone would use *paneity* at all, ever.

Nevertheless, the intrepid compilers of the *OED* somehow were able to dig up three citations for the word, all thoroughly banal (no surprise there). The most recent, dated 1782, is from Joseph Priestley (how fitting), in which he manages to swallow in one sentence not only *paneity* but the equally ludicrous **vineity** (vi-NEE-i-tee, the quality of being wine) in an apparent assessment of the flavors of communion. "There did remain a certain paneity and vineity," writes Priestley—in other words, the wafer tasted wafery and the wine winy. Gee, what did he expect, chocolate truffles and brandy? Immaculate indigestion?

Yet, if you think about it, you have to admit that *paneity*, an utterly ridiculous word, could have myriad applications in today's utterly ridiculous world. Just let your mind loaf a moment and consider the possibilities.

For example, I can see the late Julia Child garrulously advising us how to pamper an intractable lump of dough until it has reached optimum paneity.

I can see an infomercial for one of those trendy bread-making machines, with the talking head extolling the miraculous virtues of the product: "Only the fabulous Loafamatic gives you instant flour power and perfect paneity every time!"

I can see Batman and Robin suspended over a swirling vat of yeasty goo. As the evil Joker **cachinnates** in the background, the Boy Wonder exclaims, "Holy paneity, Batman! It's dough or die now!" (*Cachinnate,* pronounced KAK-i-nayt, means to laugh loudly and uncontrollably.)

And finally, as the father of a four-year-old who watches her fair share of television, I can see how an entire nation of parents of young children can have their brains baked into bland paneity by the Wonder bread puerilism of Barney, the dough-bellied dinosaur sensation. (And *puerilism*, from Latin *puerilis*, childish, is the *perfect* word for that purple plumposity, don't you agree? For as the shrinks like to say, it denotes the manifestation of immature behavior in an adult, especially as a symptom of mental illness.) Someday, I'm convinced, some crazed parent will kidnap that insufferable, giggly creature and subject him to **corsned,** the ordeal by bread.

According to Susan Kelz Sperling in *Poplollies and Belli-bones,* **corsned** (pronounced like *coarse Ned*) was "a medieval test to determine guilt. The accused was ordered to swallow an ounce of bread consecrated by a priest with an exorcism. If he went into convulsions he was pronounced guilty, but if he had no reaction he was proclaimed innocent."

Enough said about bread. It's time for an appetizer—otherwise known as an **opsony** (AHP-suh-nee) or **opsonium** (ahp-SOH-nee-um), any food eaten with bread as a relish.

APPETIZERS

As you make your way through the rest of this wordfeast, nibbling each verbal **viand** (VY-und, an item of food, especially a delicious one), you may want to assume a relaxed posture more suitable for intellectual ingestion. I'm referring, of course, to the act of **accubation** (AK-yoo-BAY-shin).

Accubation, as all **aristologists** (experts in the art of dining) know, is the practice of eating or drinking while lying down, usually on the belly or resting on one elbow, after the manner of the ancient Greeks and Romans (and probably a bunch of other ancient types as well). Unfortunately, in our fast-paced, fast-food-addicted times, the leisurely art of accubation has gone the way of the record player and rotary telephone. Now most people eat on the go, a practice that might be called "transitive ingestion," or to coin a single word, *agitoalimentation* (from Latin *agitare,* to move quickly, and *alimentation,* the act of providing nourishment). Today the only surviving accubators are hospital patients and couch potatoes.

You've heard of the Italian antipasto, the appetizer (often a salad with meats and cheese) eaten before the second course, which is traditionally a dish of pasta. Did you know that from *antipasto* comes an English word you can use to describe anything taken before the main course? **Antipastic** (AN-tee-PAS-tik) means pertaining to appetizers or hors d'oeuvres, or to the eating of them, as in, "Their *antipastic* indulgence left them too farctate to enjoy the rest of their meal." (**Farctate,** pronounced FARK-tayt, means stuffed, crammed to the gills.)

Here's a tip for your next romantic dinner: At the beginning of the meal, try suavely proposing a little antipastic experimentation. You never know: If the viands are tasty and the mood is right, it might lead to some intimate accubation.

Main Course

It's time now for the **bellytimber**, a delightful and unde-
servedly obsolete word meaning hearty, nourishing food. If I
were a restaurateur, I'd open a place called Bellytimber and bill
it as "the home of the **opsomaniac**, the **oligophagous**, the **gastrophile**, and the **grandgousier**." Those four grand words
describe different kinds of eaters, of which you may be one.

If you're crazy about a certain food, loving it to the point
of madness, then you're an **opsomaniac** (AHP-suh-**MAY**-nee-
ak). If you're like my daughter, who fancies meat and potatoes
but who would rather engage in geophagy than choke down a
vegetable, then you're **oligophagous** (AHL-i-**GAHF**-uh-gus),
meaning you eat only a few kinds of food. (*Geophagy* is the act
of eating dirt or clay.) If you're a **gastrophile**, you live to pamper your stomach with good food. And if you're a **grandgousier** (grahn-gooz-YAY), then your favorite meal is the
all-you-can-eat special, for the grandgousier will eat anything
and everything, especially to excess.

As you may imagine, the grandgousier is by no means the
only glutton in the language. Other grandiloquent words for
hearty eaters include **trencherman**, **gourmand**, **gormandizer**,
and **barathrum** (BAR-uh-thruhm), which has a decidedly unap-
petizing etymology.

The *barathrum* was a rocky pit outside the walls of ancient
Athens into which the dead (and occasionally live) bodies of
criminals were thrown. Later the word was applied to the
proverbial bottomless pit, hell, and eventually it came to be
used figuratively of a person like a bottomless pit—hence, a
voracious eater.

Here's a heaping plateful of words about eating and eaters:

cleptobiosis: (KLEP-toh-by-**OH**-sis) the act of plundering food.
> A late-night refrigerator raid is an act of cleptobiosis.
> *Cleptobiotic* is the adjective. See **lestobiosis** below.

edacity: (ee-DAS-i-tee) voracious appetite.
> *Edacious*, voracious, devouring, is the adjective.

fletcherize: to chew each bite of food at least thirty times; to masticate thoroughly.

This word is the gift of the language of one Horace Fletcher, a nineteenth-century American author and nutritionist who promulgated a theory of eating only when hungry (now there's a concept) and chewing one's food thoroughly before swallowing. The theory, called Fletcherism, was popularized in this grisly—or perhaps that should be gristly—bit of cautionary verse by the famous humorist and poet, Hogden Gnash:

EPITAPH FOR A HAPLESS EATER

The wretch who 'neath this tombstone lies,
With maggots feasting on his eyes,
Failed to chew his steak and fries,
And choked his way to a swift demise.

The lesson here contains no surprise:
He who eats too fast is he who dies.
So remember, all you gals and guys,
Before you swallow, fletcherize!

Especially zealous fletcherizers adhere to an even more rigorous method of mastication known as **poltophagy** (pahl-TAHF-uh-jee). This word, which comes from the Greek *poltos*, porridge, and *phagein*, to eat, pertains to the act of chewing food until it is the consistency of soup.

groak: to stare silently at a person who is eating in the hope of being given some of the food.

I'm no scientist, but I'm willing to bet there's a special gene in the chromosomes of dogs that makes them groak. Every mutt I've ever known has an uncanny proclivity for unabashed groaking. See **scaff** below.

jejunator: (JEE-juh-NAY-tur) a person who fasts.

lestobiosis: (LES-toh-by-OH-sis) the act of pilfering food.

Stealing cookies from the cookie jar is the classic act of *lestobiosis*. *Lestobiotic* is the adjective.

limosis: (ly-MOH-sis) This is the medical term for, as the *Century Dictionary* puts it, "a depraved or morbidly ravenous appetite caused by disease." See **parorexia** and **pica** below.

mellisugent: (MEL-i-SYOO-jint) honey-sucking, a word aptly applied to that roly-poly, cuddly, *mellisugent* little fellow, Winnie the Pooh.

mung: chicken feed.

nidor: (NY-dur or NY-dor) the savory aroma of cooked food, especially meat.

Nidor is a good word to use when you're hanging around the barbecue with your friends, sniffing the sialogogic odors coming from the grill. (Remember the noun *sialogogue* from the beginning of this chapter? The adjective *sialogogic*, pronounced sy-AL-uh-**GAHJ**-ik, means "promoting salivation.")

The rare adjective **nidorous** may mean "resembling the odor or flavor of cooked meat" *(Century)*, or "rankly odorous" *(Webster 2)*, or smelling of "cooked or burnt animal substances" *(OED)*. The extremely rare (but wonderful) word **nidorosity** means "eructation [belching] with the taste of undigested meat" *(Century)*. The *omophagist* (next entry) is likely to suffer from nidorosity. See **smellfeast** below.

omophagist: (oh-MAHF-uh-jist) a person who eats raw flesh.

This is a great word to use for anyone whose behavior is draconian, Machiavellian, or outright bloodsucking. For example, I once had an omophagist for a landlord—hasn't everyone? And let's not forget the other universally despised raw-flesh-ripper: the boss. The adjective is **omophagous** (oh-MAHF-uh-gus), eating raw flesh. I've seen some *omophagous* divorces, and I've attended many a family gathering punctuated by *omophagous* gossip.

parorexia: (pa-ror-REKS-ee-uh) perverted appetite; a craving for strange, offensive, or indigestible foods. Parorexia (also called *allotriophagy*, uh-LAH-tree-**AHF**-uh-jee) comprises anorexia, bulimia (byoo-LIM-ee-uh), **limosis, geophagy, phagomania, pica,** and other eating disorders.

phagomania: (FAG-oh-**MAY**-nee-uh) insatiable hunger. Also called **acoria** (uh-KOR-ee-uh).

The related word **polyphagia** (PAHL-i-**FAY**-jee-uh) means excessive or compulsive eating.

pica: (PY-kuh) In zoology (which everyone knows is pronounced *zoh*-ology, not *zoo*-ology), *Pica* designates the genus containing the magpie, a bird renowned for its rapacious nature and omnivorous appetite. In medicine, *pica* is used for a craving for unnatural or indigestible food, such as chalk, ashes, mud, paint chips, or coal. **Geophagy** (jee-AHF-uh-jee), a craving to ingest dirt or clay, is a form of pica. The adjective is **geophagous** (jee-AHF-uh-gus).

Webster 2 notes that pica occurs in human beings particularly during "hysteria, pregnancy, and insanity"—otherwise known as the three stages of parenthood or the three stages of writing a book. (Gee, no wonder I've been getting this strange urge to lick the dust off my computer keyboard.)

piddle: to pick at one's food, eat like a bird (from Swedish dialect).

Another verb, to **pingle** (from English and Scottish dialect), means to fiddle or trifle with one's food, showing little interest or appetite.

scaff: to beg or sponge food.

Scaffing is often preceded by groaking.

smellfeast: a person who has an annoying habit of dropping in uninvited at mealtimes. Another word for this type of moocher, enshrined in the great *OED*, is *lickdish*.

Among the *OED*'s citations for *smellfeast* is a 1664 quotation from the philosopher Henry More: "Like so many smell-feasts they hankered near the Altars to enjoy the nidorous fumes."

The *OED* traces *smellfeast* back to 1519, but I uncovered a much earlier citation in the prologue to *The Culinary Tales*, a piquant epic by an obscure fourteenth-century poet named Geoffrey Saucer (sometimes spelled Saucier):

> Whan that April, in hir kitchen sweete,
> Hir goode stewe hath prepared for to eate,
> And boiled it all day longe in swich licour,
> Until me tongue doth hangen down to the floore;
> Whan that the streete reeke with the soote smelle
> Inspired by the contentes of hir stewe so swelle—
> With tendre taters, carrotes, onyonne,
> Halve a cors of Ram so yonge,
> And smale fowles no longer maken melodye,
> All bubbling in hir caldron in harmonye—
> Thanne do I longen to goon by April's doore
> To aske if she needeth something from the stoore,
> And pray that blisful cooke will invyte me inne.
> Yea, I am a *smellfeast,* but is that a sinne?

snapsauce: a person who purloins food, steals the last bite when no one's looking, or crassly licks his fingers while eating.

sneeze guard: the plastic shield around a salad bar or in front of the food trays in a cafeteria line.

tachyphagia: (TAK-i-**FAY**-juh) fast eating.

xerophagy: (zeer-**AHF**-uh-jee) a diet of bread and water.

In its strict sense, *xerophagy* refers to a type of religious fast in which the *jejunator* (see above) consumes only bread, salt, water, and unseasoned vegetables.

Some Dessert?

Now that you've ingested that verbal bellytimber, here are a few **postprandial** (after-dinner) delicacies to clear your palate:

alliaceous: (AL-ee-**AY**-shus) smelling like garlic or onions.

bard: to wrap meat in strips of bacon before cooking.

basin: the small depression or dimple at the bottom of an apple, pear, or other similar fruit. The basin is opposite the stem end of the fruit.

cenatory: (SEN-uh-tor-ee) pertaining to dinner or supper. See **jentacular** below.

comestion: a devouring by fire.

    The next time you accidentally grill or broil the beef beyond recognition, instead of mumbling, "Honey, I shrunk the steak," try announcing grandly, "Sweetheart, we have achieved *comestion!*"

devorative: (de-VOR-uh-tiv) made to be swallowed without chewing, capable of being swallowed whole.

    This is the perfect word to describe an irresistibly sensual man or woman. Or you could use it for anything ingested in one great gulp: "Hank enjoyed lightweight, *devorative* thrillers"; "Andrea found algebra and geometry *devorative*, but calculus gave her plenty to chew on."

dysphagia: difficulty swallowing, a word that could readily be applied to intellectual ingestion.

graminivorous: (GRAM-i-NIV-or-us) eating grass.

jentacular: pertaining to breakfast.

lubber-wort: food without nutritive value; junk food.

MIDNIGHT SNACK

Still hungry? Want to munch on some more verbal trivia? Here's a pop quiz from the where's-the-beef department: If a vegetarian eats no meat, and a **vegan** (VEE-gin) eats no animal products in any form, what do you call a vegetarian who will eat dairy products? And what do you call a vegetarian who will eat both dairy products and eggs? Answers appear at the end of the chapter.

LEFTOVERS AND HANGOVERS

Some of my all-time favorite food words would make Emily Post retch. Heck, some of them make me gag too, but that doesn't diminish the fact that they're still great words with perfectly proper uses. They're not for the lily-livered, and some are tough to choke down, but they're worth every bite. So, follow me now down the intestinal tract of language.

Our first specimen is **inmeat,** the edible viscera (the heart, liver, kidneys, intestines, etc.) of any animal, prepared for human consumption. Next on our list of leftovers are **gubbins,** fish scraps, and **chankings** (rhymes with *spankings*), a word I am eager to rescue from the Great Dumpster of English. *Chankings* means food that you spit out—or, as *Webster 2* puts it more delicately, "pieces rejected from what is chewed," such as fish bones, gristle, seeds, pits, stems, skin, those peppercorn chunks in salami, and so on. It's been a while since I checked my Emily Post, but I don't recall her dishing out any advice on the polite disposal of chankings.

Now let's consider those bits of burnt fat and skin and meat left in your frying pan or roaster or stuck to your grill. Did you know there's a word for those scuzzy scraps? To be exact, there are at least six words, or variations on the same word: **crettins, crittens, critlings, crautings, critouns,** and **cracklings** (the form commonly used in the United States).

Some wag once said that cottage cheese was a food that looked as though it had already been eaten. The word for food that has been swallowed and partially digested is **chyme** (KYM). Specifically, *chyme* refers to food that has been subjected to gastric juices in the stomach, reduced to a semifluid mass, and expelled into the small intestine. It's something you don't want to see if you can avoid it.

Before it's time for chyme, there has to be a **bolus** (BOH-lus), a soft, round lump of chewed food ready for swallowing. *Bolus* is also used in veterinary medicine for a lump of medication or a big fat pill. And speaking of medicine, the next time you're feeling queasy or you've got the **lurgies** (LUR-geez), an English dialectal word that means, in American parlance, "the hangover blues," you'll want to stick to Alka-Seltzer or Pepto-Bismol and stay away from the **slibber-sauce,** which refers to any messy, repulsive, nauseating concoction, especially one used for medicinal purposes. As they say in that colorful California dialect known as Valleyspeak, "Gag me with a spoon."

If a disgusting dollop of slibber-sauce and a heaping plate of **maw-wallop** (badly cooked, messy food) don't make you want to toss your cookies, then your stomach is strong indeed. I doubt, however, that even the most ironclad alimentary canal or chalcenterous* grandgousier could withstand the pernicious effects of **sitotoxism** (SY-toh-**TAHKS**-iz'm), poisoning from vegetables; or of **cagmag** (KAG-mag), spoiled food, especially unwholesome or decayed meat.

Neither are the viscera immune to an occasional bout of **borborygmus** (BOR-bor-**RIG**-m<u>u</u>s), the rumbling sound of gas passing through your intestines, also known as **gurgulation.** And when borborygmi strike, how do you spell relief? In this grandiloquent guide we reach for the word **carminative** (kar-MIN-uh-tiv), which as a noun means a medication that expels gas from the bowels and as an adjective means serving to expel gas from the bowels. (A synonym for the noun is **physagogue,** pronounced FIS-uh-gahg.)

And on that excretory note, dear reader, I shall evacuate this chapter before you become **crapulent, crapulous,** or **crop-sick,** all of which mean ill from overindulgence in food or drink, or both. The chefs at La Maison Prolixe have dished up but a smidgen of all the verbal delights to be tasted in this book, and I want you to have a hearty appetite for the grandiloquent cornucopia to come.

Answers to the "Midnight Snack" Pop Quiz

lactovegetarian and **lacto-ovo-vegetarian,** respectively.

---

*Having bowels of brass (a word from chapter 1, remember?).

❖

EROTOGRAPHOMANIA*

The Hottest Highfalutin Words About Love and Sex

They give an "X" rating to flicks
Where sex is the center of kicks,
While violence and war
Are considered fit for
Small children no older than six.
—NORMAN W. STORER

This chapter contains verbally explicit adult material that may titillate your intellectual erogenous zones. Reader arousal is advised.

In naked English, that means you're about to read a bunch of highbrow smut. So slip into something more comfortable and prepare for a torrid tour of the red-light district of language.

Before we begin, let's check your prurient pulse. If it's racing with erotomaniacal expectation—in other words, if your heart is pounding with desire and you're drooling like a dog in heat—that's good. You're ready for my amorous verbal advances. However, if your libido is lagging, if you are a victim of **acedolagnia** (uh-SEE-doh-**LAG**-nee-uh), complete indiffer-

---

*__erotographomania:__ (e-RAHT-uh-GRAF-uh-**MAY**-nee-uh) a mania for writing ardent love letters, or an obsession with erotic writing.

ence to sex, or if you just can't relax and loll for a few pages in a brothelful of lascivious lex, then I must issue the following Surgeon's Genital Warning:

> If you are a person who cannot be wooed
> By a wanton and wanderlust word in the nude;
> If you are inclined to come wholly unglued
> By visions of firm, well-built words being viewed;
> And if you are not, as they say, in the mood
> For libidinous language that's masterfully spewed;
> I don't wish to be sued, or royally screwed,
> Or eschewed as a lecherous dude by some prude.
> So please, my dear reader, if you think this is lewd,
> You're free to read something less sexually imbued.

In the following pages I shall travel to the limits of lustful impropriety to teach you every word you always wanted to know about sex but were afraid to grasp. We shall begin with a brief look at different types of lovers, then proceed to disrobe various words for desire, arousal, flirtation, seduction, and the protean act of **subagitation** (SUHB-aj-i-TAY-shin, sexual intercourse). After that we will take a passing glance (or make a glancing pass) at marriage and its frequent consequence (having kids) and conclude with a button-popping peep show of sexual hang-ups, disorders, and other eccentricities.

If you indulge in a little linguistic **oculoplania** (AHK-yoo-loh-PLAY-nee-uh), the act of letting the eyes wander lustfully while assessing someone's physical charms, I am sure you will see that I have handled this ticklish topic with admirable **abrophrenia** (AB-roh-FREE-nee-uh), the graceful expression of thoughts and feelings about love or sex. In fact, I am certain that by the end of your tender tryst with this chapter you will have achieved complete verbal gratification. Then you can share the intimate pleasures of your sexy new lexicon with a **poplolly**, that special person dear to your heart—otherwise known, in pop psychological parlance, as your "significant other."

LOVERS' LANE

One of the most troublesome language problems of our sexually more aboveboard times has been finding a suitable term for a lover who is not a spouse. The problem has been further complicated by the need to find a term that embraces all forms of unmarried intimate arrangements—live-in and live-out, committed and casual, straight and gay. The expression "significant other," though cloyingly trendy, appears to fill the bill, but is it the best locution on the market? Let's see.

Some time ago the U.S. Census Bureau, in its infinite bureaucratic wisdom, came up with **POSSLQ** (PAHS'l-kyoo), an acronymic appellation that stands for "*p*erson of the *o*pposite *s*ex *s*haring *l*iving *q*uarters." The obvious problem with POSSLQ is that it fails to include same-sex couples as well as any amorously involved unmarried couples who are not living together. **Quasi-conjugal dyad** (KWAY-zy KAHN-ju-gul DY-ad), perhaps the best of many nonce-terms coined in response to the bureaucratic ineptitude of POSSLQ, does a better job of covering all the bases, but it exudes a clinical aroma, the unsavory smell of "technospeak," just as "significant other" has the rancid odor of the solipsistic self-help set.

So is there a word that isn't fuzzy or facetious or pseudosophisticated, one that can be used in the bedroom or the boardroom, over dinner with your parents or at a cocktail party with your peers? *Poplolly* (c. 1570–1850) has potential, but I admit it sounds too sweet for general use: "Jim, this is Sally, my supervisor at work. Sally, this is my . . . uh, poplolly, Jim." No way.

The most socially acceptable term I have found for an intimate companion is **amari** (ah-MAH-ree). Coined by poet Cynthia MacDonald, *amari* appears in Jack Hitt's *In a Word: A Dictionary of Words That Don't Exist but Ought To;* it combines the Greek privative prefix *a-*, not, and the Latin *maritare*, to marry (with a suggestive similarity to the Italian *amore*, love), to denote a sexual partner to whom one is not married. *Amari* may be a dark horse in the race against the ugsome "significant other," but it certainly has my bet for the better word.

Let me introduce you now to some interesting *amaries* (as I presume the plural would be formed in English), along with a few other kinds of lovers—licit, illicit, and explicit.

bedswerver: an unfaithful spouse or partner.

catamite: (KAT-uh-myt) a boy who serves or is kept as a lover by a man. *Catamite* comes from *Catamitus,* the Latin name for Ganymede, the young cup bearer to the Greek Olympian gods, and has been used in English for four hundred years.

cavalier servente: (kah-vahl-YAIR sair-VEN-tay) a married woman's lover, especially a gallant or glamorous single man who everyone knows is accompanying a married woman in public and servicing her in private. In the novel *Youngblood Hawke,* Herman Wouk writes, "He was Frieda Winter's *cavalier servente,* a young man openly attending a married woman with her husband's knowledge."

    Another foreignism for an unmarried man who is amorously and openly attentive to a married woman is **cicisbeo** (CHEE-chiz-**BAY**-oh or si-SIS-bee-oh).

concubine: (KAHNG-kyoo-byn) a woman who lives and makes love with a man to whom she is not married.

hetaera: (he-TEER-uh) In ancient Greece, a high-class mistress or concubine who consorted with men of wealth and culture; in contemporary usage, a woman who uses her physical charms to climb the social ladder.

insignificant other: someone with whom you have a short-term or an off-and-on love affair; a person you get involved with "on the rebound" or with whom you have casual, uncommitted, or indifferent sexual relations (my nonce-term).

keeperess: a woman who keeps a man, supporting him financially for the purpose of carrying on an adulterous affair. The man in this relationship is called a "kept man."

meacock: a meek or effeminate man who dotes on his wife or who is dominated by her; a henpecked husband.

nestcock: the old term for a househusband, a man who stays at home and manages the house while his wife goes to work.

ocnophile: a codependent lover; a smothering, obsessive partner.

puellaphilist: (p(y)oo-EL-uh-FIL-ist) a lover of girls.

significant udder: a person you "milk" for the transitory relief of intimate companionship, but with whom you are not interested in having a serious relationship (my nonce-term).

spoffskins: a woman with a dubious sexual history who shacks up with a man and poses as his wife.

wittol: (WIT'l) a man who meekly or tacitly accepts that his wife, the *wittee*, is committing adultery.

Everyone knows a virgin is someone who hasn't had sex, especially a woman—so is there a word that applies exclusively to a virgin man? You bet: **nullimitus** (nuh-LIM-i-tus), from the Latin *nullus*, none, and *emittere*, to send out, let loose. Literally, a nullimitus is a guy who hasn't yet let loose.

And what about the woman and man who have had lots of sex with many different partners? What do you call them? (In the age of AIDS, *stupid* comes to mind, but I digress.) A sexually promiscuous woman is a **multicipara** (MUHL-ti-SIP-uh-ruh), from the Latin *multus*, many, and *recipere*, to receive, literally "one who has received many." A sexually promiscuous man is a **multimitus** (muhl-TIM-i-tus), from *multus* and *emittere*, literally "one who has had many emissions."

ALL ABOUT DESIRE

We tend to think of the male sex as the one more prone to experience and manifest excessive sexual desire, but it's interesting to note that the voluminous *Webster 2* (1934) contains more words for unbridled lust in women.

For men, there are three words and two variants: **gynecomania** (GY-nuh-koh-MAY-nee-uh); **tentigo** (ten-TY-goh); and **satyriasis** (SAT-i-RY-uh-sis), with the variants **satyrism** (SAT-i-riz'm) and **satyromania**. For women, there are at least six discrete words: **nymphomania, andromania, clitoromania**

(KLIT-ur-oh-), **phallomania, hysteromania** (HIS-tur-oh-), and **uteromania.**

The general term for abnormally strong sexual desire, usually for a specific person, is **erotomania** (i-RAH-tuh-**MAY**-nee-uh).

Who invents these sex-crazed words? Probably a bunch of gynecomaniacal linguists fantasizing about finding an andromaniacal playmate, or maybe some eggheaded **phanero-lagniast** (FAN-ur-oh-**LAG**-nee-ast), a shrink who studies the manifestations and gradations of human lust. Your twisted guess is as good as mine. All I know is that the faceless phanerolagniasts of this world have been defining and refining the nomenclature of desire for centuries, and today there's a word for just about every form of lust and lustful behavior that you can imagine. So, grab your favorite **philter** (love potion or charm) and get ready for an unexpurgated expedition into the most exotic erotic territory in the English language.

ablutoskepsis: (uh-BLOO-toh-**SKEP**-sis) sexual excitement derived from secretly watching a person (or persons) bathing naked. See **lavacultophilia** below.

agnuopia: (AG-n(y)oo-**OH**-pee-uh) a salacious and submissive stare, the notorious come-hither look.

Take care to distinguish *agnuopia* from its homophone, *Agnewopia*, which denotes the peculiar condition in which one views the world as if through the eyes of former Vice President Spiro T. Agnew. Compare **belgard** below.

altocalciphilia: (AL-toh-KAL-si-**FIL**-ee-uh) sexual desire for a person (not necessarily a woman) wearing high heels.

anililagnia: (AN-i-li-**LAG**-nee-uh) attraction to old women.

antaphrodisiac: (ant-AF-roh-**DIZ**-ee-ak) something that reduces or inhibits sexual desire.

apodyopsis: (AP-oh-dy-**AHP**-sis) the act or habit of mentally undressing a person or fantasizing about what he or she looks like naked. Compare **gymnophoria** below.

basorexia: (BAY-zuh-**REK**-see-uh) an overwhelming desire to kiss or neck. See **philemalagnia** below.

belgard: (bel-GAHRD) a loving or longing look (from the Italian *bel guardo*).

bemascopia: (BEE-muh-SKOH-pee-uh) sexual excitement derived from observing a woman's legs as she walks or climbs steps.

brachycraspedonia: (BRAK-i-KRAS-puh-DOH-nee-uh) sexual excitement aroused by ogling women in short or tight skirts.

This lecherous limerick by Norman W. Storer displays a clever blend of bemascopia and brachycraspedonia:

> While strolling along by the Thames,
> I delight in the height of girls' hhames;
> If they were much higher,
> I'm sure I'd catch figher—
> I *do* like a shapely fhame's sthames!

brassiroregia: (bruh-ZEER-i-REE-jee-uh) salacious interest in brassieres.

cacocallia: (KAK-uh-KAL-ee-uh) the paradoxical state of being ugly but at the same time sexually desirable.

callicacia: (KAL-i-KAY-shee-uh) an amorous mental state in which the unattractive aspects of or qualities in your partner seem appealing and arousing.

cheiloproclitic: (KY-loh-proh-KLIT-ik) attracted to the lips.

chorotripsis: (KOR-oh-TRIP-sis) sexual excitement derived from body friction while dancing.

cingulomania: (SING-gyoo-loh-MAY-nee-uh) a strong desire to hold a person in your arms.

Cleopatralagnia: sexual excitement derived from watching a woman recline in the seductive manner of Cleopatra.

colpkinophilia: (kahlp-KY-nuh-FIL-ee-uh) an attraction to small-breasted women.

coxinutant: (KAHK-si-N(Y)OO-tint) having a seductive sway in the hips when walking.

cyesolagnia: (sy-EE-suh-LAG-nee-uh) attraction to pregnant women.

dishabilloerigesis: (DIS-uh-BIL-oh-er-i-JEE-sis) stripping one's clothes off seductively to arouse an observer to passion.

> My love could write a lengthy thesis,
> Full of sexy exegesis,
> On how my love for her increases
> When she performs, in bits and pieces,
> *Dishabilloerigesis.*
>
> —E. E. SQUIRMINGS

ecdemolagnia: (ek-DEE-moh-LAG-nee-uh) a condition in which one feels more hot to trot in a place other than home.

The Wizard of Oz taught us that "there's no place like home," but many couples know that a sojourn in another country or even an overnight stay in a sleazy motel can induce some extremely pleasant ecdemolagnia.

gerontolagnia: (je-RAHN-tuh-LAG-nee-uh) strong sexual desire in an older man.

gerontophilia: (je-RAHN-tuh-FIL-ee-uh) attraction to old folks.

gomphipothic: (GAHM-fi-PAH-thik) sexually excited by the sight of a lovely set of teeth.

> Those grimlipped old folks in *American Gothic*
> Seem especially dour if you're *gomphipothic.*
>
> —PHIL A. KAVATI

Gomphipothic has been traced back to an obscure thirteenth-century epic masterpiece by the unsung Italian poet Donte.

grapholagnia: (GRAF-uh-LAG-nee-uh) an urge to look at dirty pictures.

gymnocryptosis: (JIM-noh-krip-TOH-sis) telling others about your intimate sexual experiences. The word may apply to women or men, and does not necessarily imply boasting.

gymnogynomania: (JIM-noh-GY-nuh-MAY-nee-uh) the obsession of the "peeping Tom"; male voyeurism. A male voyeur is called a *gymnogynomaniac.*

gymnophoria: (JIM-noh-**FOR**-ee-uh) the sense that someone is mentally undressing you, or that a person is viewing you naked even though you are clothed. See **apodyopsis** above.

gynonudomania: (GY-noh-N(Y)OO-duh-**MAY**-nee-uh) an overwhelming urge to tear off a woman's clothes.

> A transvestite from Old Transylvania
> Would brook no *gynonudomania.*
>> He/she said, "Rip my clothes,
>> Or put runs in my hose,
> And I'll take off my spike heels and brain ya!"
>>> —FRAN C. PANTZ

gynotikolobomassophilia: (gy-NAHT-i-koh-LOH-boh-MAS-uh-**FIL**-ee-uh) a proclivity for nibbling on women's earlobes.

haptepronia: (HAP-tuh-**PROH**-nee-uh) the inclination to respond favorably to amorous advances; colloquially, the state of being hot to trot.

hirsutophilia: (hur-S(Y)OOT-uh-**FIL**-ee-uh) attraction to hairy men.

hymenorexis: (HY-men-uh-**REK**-sis) the act of deflowering a virgin—what precocious adolescent males call "devirginization."

hypnerotomachia: (HIP-nur-oh-tuh-**MAK**-ee-uh) This extremely rare word denotes something everyone at one time or another has experienced: "the struggle between sleep and sexual desire" (Norman W. Schur, *1000 Most Obscure Words*).

imparlibidinous: (im-PAHR-li-**BID**-i-nus) unequal in sexual desire.

   The word applies to a couple where one person is more ardent and eager to have sex than the other.

korophilia: (KOR-uh-**FIL**-ee-uh) attraction to young men or boys.

krukolibidinous: (KROO-koh-li-**BID**-i̯-nu̯s) crotch-watching; having one's gaze fixated on the crotch.

KRUKONFESSION

Perhaps it's the sinful forbiddenness
Of a person's most personal hiddenness
That makes me so *krukolibidinous*.
—J. ALFRED TRUESCHLOCK

lavacultophilia: (LAV-uh-KUHL-tuh-**FIL**-ee-uh) a desire to ogle people wearing bathing suits. See **ablutoskepsis** above.

libidopause: (li̯-BID-uh-pawz) the time of life when the libido wanes and interest in sex declines—i.e., either advanced age or shortly after marriage.

    Libidopause applies to both sexes. See **viripause** below.

lygerastia: (LY-jur-AS-tee-uh) the condition of those who become amorous only when the lights are low or out. (The word means literally "twilight lover.")

matronolagnia: (MAY-truh-nuh-**LAG**-nee-uh) attraction to older women, especially mature women who are married or widowed and who have borne children (i.e., matrons).

matutolagnia: (muh-T(Y)OO-tuh-**LAG**-nee-uh) an urge to have sex in the morning.

melolagnia: (MEL-uh-**LAG**-nee-uh) amorous feelings inspired by music.

nanophilia: (NAN-uh-**FIL**-ee-uh) sexual attraction to short people.

neanilagnia: (nee-AN-i̯-**LAG**-nee-uh) sexual attraction to teen-agers, also called **neanirosis.**

    Neanilagnia and *neanirosis* come from the Greek *neanikos,* youthful, and both words apply to boys or girls. For sexual attraction to teenage or pubescent girls, we have **lolitalagnia** or **lolitaphrenia** (inspired by Humbert Humbert's obsession in Vladimir Nabokov's novel, *Lolita*).

philemalagnia: (fi̯-LEE-muh-**LAG**-nee-uh) sexual excitement derived from kissing. See **basorexia** above.

prenuptiophrenia: (pree-NUP-shee-uh-**FREE**-nee-uh) in persons about to be married, the buildup of sexual excitement that precedes the wedding and consummation of the union.

> Two lovers—betrothed—in Armenia—
> Had a case of—pronounced neurasthenia.
> Before they could wed—
> They were taken to bed—
> Diagnosis:—*prenuptiophrenia*.
>   —EMILY SHTICKINSON

self-agglandize: (-uh-GLAN-dyz) to make oneself more physically attractive by artificial means such as cosmetic surgery, crash dieting, implants, weight training, or hormone treatments. (Coined by journalist Michael Globetti.)

sphallolalia: (SFAL-oh-LAY-lee-yuh) flirtatious talk that does not lead to amorous action.

sthenolagnia: (STHEN-uh-LAG-nee-uh) sexual desire aroused by witnessing an exhibition of strength or physical prowess. The word may apply to men or women.

threpterophilia: (THREP-tur-oh-FIL-ee-uh) attraction to female nurses.

tibialoconcupiscent: (TIB-ee-AY-loh-kahn-KYOO-pi-sint) having a lascivious interest in watching a woman put on stockings.

trichoerethism: (TRIK-oh-ER-uh-thiz'm) sexual excitement aroused by a person's hair.

tripsolagnophilia: (TRIP-suh-LAG-nuh-FIL-ee-uh) the desire to obtain sexual pleasure from massage.

vernorexia: (VUR-nuh-REK-see-uh) a romantic or sexually aroused mood inspired by the coming of spring; also called **vernalagnia,** and colloquially known as "spring fever."

> I always have increased desires
> Whenever I smell autumn fires.
> Winter, because it is colder,
> Often makes me a little bit bolder.
> And summer, so sticky and hot,

Makes my hormones erupt on the spot.
But in springtime I feel so much sexia,
For nothing can match *vernorexia!*
—ROBERT LEWDEST SPRINGHASPRUNG

vesthibitionism: (VES-ti-**BISH**-i-niz'm) in a woman, the flirtatious display of some portion of an undergarment—such as a bra strap, slip, garter belt, or lacy chemise or camisole—to arouse sexual interest. The pop singer (and sometime actress) Madonna has almost single-handedly made vesthibitionism a contemporary fashion phenomenon.

viricapnity: (VI-ri-**KAP**-ni-tee) the aura of virile sexuality presumed to emanate from a man who is smoking.

Not long ago, the viricapnity quotient of stars such as Humphrey Bogart, Clark Gable, William Holden, and Marlon Brando was Hollywood's stock in trade. Today, however, the man who lights up as a way to lure a lover is likely to have his lust extinguished and see his amorous aspirations go up in smoke when he is escorted not into the bedroom but out the front door.

I have been unable to find an equivalent term meaning the sexual aura surrounding a woman who is smoking, so I will coin one: **feminocapnity** (FEM-i-noh-**KAP**-ni-tee).

viripause: the time of life when a man loses interest in sex or loses the ability to perform.

I heard this word used in a report on the TV show *20/20* (February 24, 1993). To my knowledge, it has not yet been recorded in any dictionary.

ximelolagnia: (ZY-muh-luh-**LAG**-nee-uh) a desire to ogle women who are sitting with their legs crossed.

We shall close this licentious section with a peek at a few almost unutterable words for incestuous desire:

for a mother: matrolagnia (MA-truh-**LAG**-nee-uh)
for a daughter: thygatrilagnia (thy-GA-truh-**LAG**-nee-uh)
for a niece: adelphithymia (uh-DEL-fi-**THY**-mee-uh)

for a sister: adelphepothia (uh-DEL-fi-**PAH**-thee-uh) or **sorori-lagnia** (suh-ROR-i-**LAG**-nee-uh)
for a father: patrolagnia (PA-truh-**LAG**-nee-uh)
for a brother: fratrilagnia (FRA-truh-**LAG**-nee-uh) or **casi-meria** (KAS-i-**MEER**-ee-uh)
for a nephew: adelphirexia (uh-DEL-fi-**REK**-see-uh)

With all the words for forbidden fruit out there you'd think there'd be one for erotic interest in a son. Alas, though I searched high and low, all I could find was the feckless and Freudian *Jocasta complex*. Allow me, then, to offer **filiolagnia** (FIL-ee-uh-**LAG**-nee-uh), from the Latin *filius*, a son, and the Greek *lagneia*, lust.

A SOUPÇON OF SARCOLOGY

Sarcology (sahr-KAHL-uh-jee) is the study of the soft or fleshy parts of the body. It's an anatomical term, but to anyone with an ear for the erotic it fondly embraces a soft-core aspect of sexuality worthy of discussion here.

You don't have to be a softheaded sarcologist to see that the tantalizing display of tightly clad, partly clad, or occasionally unclad breasts and buttocks makes big bucks for the magazine, motion picture, and television industries. For example, where would *Sports Illustrated* be without its annual callimammapygian swimsuit issue? What would *Cosmopolitan* be without a bathy-colpian goddess gracing the cover? How much money would a romantic film make if its male lead is steatopygic, compared with one featuring the callipygian charms of stars like Robert Redford, Jeff Bridges, and Harrison Ford? And how can you possibly understand what the heck I'm talking about unless I define all these pygophilous, bustluscious words?

bathycolpian: (BATH-i-**KAHL**-pee-in) having an ample bosom with deep cleavage.
bustluscious: (exposes its meaning) having a luscious bust.

callimammapygian: (KAL-i-MAM-uh-**PIJ**-ee-in) having beautiful breasts and buttocks.

callipygian: (KAL-i-**PIJ**-ee-in) having sexy buns.

pygophilous: (py-GAHF-i-lus) bun-loving.

steatopygic: (STEE-uh-tuh-**PIJ**-ik) having a fat behind.

But back to my point: If pop culture stopped serving up a steady sarcological diet of alluring **nutarians** (women with attractively bouncing breasts) and impeccable **pygobombes** (men or women with sexy, well-rounded rumps), where would we be? Probably at the opera, watching a **megamastous** mezzo soprano wail about unrequited love with a steatopygic, barrel-chested baritone. (**Megamastous,** pronounced MEG-uh-**MAS**-tus, means Dolly Partonesque, having an extremely well-endowed bosom.)

Let's face it. No matter where you go, you're going to have somebody's flesh in your face. It's not an altogether unpleasant prospect, especially when you have a few choice sarcological terms at your command. Here are a few more words you can use to spice up a conversation with your main squeeze:

callibombe: (**KAL**-i-bahm) the state of having sexy body curves, or a person with such an attractive shape.

> I once was coolest of the Cool,
> And never once did play Love's fool.
> I had Sangfroid, I had Aplomb—
> I lost them to a *callibombe*.
> —ALEXANDER GROPE

callicolpian: (KAL-i-**KAHL**-pee-in) having beautiful breasts.

callimazonian: (KAL-i-muh-**ZOH**-nee-in) a woman with beautiful breasts.

colpocoquette: (KAHL-puh-koh-**KET**) a woman who knows she has an attractive bosom and who makes good use of its allure.

colposinquanonia: (KAHL-puh-SIN-kwah-**NOH**-nee-uh) placing the breasts above all other physical attributes in one's estimation of the attractiveness of a woman (from the Greek *kolpos,* bosom, and the Latin *sine qua non,* an indispensable thing, essential condition).

colpotantia: (KAHL-puh-**TAN**-shee-uh) the act of drawing attention to the breasts to arouse sexual interest.

glutolatrous: (gloo-**TAHL**-uh-tr<u>u</u>s) worshiping the buttocks. The glutolatrous person loves anything *natiform* (NAY-t<u>i</u>-form), resembling the buttocks.

mammaquatia: (MAM-uh-**KWAY**-shee-uh) the bobbing or jiggling of a woman's breasts when she walks, dances, or exercises.

mazotropism: (MAY-zuh-**TROHP**-iz'm) the ability of a woman's breasts to turn heads.

quatopygia: (KWAY-tuh-**PIJ**-ee-uh) shaking one's booty.

schizoscopia: (SKIT-suh-**SKOH**-pee-uh) the act of leering surreptitiously at a woman's exposed cleavage.

To amply round out this section on sarcology, here is one more word of bathycolpian proportions: **poitrinographia** (POY-tr<u>i</u>-noh-**GRAF**-ee-uh), an inordinate interest in writing about breasts.

> If your lover's a poet with *poitrinographia,*
> He'll only be able to write about half a ya.
> —Ophelia Derriere

LET'S HAVE LEX

Now that you've had an opportunity to ogle and pet a haremful of flirtatious language, I trust you are sufficiently aroused to forgo further verbal foreplay. In short, it's time to hit the hifa-lutin hay and make word whoopee.

Below you will find a pantload of preposterously precise terms for **cubicular** (in the bedroom) and extracubicular activity. Like the words you've courted thus far, most are polysyllabic *objets d'amour* from Latin and Greek. But of course you already know that in this book, love is a many-syllabled thing.

Here, before your naked eyes, are the grandest grandiloquent gems of coital engagement—diamonds in the buff:

acokoinonia: (AK-oh-koy-**NOH**-nee-uh) sex without passion or desire.

> The insensitive lovers I've knownia
> Might as well have had sex all alonia.
> What is love if it's *acokoinonia?*
> Lots of grunts, but not one single groania.
> —ANAÏS NUMB

acritition: (AK-ri-**TISH**-un) sex without orgasm.

agonophilia: (AG-ahn-uh-**FIL**-ee-uh) in a man, a preference for lovemaking in which the woman pretends to struggle before acquiescing to sexual intercourse.

allomulcia: (AL-uh-**MUHL**-see-uh) the act of imagining during sex that your partner is another, more desirable person.

amomaxia: (AM-uh-**MAKS**-see-uh) lovemaking in a parked car.

amychesis: (AM-i-**KEE**-sis) the involuntary act of scratching or clawing your partner in the heat of passion; also called **chelonia** (ki-**LOH**-nee-uh).

anthorexia: (AN-thuh-**REK**-see-uh) the act of setting a romantic mood (with flowers, a candlelight dinner, etc.).

artamesia: (AHR-tuh-**MEEZ**-ee-uh) incomplete sexual gratification caused when your partner reaches the peak of pleasure too fast.

brachycubia: (BRAK-i-**K(Y)OO**-bee-uh) a swiftly executed bout of coitus, short but not necessarily sweet. The old slang term for this is a "dog's match."

cataglottism: (KAT-uh-**GLAHT**-iz'm) a tongue-kiss.

coitobalnism: (KOH-i-toh-**BAL**-niz'm) sex in the bath or shower.

coitus diurnus: sex during the day.

coitus nocturnus: sex at night.

coitus pergratus: mutually gratifying sex. Also called **deupa-reunia** (D(Y)OO-pa-**ROO**-nee-uh). See **meupareunia** below.

coitus sordidus: sex for money.

copulescence: (KAHP-yoo-**LES**-ints) the afterglow of successful sex (coined by writer and word maven Lewis Burke Frumkes).

dasofallation: (DAS-oh-fuh-**LAY**-shin) sex in the woods.

dermagraphism: (DUR-muh-**GRAF**-iz'm) the practice, common among adolescents, of creating livid marks or bruises on the skin (colloquially called *hickeys* or *love bites*) while engaged in an ardent necking session.

In medical jargon, the hickey is called a "passion purpura." The fervent form of necking in which kissers inflict their brutal love bites is aptly called **vampirophilemia** (vam-PY-roh-fi-**LEE**-mee-uh).

deuterition: (D(Y)OO-tur-**ISH**'n) a second round of sexual intercourse. See **lagnodomnia** below.

discinctophilia: (di-SINGK-tuh-**FIL**-ee-uh) a preference for partial nudity during sex—or a preference for being partly dressed, if you prefer the glass half full.

fawnicate: to fondle or caress.

lagnodomnia: (LAG-nuh-**DAHM**-nee-uh) delaying orgasm until your partner has achieved gratification.

> If *lagnodomnia*
> Gives you insomnia,
> Then make it your mission
> To perform *deuterition*.
> —JOHN HALF-DONNE

lagnolysis: (lag-NAHL-uh-sis) thorough release of sexual tension.

meupareunia: (M(Y)OO-pa-**ROO**-nee-uh) sex that gratifies only one partner.

orthostatic coitus: sex performed standing up.

paneunia: (pan-YOON-ee-uh) sexual promiscuity; the wanton pursuit of sexual gratification.

philematology: (fi-LEE-muh-**TAHL**-uh-jee) the art of kissing.

polyvaleur: (PAH-lee-vuh-**LUR**) a man who can have sex several times a night or have more than one orgasm during sexual intercourse. See **univaleur** below.

recumbofavia: (ri-KUHM-boh-**FAY**-vee-uh) a preference for having sex while lying down.

sphalmorgasmy: (SFAL-mor-GAZ-mee) The *Lecher's Lexicon* defines this word as "an incomplete or otherwise unsatisfactory orgasm" (from the Greek *sphalma*, frustration, and *orgasm*).

Sphalmorgasmy reminds me of the time I saw a computer philosophize about love. In the early 1980s, when personal computers were just beginning to boom, I had the opportunity to review one of the first computerized thesaurus programs. It was an unwieldy, woefully uncomprehensive beast compared with the instant synonymic gratification available today. You typed in the word you wanted synonyms for—*erudite,* for example—and if it wasn't a keyword in the database, the computer would display a message like this: " 'ERUDITE' NOT FOUND. SHOULD BE BETWEEN 'ERROR' AND 'ERUPT.' "

After monkeying with the program for a while I became irritated because it seemed that every other word I entered generated an "*X* not found, should be between *Y* and *Z*" response. Finally, exasperated, I typed in the word *fuck*. To my astonishment—and I am not kidding you here—the computer shot back with this amazing apothegm: " 'FUCK' NOT FOUND. SHOULD BE BETWEEN 'FRUSTRATE' AND 'FULFILL.' "

succubovalent: (suh-KYOO-boh-**VAY**-lent) able to have sex only when lying beneath your partner.

synorgasmia: (SIN-or-**GAZ**-mee-uh) simultaneous orgasm.

> Who says sex has no razzamatazzmia?
> Have you ever achieved *synorgasmia?*
> —ELECTRA FRIED

timotrudia: (TIM-uh-**TROO**-dee-uh) sexual timidity or bash-
    fulness.

typhlobasia: (TIF-luh-**BAY**-zee-uh) kissing with the eyes closed.

univaleur: (YOO-nee-vuh-**LUR**) a man who can have sex only
    once a night (or day) or who has one orgasm per encounter.

xeronisus: (ZEER-uh-**NY**-sus) unsatisfactory sexual inter-
    course due to the inability to reach orgasm.

FIRST COMES LOVE, THEN COMES MARRIAGE . . .

Most people use the word *nubile* (N(Y)OO-bil) to describe a
young woman with a sexually attractive, well-developed figure.
("*His jaw dropped to his drawers at the sight of her naked, nubile
body splayed across the bed.*"—Danielle Squeel.) Dictionaries
duly note this sensual sense, but the traditional meaning, which
you will also find in any dictionary, is ready to wed, sexually
mature, and of an appropriate age to marry.

    Is there an equivalent term for a young man? You bet.
Viripotent (vi-RIP-uh-tint), from the Latin *vir,* man, and
potent, means able to copulate with a woman—hence, in the
mores of yore, ready to marry. Since the 1500s the word has
also been used as a synonym for *nubile;* in this sense, a *viripotent* woman is mature enough to have sex with (and therefore
marry) a man.

    When a nubile young woman and a viripotent young
man fall in love and decide to marry, they usually enter into
that obligation trusting that neither partner will prove to be a
bedswerver who commits **spousebreach.** That's the old (and
far more expressive) term for adultery, which to my ear
sounds as if it means "something only adults do," which I
suppose it is.

    Once wed, our once-nubile-and-viripotent lovers should
hope their union is not **sexogamy** (seks-AHG-uh-mee), a marriage founded only on sexual attraction, or worse, **agenobiosis**
(AJ-uh-noh-by-**OH**-sis), a sexless marriage. Such troubled cou-
plings often lead to **diasteunia** (DY-uh-**ST(Y)OO**-nee-uh), the

practice of sleeping in separate beds, and a severe case of **cagamosis** (KAG-uh-**MOH**-sis), marital unhappiness.

All of these problems can be avoided, of course, if you remain an **agamist** (AG-uh-mist), an unmarried person. But if you're not sure you want to stay single, and assuming you are not afflicted with **misogamy** (mis-AHG-uh-mee), aversion to marriage, don't worry. You can always change your mind and experience all those marvelous marital woes at an advanced age by opting for **opsigamy** (ahp-SIG-uh-mee), tying the knot late in life.

At whatever age you decide to marry or cohabit, the predominant question is, how do you select your mate? If it's by **geneclexis** (JEN-i-**KLEK**-sis), then you are making your selection solely on the basis of physical appearance, without regard for intellect or character. The opposite practice, that of selecting a partner based on intelligence and character without regard for physical attractiveness, is called **noeclexis** (NOH-i-**KLEK**-sis).

If you can't find a suitable partner, before you get desperate and go on *Love Connection* you can consult a **proxenete** (PRAHK-suh-neet), a professional matchmaker—or, in the parlance of today's mating ways, a dating service.

Whatever you do to locate your lifemate, here's hoping it results in **homogamosis** (HOH-moh-ga-**MOH**-sis), a marriage between well-matched persons, as opposed to **heterogamosis** (HET-ur-oh-ga-**MOH**-sis), a marriage in which the partners are grossly incompatible.

Another factor to consider in selecting your spouse is class—or as we say today, upward or downward mobility. If you aspire to **hypergamy** (hy-PUR-guh-mee), then you want to marry someone at or above your social station. If you don't care what the Joneses think, then it won't bother you if your union is **morganatic** (MOR-guh-**NAT**-ik), with a person from a lower class. Historically, *morganatic* refers to a marriage between a member of the nobility and a commoner in which the aristocrat's titles and property cannot be inherited by the ignoble spouse or the half-noble, half-common offspring. Finally, if you're so downtrodden that anything looks like up, you can opt for a **Westminster wedding,** a match between a whore and a rogue.

Whether you marry up, down, laterally, or collaterally (which in one of its senses means of the same stock but from a different family line—for example, a first or second cousin), once you're hitched you'll have to find a place to **nidificate** (NID-i-fi-kayt), build a little nest.

Young newlyweds who are setting up shop have always had to make ends meet on a slender budget, but with today's ever-tightening domestic belts there has been a modest revival of an old custom from our pre-urbanized, agricultural days: **matrilocal** marriages, where the couple lives with the wife's parents, and **patrilocal** marriages, where they live with the husband's parents.

Residing matrilocally or patrilocally has its drawbacks, however, and may lead to serious hang-ups like **agrexophrenia** (uh-GREKS-uh-FREE-nee-uh), the inability to have sex because you fear someone is nearby and may overhear you, and **soceraphobia** (SOH-sur-uh-FOH-bee-uh), aversion to your in-laws. So count your blessings if you and your mate can manage to dwell **superextraparentalocally,** my nonce-term for "as far away from one's parents as possible."

Here are some more marital words worth wedding to your brain:

alphamegamia: (AL-fuh-muh-GAM-ee-uh) marriage between a young woman and an older man.

Isonogamia (EYE-suh-nuh-GAM-ee-uh) denotes the most common matchup—between persons of the same or almost the same age. **Anisonogamia** (an-EYE-suh-nuh-GAM-ee-uh) and **dysonogamia** (DIS-uh-nuh-GAM-ee-uh) both denote marriage between persons of unequal age, especially when there is a considerable age difference.

I'm dismayed there doesn't seem to be a word for marriage between an older woman and a young man, so I shall propose **anilojuvenogamy** (AN-i-loh-JOO-vin-AHG-uh-mee), formed from the Latin *anilis*, pertaining to an old woman, *juvenis,* a young man, and Greek -*gamy,* marriage.

aterpsist: (ay-TURP-sist) someone who believes in having sex only for the purpose of producing offspring.

azygophrenia: (AZ-i-guh- or uh-ZY-guh-FREE-nee-uh) a neurotic condition brought on by living a lonely single life.

digamy: (DIG-uh-mee) a legal second marriage, after divorce or after one's spouse has died, also called **deuterogamy** (D(Y)OO-tur-**AHG**-uh-mee).

> After the familiar *bigamy* come **trigamy** (TRIG-uh-mee), marriage to three persons at once or a third marriage, and **quadrigamy** (kwah-DRIG-uh-mee), marriage to four persons at the same time or a fourth marriage.

exogamy: (eks-AHG-uh-mee) marriage outside one's social group.

> Examples of *exogamy* include interfaith and interracial marriages—the latter also known by the pejorative term **miscegenation** (mi-SEJ-i-NAY-shin). Marriage within one's social group is called **endogamy** (en-DAHG-uh-mee).

gamomania: (GAM-uh-MAY-nee-uh) an urge to make outrageous or extravagant proposals of marriage.

levirate: (LEV-ur-it) the marriage of a woman to her husband's brother (also called **leviration**). See **sororate** below.

mariticide: (muh-RIT-i-syd) the murder of a husband by his wife. See **uxoricide** below.

maritodespotism: (MAR-i-toh-DES-puh-tiz'm) ruthless, tyrannical behavior in a husband. The corresponding adjective is **maritodespotic.** See **uxorodespotism** below.

maritorious: (MA-ri-TOR-ee-us) excessively devoted to a husband, especially in a self-effacing or submissive way. See **uxorious** below.

monandry: (muh-NAN-dree) the practice of having one husband at a time.

> Women who are **monandric** (muh-NAN-drik) are also known as *chronic wedbetters* They follow the advice of Mark Twain, who said, "I make it a point not to smoke more than one cigar at a time."

opsimatria: (AHP-si-MAY-tree-uh) the bearing of a child late in a woman's life.

Opsimatria is on the rise among professional women, who often delay having a baby until they are well into their thirties. The corresponding term is **opsipatria** (AHP-si-PAY-tree-uh), the siring of a child by an elderly man.

pantagamy: (pan-TAG-uh-mee) literally, marriage to all; the doctrine that every man is married to every woman, and vice versa. Another word for this is **cenogamy** (si-NAHG-uh-mee), communal marriage.

polyandry: (PAHL-ee-AN-dree) marriage to several men, or having several male lovers, at the same time.

polyapopemptic: (PAH-lee-AP-uh-PEMP-tik) my nonce-word for "many times divorced" (from poly-, many, and apopemptic, pertaining to a departure, bidding farewell, valedictory).

polygyny: (pah-LIJ-i-nee) marriage to several women, or having several female lovers, at the same time.

sororate: (suh-ROR-it) the marriage of a man to his wife's sister.

uxoricide: (uks-OR-i-syd) the murder of a wife by her husband.

uxorious: (uks-OR-ee-us) excessively devoted to a wife, especially in a self-effacing or submissive way.

uxorodespotism: (uk-SOR-oh-DES-puh-tiz'm) wifely tyranny, domination of a husband by a wife. The corresponding adjective is **uxorodespotic.**

Oikonisus (oy-KAHN-i-sus), the desire to start a family, is an affliction that affects both women and men. The victims of oikonisus, being childless, can conceive only of the joys of parenthood and are blissfully unaware that as parents they will spend approximately the next two decades in a sleep-deprived, anxiety-driven daze, helplessly wringing their hands and saying "Stop that!" "Be careful!" and "No!" about 12 billion times.

If a woman has a strong desire to have a baby, her condition is called **nepiomania** (NEP-ee-uh-MAY-nee-uh). If that desire is fulfilled, it will lead either to **eutocia** (yoo-TOH-shee-uh), normal or easy childbirth, or **dystocia** (dis-TOH-shee-uh), difficult or abnormal childbirth.

Let's hope it's eutocia; however, if it's dystocia, don't despair, for not long after childbirth most women are blessed with **parturient** (pahr-CHOOR-ee-int) **amnesia,** the act of forgetting, or the ability to forget, the pain of labor and delivery. Parturient amnesia is the oblivion that preserves our species, for without it, how many women would choose to have another child? Probably about as many as there'd be men who'd volunteer for a second round of torture on the rack.

Whether you experience eutocia or dystocia—and fathers can do so vicariously—the first time you hold that newborn babe in your arms you'll probably be overwhelmed by **philoprogeneity** (FIL-oh-PROH-ji-NEE-i-tee), love for your offspring, also known by the simpler word **storge** (STOR-jee), the instinctive affection or natural love that parents have for their children. And it doesn't make much difference whether you and your partner in procreation are **arrhenotokous** (AR-e-NAHT-uh-kus), blessed with only boys, **thelyotokous** (THEL-ee-AHT-uh-kus), blessed with only girls, or **ampherotokous** (AM-fur-AHT-uh-kus), blessed with both boys and girls. For as the ancient Roman pediatrician and poet N. Loco Parentis tells us,

> When you have a little one,
> Or maybe two or three,
> All that matters, all that counts,
> Is good *pedotrophy*.

As you probably inferred, **pedotrophy** (pe-DAH-truh-fee) is the art of rearing children properly.

Hang-ups and Other Eccentricities

Are you ready for a slightly twisted tour of the seamier side of sex? You won't need any special paraphernalia for this excursion into perversion, but it wouldn't hurt to have an extra dose of

paraphilia (PAR-uh-**FIL**-ee-uh), a preoccupation with unusual or abnormal sexual practices. You never know—you might find some unspeakable proclivity of your own along the way.

Follow me now down the primrose path, and watch your prurient step!

aischrolatreia: (EYE-skroh-luh-**TRY**-uh) worship of obscenity, love of smut or filth.

anorchous: (an-ORK-us) devoid or deprived of testicles.

This word could be used to great effect to describe any man who, in colloquial lingo, "has no balls."

brassirothesauriast: (bruh-ZEER-oh-thuh-**SAW**-ree-ast) a person who collects brassieres or pictures of women wearing them.

cypripareuniaphile: (SIP-ri-puh-**ROO**-nee-uh-fyl) a lover of prostitutes. Also called a *philopornist*.

I discovered this deviant bit of *sesquipedalia verba* in a limerick by Willard R. Espy that appears in *Say It My Way:*

> Said a hooker who works out of Niles,
> "Cypripareuniaphiles
>   Are easy to please—
>   They'll pay for a squeeze,
> And double for pinches or smiles."

cryptovestiphilia: (KRIP-toh-VES-ti-**FIL**-ee-uh) a fetish for women's underwear.

The redoubtable word **melcryptovestimentaphilia** (hang on to your drawers, here comes the pronunciation: mel-KRIP-toh-VES-ti-MEN-tuh-**FIL**-ee-uh) denotes a penchant for women's black undergarments.

ecdysiophile: (ek-DIZ-ee-uh-fyl) a person who frequents strip joints or likes to watch women or men strip.

The more familiar word **ecdysiast** (ek-DIZ-ee-ast), coined by H. L. Mencken in 1940, denotes the person who strips.

ectovalent: (EK-toh-**VAY**-lint) capable of having sex only in a place other than home.

eleutherophilist: (i-LOO-thur-**AHF**-uh-list) someone who advocates free love.

erastophiliac: (i-RAS-tuh-**FIL**-ee-ak) a person obsessed with meddling in and gossiping about the sexual lives of others.

eunoterpsia: (YOO-noh-**TURP**-see-uh) the doctrine that pursuing sexual pleasure is the chief goal of life.

faunoiphilia: (FAW-noy-**FIL**-ee-uh) an abnormal desire to watch animals copulate.

    Sexual arousal derived from watching animals copulate is called **zooeroticism** (ZOH-oh-i-**RAH**-ti-siz'm). **Zooerastia** (ZOH-oh-i-**RAS**-tee-uh) is sexual intercourse with an animal.

frottage: (fraw-TAHZH) sexual excitement or gratification derived from rubbing one's body against another person, typically in a crowded public conveyance such as an elevator, bus, or train.

    A man who engages in this practice is called a **frotteur** (fraw-TUR); a woman who does so is called a **fricatrice** (FRIK-uh-tris). Another term for this behavior is **medotripsis** (MED-oh-**TRIP**-sis).

gymnopædic: (JIM-noh-**PEE**-dik) of or pertaining to naked boys.

    Historically this word applies, says the *Century Dictionary* (1914), to ancient Greek "dances and gymnastic exercises performed, as at public festivals, by boys or youths unclothed." The festivals where this naked dancing took place and the dancing itself were known as **gymnopædia** (JIM-noh-**PEE**-dee-uh).

    The Greeks had another titillating form of **terpsichore** (turp-SIK-uh-ree), dancing. The **cordax** (KOR-daks) was a chorus dance "of wanton character," says the genteel *Century*. The **cordactes** (kor-DAK-teez) were performed by wild, drunken, nude dancers as part of the annual Bacchanalia, an orgiastic feast in honor of Bacchus, the Greek god of wine.

gynecomastia: the abnormal development of breasts in a male.

hemerotism: (HEM-uh-ruh-tiz'm) sexual daydreaming.

libidacoria: (li-BID-uh-**KOR**-ee-uh) uncontrollable sexual desire in a man or woman that knows no satisfaction, no matter how often the afflicted person indulges in sex.

mageira: (muh-JY-ruh) sublimation of sexual desire or feelings of sexual inadequacy through the act of cooking.

martymachlia: (MAHR-ti-**MAK**-lee-uh) a form of exhibitionism in which a person wants to make love in front of other people. The word may apply to men or women.

maschalagnia: (MAS-kuh-**LAG**-nee-uh) a fetish for armpits.

mastilagnia: (MAS-ti-**LAG**-nee-uh) sexual pleasure derived from being whipped.

merkin: a hairpiece for the pudendum; toupee of Venus.

mixoscopy: (miks-AHS-kuh-pee) the act of secretly watching others have sex.

ozoamblyrosis: (OH-zoh-AM-bli-**ROH**-sis) loss of sexual appetite because your partner has wicked B.O.

> Love is not a bed of roses,
> Perhaps because we all have noses.
> Love's urge can choke on halitosis
> And die from ozoamblyrosis.
> —EUREKA FOWLER

The related word **halitalagnia** (HAL-i-tuh-**LAG**-nee-uh) denotes the unfortunate state of being turned off during lovemaking by your partner's bad breath.

paphian: (PAY-fee-in) pertaining to illicit love or wanton sex.

pederosis: (PED-uh-**ROH**-sis) sexual abuse of a girl.

When a man sexually abuses a boy, it's called *pederasty,* and when a man or woman sexually abuses a girl, it's known as *pederosis.* The sick state of mind in which a person lusts after children, boys or girls, is called **pederotosis** (PED-ur-uh-**TOH**-sis).

peotomy: (pee-AHT-uh-mee) what Lorena Bobbitt performed on her ex-husband; i.e., amputation of the penis.

pubephilia: (PYOO-buh-**FIL**-ee-uh) erotic interest in pubic hair.

renifleur: (ren-i-FLUR) a person who gets turned on by odors, especially body odors, and especially, notes Richard A. Spears in *Slang and Euphemism*, by the smell of someone else's urine.

Renifleur, which comes from the French and means literally "a person who sniffs," is a psychiatric term. There are three other technical terms for sexual stimulation produced by a smell, whether pleasant or repulsive: **olfactolagnia** (ahl-FAK-tuh-**LAG**-nee-uh), **osmolagnia** (AHS- or AHZ-muh-**LAG**-nee-uh), and **osphresiolagnia** (ahs-FREE-zee-uh-**LAG**-nee-uh).

sacofricosis: (SAK-oh-fri-**KOH**-sis) the practice of surreptitiously or absentmindedly fiddling with your genitalia through your pants pockets.

Among hormonally hyperactive adolescent boys, this diversion is commonly referred to as "playing pocket pool."

scopophiliac: (SKOH-poh-**FIL**-ee-ak) a person who gets sexual pleasure from looking at erotic pictures or spying on naked or scantily clad people. *Scopophilia* is the act of getting one's kicks from doing this.

The related word **gymnothesaurist** (JIM-noh-thuh-**SAW**-rist) denotes someone who collects pictures of partly clothed women or men.

sexotropic: (SEKS-uh-**TRAHP**-ik) constantly thinking about sex.

syndyasmia: (SIN-dy-**AZ**-mee-uh) the technical term for an "open marriage" or "open relationship" where each partner is free to have sex (and in some cases cohabit) with other people. *Syndyasmian* is the adjective.

tragolimia: (TRAY-guh-**LIM**-ee-uh) in a man, an overwhelming and indiscriminate urge to have sex with any woman, regardless of her looks or age.

vincilagnia: (VIN-si-**LAG**-nee-uh) having or wanting to have sex with a partner who has been tied up or chained.

volumptuous: grossly overweight after having once been attractively buxom (coined by writer and editor Colin Harrison).

Often, due to fad-dieting, a person will vacillate

between voluptuousness and volumptuousness. Contemporary celebrities who fall into this category include Liz Taylor, Delta Burke, and Oprah Winfrey.

AFTERPLAY

It's time now to wind down from all this linguistic rapture with some verbal afterplay. Try answering these sexy questions:

Have you ever been someplace where there were few or no men—a convent, for example? How about a place where there were few or no women—say, the Dallas Cowboys' locker room? Did you know there are specific words for such sexual scarcities? **Spaneria** (span-EER-ee-uh) means a dearth of men, and **spanogyny** (span-AHJ-i-nee) means a dearth of women.

Have you ever witnessed a public display of **genitojacosis** (JEN-i-toh-ja-KOH-sis)? If you've had your eyes open at any time since the 1950s, there's no way you could have missed it. *Genitojacosis* is a sexually suggestive thrusting of the hips. It's a standard maneuver among ecdysiasts (striptease artists) and erotic dancers that has also been used with unabashed effectiveness by numerous pop music stars such as Elvis Presley, Mick Jagger, Michael Jackson, Madonna, and Beyonce.

If menopause is the time in a woman's life when menstruation ceases, what's the word for the time in her life during which she is menstruating? It's **menacme** (muh-NAK-mee). How about the time when she begins menstruating? That's **menarche** (muh-NAHR-kee). And what about the time before a girl or boy reaches puberty? No, I'm not going to let you get away with calling that childhood. In this grandiloquent guide, it's **impuberty**.

Have you ever seen Adam and Eve depicted without their **antipudic** (AN-ti-PYOO-dik) attire? Unless you happen to be into obscure biblical smut, I doubt it. Adam and Eve *sans* antipudic attire would be wearing their birthday suits, *sans* fig leaves, for *antipudic* means "serving to cover the private parts."

(By the way, the word for a fig leaf used to cover the genitalia is **thrion,** pronounced like *three on.*)

Okay, now it's time for true confessions. Remember the word *krukolibidinous?* It means "crotch-watching." With that as your clue, answer me truthfully: Have you ever assessed someone's **medectasia** (MED-ek-**TAY**-zhee-uh)? If so, then you have ogled a man's crotch, for *medectasia* means the bulge in the crotch created by a man's privates, as seen through whatever item of clothing happens to cover the area at the moment.

Finally, have you ever (and I'll admit that I have on not a few occasions) looked at a lissome magazine model sporting a French-cut bikini or scanty lingerie and marveled at her perfect pubic depilation? There's not a hair in sight! Of course, as I've marveled I've also wondered whether there was a word for that **glabrous** (GLAB-r̲u̲s̲, smooth and hairless) genital state. Luckily, before I pulled out my own hair, I found it: **acomovulvate** (uh-KOH-moh-**VUHL**-vayt). This sleek word combines *acomia* (uh-KOH-mee-uh), baldness, and *vulva* to describe the condition of a woman who has no hair (or at least no visible hair) in her genital area.

And with those bald remarks, dear reader, it's time to recover our antipudic attire and re-cover our private parts. For we must proceed now to our next grandiloquent lesson in life—a subject in polar opposition to love and lovemaking, but one almost as dear to my heart.

❖

CHAPTER FOUR

BILLINGSGATE 101

When You'd Rather Flite Than Fight

> There is nothing that's quite so delicious
> As a quip that is perfectly vicious.
>   I've always exulted
>   When someone's insulted—
> Who needs sex when you can be malicious?
> —G. B. PSHAW

Are you a **breedbate,** someone who likes to start arguments or stir up quarrels? Are you also **maledicent** (MAL-e-DY-sint), addicted to vicious, abusive speech? If you answered yes to those questions—or more pertinently, "Yes, you **sebaceous, ophiophagous clodpate**"*—then you've come to the right chapter. Herein you will find more than enough virulent verbal ammunition to use the next time you choose to flite rather than fight.

To **flite** (also spelled *flyte*) means to quarrel or brawl in words, and the noun **fliting,** according to *Webster 2,* refers to "an exchange of invective, abuse, or mockery," especially one "set forth in verse between two poets."

---

*Translation: *sebaceous* (suh-BAY-shus), slimy, oozing fat or grease; *ophiophagous* (AHF-ee-AHF-uh-gus), snake-eating; *clodpate,* a combination of a clod and a blockhead.

Poets trashing each other? I might actually pay to see that. Better yet, why limit it to poets? Can't you imagine a TV show called *Fliting for Your Life* where celebrities and comics put each other down and cut each other up? Just think of the potential matchups! There's no doubt about it: A show featuring a vicious mix of highbrow slander, middlebrow mudslinging, and lowbrow "Yo' mama" contests would dominate the Nielsens.

But let's step back for a moment to the sixteenth century when, for some obscure reason, public fliting sessions among Scottish poets became a popular pastime. Why did they do it? Maybe the poets back then were so woefully unpublished and underemployed (my, how things haven't changed) that they resorted to vilifying each other to gain notoriety. Describing those duels of derision, Sir Walter Scott wrote that "flytings consisted of alternate torrents of sheer **billingsgate** poured upon each other by the combatants."

Every budding breedbate who aspires to flite and hopes to master the ungentle art of disparagement and defamation should have a thorough knowledge of *billingsgate,* obscene and abusive language. The word comes from the name of an old fish market in London infamous for foul-mouthed characters whose manner of conversing apparently was more malodorous than the merchandise.

Long before billingsgate and the feisty flitings of the Scots there was a form of lewd, abusive jesting known as **Fescennine verses** (FES-uh-nin or FES-uh-nyn). This coarse brand of poesy originated in the Etruscan city of Fescennia and later became popular in Rome. According to the *Century Dictionary,* Fescennine verses were "of a personal character, extemporized by performers at merry-meetings, to amuse the audience." The *Columbia Encyclopedia,* third edition, calls them "ancient Italian doggerel lines, bantering and scurrilous, originally chanted at rustic festivals—perhaps to avert the evil eye."

Could Fescennine verses be the rhetorical mother of all modern ribaldry? It's tempting to think so. One thing I'm sure of, though, is that the ancient Italian penchant for poetic irreverence lives on in two fine English words: the adjective **fescen-nine**, obscene, licentious, scurrilous, and the noun **fescenninity** (FES-uh-**NIN**-i-tee), that which profanes or provokes.

And now, with that preamble out of the way, it's time for Billingsgate 101—the course that will transform you from a dreary, dunderheaded reader into a venom-spewing virtuoso of **opprobrious, calumnious, vituperative, thersitical,** and **vilipendious** (read "insulting and abusive") English words.

Surly General Warning: If you are faint of heart, if you were brought up to speak well of others regardless of how much you detest them, or if the subject of insolent speech leaves you **mopsical** (having a dopey, idiotic expression on your face—rhymes with *Popsicle*), then I advise you to take this book back to where you bought it and demand to pay for it again.

A PIE FOR AN EYE

Imagine yourself confronting the object of your contempt. You utter the rhetorical question, "You know what *you* are?" and the object of your contempt, being contemptible as always, sneers back, "No, what *am* I?" How do you follow up?

Unfortunately, most people, on account of their deficient vocabularies, would splutter a vulgar expletive that would result in a punch in the nose or a spot in the unemployment line. Obviously that won't do for you. Your goal is not to get beat up or booted out the door, but to live to flite another day. You want to nonplus your opponent with the most colorful and inscrutable words possible. You want your abusive banter to baffle and bewilder. For then, when your poor victim's jaw drops in mopsical astonishment, you can **geck** (toss your head with scornful pride) and stride away triumphant.

Geck (an old Scottish dialectal word) is also a useful noun meaning an expression or gesture of scorn or contempt. The perfect geck, of course, is one that will **dilacerate** (di-LAS-ur-ayt) or **dilaniate** (di-LAY-nee-ayt) your adversary, tear him to pieces or rip her to shreds. If you want to earn your B.A. in billingsgate, your doctorate in denigration, and become a grand master of the grandiloquent geck, the first lesson you must learn is how to attack the person you wish to put down. As the ancient Roman philosopher E. Coli advised in his saber-toothed treatise on affrontery, *Par Pari Refero* ("tit for tat"),

> *Lex talionis* is the law of the pack:
> When you are hurt, you must hurt back.
> To frustrate your enemies when you're attacked,
> Mock how they look, what they are, how they act.

SLOBS AND FOPS

What would you call the guy who wears socks that don't match, who always has a shirttail hanging out, who picks his nose at the dinner table, and whose hair looks matted and greasy even after a shower? This sloppy fellow is known as a **grod.** And what about his female counterpart—the woman who looks as if she combed her hair sometime last week, whose purse is overflowing with gum wrappers and used tissues, and who always has chipped nail polish and a run in her stocking the size of the Mississippi River? She's a **groddess,** of course.

Cleanliness may be next to godliness, but the squalid world is teeming with all manner of grods and groddesses just waiting for you to mop them up and take them to the cleaners. Here are some "dirty" words to describe the draggle-tailed people you know:

beagle: a man who dresses oddly or grotesquely.
callet: a drab, untidy woman.
dratchell: a slovenly, lazy woman.
drazel: (DRAZ'l) or **drossel** (DRAHS'l): a filthy, vagrant slut.
feague: (rhymes with *league*) a dirty, lazy man.
jeeter: a rude, uncouth slob.

muck-scutcheon: a filthy, bedraggled person.
shabbaroon: a poorly dressed fellow.
slammock (or **slummock**): an awkward slob.
slattern: a slovenly woman or girl; also, a prostitute.
slubberdegullion: a boorish, contemptible slob.
tatterdemalion: (TAT-ur-duh-MAYL-yun) an unkempt person
    who wears shabby or ragged clothing. The word may also
    be used as an adjective.

On the other side of the cleanliness coin are the **fops** and **dandies,** conceited men preoccupied with the style of their hair, the cut of their clothes, and the make of their cars. Perhaps the most exaggerated example of this self-important, preening breed is the **prickmedainty,** a man or woman who is compulsively fastidious about dress, appearance, and manners.

A man whose vanity is so exaggerated that it's laughable is called a **coxcomb** (from "cock's comb," the cap worn by professional jesters in the Elizabethan era.) If the coxcomb is a jabbering fool given to pretentious displays, he's a **popinjay.** If the arrogant fop makes saucy remarks and impertinent advances, he's a **princock** or **princox.** A woman who is impudent and vain is called a **gaukie** (GAW-kee).

Has a foolish, fussy man been dumping on you lately? You can rain on his parade by calling him a **fribbler** or a **twiddlepoop.** Has a frivolous female airhead accused you of being uncool? Frost her eyeballs by calling her a **frippet** or a **fizgig.** Need some verbal firepower to flatten an obnoxious stuffed shirt? Try the supremely supercilious **flapadosha,** which applies to any vain, ostentatious, shallow person.

OBESE ABUSE

I know it's politically incorrect these days to give the overweight grief, but c'mon— this is a chapter on insults, so give me a big fat break. If some rotund rat has been busting your chops and cooking your goose, you have to fight back, and calling the person "calorically challenged" just won't cut the blubber. No, what you need are some beefy, bombastic words that will really kick the cellulite out of the corpulent creep.

Let's begin with a few adjectives. **Adipose** (AD-i-pohs) and **pinguid** (PING-gwid) are the generic grandiloquent terms for fat or fatty. If you want to get more specific about the pinguid particularities of your **abdominous** (ab-DAHM-i-nus, big-bellied) antagonist, try **lardaceous** (lar-DAY-shus), abounding in lard; **butyraceous** (BYOO-ti-RAY-shus), resembling butter; or the exquisitely slimy **sebaceous** (suh-BAY-shus), consisting of fat or grease or secreting fat or grease. If your obese opponent has a scuzzy look and a slippery mien, then the word you need is **oleaginous,** having an oily appearance, a smarmy manner, or both.

In the noun department we have an ample selection for those carrying an oversized load. There are the **gorbellies, gundyguts, greediguts, swillbellies,** and **bellygods,** whose gluttony is matched only by their offensive table manners. Then we have the **porknell,** someone as fat as a pig; the **pangut,** someone who is literally all gut; and the **tenterbelly,** someone with a grossly distended abdomen (the word refers to the old method of stretching out cloth on hooks). And if you really want to batter and fry your fat foe, the most scathing and comprehensive epithet by far is **fustilugs,** a fat, clumsy, lazy, filthy slob.

FLITING THE FLUTCH

Is there a lazy person in your life—some shiftless grod who needs a little verbal shock therapy? Time-honored terms of opprobrium for sluggards and deadbeats include **drotchel, drumble, jaffler, loblolly, lollard, lollpoop, scobberlotcher,** and **ragabash,** which may apply either to one lazy bum or to a congregation of lazy bums. Among my favorite terms of abuse for the indolent are **fainéant** (FAY-nee-int), an irresponsible loafer (the word may also be used as an adjective); **gongoozler,** a person who stares idly at nothing or who loiters in the street gawking at everything; and **flutch,** a world-class couch potato.

TEASERS FOR THE BRAINLESS

Stupid is one of the first words to enter our vocabulary of insults. We acquire it at about the age of three, when we become starkly aware that no matter how much we complain or cry, we can't always do what we want and we won't always get what we want. Forever after, our experience is divided into two classes: that which gratifies us, which is good, and that which thwarts our gratification, which is stupid.

Parents are the first stupid people we must contend with, but they are easily mastered. Siblings present more of a challenge, especially if they are of the older, malevolent variety. Then there is school, where the first thing we learn is that our teacher is almost as stupid as our parents (which explains why the second thing we learn in school is how to make spitballs). By the time we reach adolescence, we are convinced that the cruel lot of destiny has ordained that we must suffer and toil among the stupidest people on earth—our fellow teens. As adults we become only more painfully aware that human stupidity is rampant, and we learn that to survive we must vigilantly defend ourselves against its pernicious influence.

As a result, we develop a well-stocked storehouse of words and expressions for stupid people. Unfortunately, many are coarse or obscene, and many more are household variety digs as hackneyed, sophomoric, and banal as the gaping fools and grinning dolts they are meant to deride. The following selection of words should help you raise your IQ (Invective Quotient) when you find it necessary to insult the intellectually impaired:

anencephalotrophia: (AN-en-SEF-uh-luh-**TROH**-fee-uh) atrophy of the brain.

Anencephalia (an-EN-se-FAY-lee-uh) is the condition of brainlessness, and *anencephalic* (an-EN-se-FAL-ik) means having no brain. Compare **pantanencephaliac** below.

balatron: (BAL-uh-trahn) a babbling buffoon; a prattling clown.

The adjective is *balatronic* (BAL-uh-**TRAHN**-ik).

Boeotian: (bee-OH-shin) an ignorant, uncultured person.

Boeotia was a division of ancient Greece, a region "known for its thick atmosphere," says the *Century Dictionary*. According to the snobbish Athenians, this torpid climate was "supposed to communicate its dullness to the intellect of the inhabitants." Although three of Greece's greatest men of letters—Hesiod, Pindar, and Plutarch—were native Boeotians, Athenian city slickers reveled in reviling these simple country folk.

The word may also be used as an adjective, as in the phrase *Boeotian ears*, ears unable to appreciate fine music or poetry.

clodpate: a combination of a clod and a blockhead.

clumperton: a clownish, clumsy lout.

coof: a simpleton, ninny.

dizzard: a thickheaded person, a numbskull.

dotterel: a silly, gullible person; a senile person.

gawkhammer: a clumsy boob.

gomeril: (GAHM-ur-ul) a half-wit.

goop: an inconsiderate boor, ill-mannered clod.

grinagog: a person with a stupid, gaping grin.

grobian: a rude, clownish, blundering oaf.

gudgeon: a foolish, gullible person, easily tricked or cheated.

gump: a complete nitwit.

Now you know the meaning of the name *Forrest Gump*.

hoddypeak: an egregious blockhead.

lobcock: a stupid, clumsy, lazy person.

looby: an awkward, ignorant person.

loord: a dull, witless person.

mattoid (MAT-oyd) 1. a person degenerate or half-mad from birth. 2. a person with a congenitally abnormal brain.

mome: (rhymes with *home*) a stupid, boring person; also, a captious critic, as, "the Boeotian *momes* of academe."

oligóphrenic: (AHL-i-goh-**FREN**-ik) severely deficient mentally (literally "having a small mind"). Synonym: *cacophrenic.*

pantanencephaliac: (PAN-tuh-NEN-suh-**FAY**-lee-ak) a person born without a brain, like the Scarecrow in *The Wizard of Oz.* *Pantanencephalia* means total absence of brain.

parvanimity: (PAR-vuh-**NIM**-i-tee) the state or quality of having a petty, inferior, ignoble mind.

> *Parvanimity* is the antonym of *magnanimity*. Usage example: "My supervisor is a paragon of *parvanimity*."

puzzlepate: a person confused by simple ideas.

quoob: an eccentric fool (a combination of *queer* and *boob*).

sumph: a stupid, sulking oaf.

unasinous: (yoo-NAS-i-nus) equally asinine, equivalent in stupidity.

> *Unasinous* may be applied to persons, ideas, or things, as in "*unasinous* TV soap operas" or "Republicans and Democrats are *unasinous*."

BEGGARS, THIEVES, SPONGERS, AND OTHER SCOUNDRELS

Now that you know how to bamboozle a Boeotian, express contempt for a quoob, show the door to a dizzard, and stump a gump, it's time to fortify your vocabulary with scurvy words for the scurrilous and depraved.

English is rife with expressive terms for rascals and rogues. Many date back to the time of Shakespeare and even to Chaucer's day. Many others are the product of nineteenth-century American underworld slang and eighteenth-century

British cant (the secret lingo of beggars, thieves, and tramps). In short, there's a word for every knave you know, so find your favorite villain in the list below:

autem divers: pickpockets who prey on churchgoers.

autem mort: According to the *1811 Dictionary of the Vulgar Tongue*, "a female beggar with several children hired or borrowed to excite charity."

bezonian: an indigent scoundrel who begs and pilfers to get by.

bug-hunter: a robber of people who are drunk.

clapperdudgeon: a beggar born of beggars; also, a beggar who bangs on a dish or cup.

cosherer: one who lodges and eats at the expense of someone else, especially a relative.

dommerer: a beggar who fakes that his tongue has been cut out or that he was born deaf and dumb.

efter: a thief who robs theater patrons during a performance.

footpad: the old term for a mugger, someone who robs you on foot. Also called a **lowpad** or a **ladrone** (luh-DROHN).

gaberlunzie: (gab-ur-LUN-zee) a wandering beggar, harmless hobo; also, a beggar licensed to accept alms or public charity.

gyrovague: (JY-roh-vayg) a vagrant monk who begs and sponges. The *gyrovagues*, or *gyrovagi* (JY-roh-**VAY**-jy), were a despised class of mendicant monks in the Dark Ages who had "no definite occupation," says the *Century Dictionary*. They wandered from monastery to monastery, subsisting on the charity of their brethren and strangers.

kirkbuzzer: a robber of churches (from Scottish *kirk*, church).

mollbuzzer: a pickpocket or purse-snatcher who preys on women.

mumblecrust: a toothless beggar.

palliard: (PAL-yurd) a tricky beggar whose parents were also tricky beggars.

Pecksniff: a hypocritical, unctuous, devious rascal who preaches virtue while pursuing his own selfish interests. The word comes from a character in Dickens's *Martin Chuzzlewit*.

pettifogger: an unscrupulous or incompetent lawyer.

The term connotes all conceivable forms of shiftiness and chicanery.

rabiator: (RAY-bee-AY-tur) a man who likes to fight or who perpetrates violent crimes.

shnorrer or **schnorrer:** (SHNOR-ur, rhymes with *snorer*) a professional panhandler or chiseler, especially one who is clever, pushy, and a smooth talker.

Shnorrer entered English from Yiddish in the late 1800s. According to Leo Rosten in *The Joys of Yinglish*, the *shnorrer* "was not apologetic; he did not fawn or whine. He regarded himself as a professional. He did not so much ask for alms as *claim* them." To illustrate the point, Rosten offers this amusing anecdote: "The *shnorrer* stopped the alrightnik [an ostentatiously successful person] and held out his palm. 'I,' said the alrightnik, 'don't hand out money on the street.' 'So what should I do,' asked the *shnorrer*, 'open an office?' "

snaffler: a horse thief or highwayman.

A *snaffle* is a bridle bit for a horse, and the word *snaffler* evolved from the thief's method of accosting his victim by seizing the snaffle to stop the horse's progress. The modern equivalent of the snaffler is the beggar (or sometimes the thief) who comes up to your car while you're at a stoplight, wipes your windshield with a filthy, greasy rag, and then demands a handout.

sorner: a person who takes advantage of someone's hospitality, especially by wheedling the host into providing free room and board. *Sorning*, says the *OED*, is "the action or practice of exacting free quarters and maintenance, or of living at the expense of others."

thigger: a cross between a *gaberlunzie* and a *sorner*, with a dash of the *shnorrer* thrown in.

Thiggers are characterized by their more genteel approach to the task of cadging and mooching, and by the fact that they often have an established clientele upon whom they make regular calls.

ARE YOU A SNARGE?

If you've come this far in this caustic chapter, I'm sure it won't surprise you if I state categorically that the world is full of people who, for a variety of reasons (some of them inexplicable), are nasty, obnoxious, insufferable, disgusting, reprehensible, immoral, ignominious, vile, or worthless.

I have no proof, dear reader, that you are not one of these wretched folk. Nevertheless, since in your infinite wisdom and generosity you have seen fit to purchase my book, I shall give you the benefit of the doubt and proceed on the assumption that whatever you are, it is inevitable that every so often you will have an unpleasant encounter with a contemptible creature. At such times you will find it necessary to put your vocabulary of abuse to work. In the following list you should find an appropriate geck for any unfortunate snarge who gets in your way.

beldam: a foul, loathsome old woman.
blellum: an idle, boring chatterer.
buffarilla: an extremely ugly young woman (a blend of *buffalo* and *gorilla*). Synonyms include *scag*, *scank*, and *bowzer*.
caitiff (KAY-tif): a despicable, wicked, or cowardly person.
crambazzle: a worn-out, dissipated old man.
cullion: a rude, disagreeable, mean-spirited person.
droud: (rhymes with *brood*) an oafish woman.
fag-ma-fuff: a garrulous old woman.
flyndrig: an impudent or deceiving woman.
fritlag: a worthless, good-for-nothing man.
fudgeon: a squat, fussy person.
galligantus: a tall, gangling, awkward person.
guttersnipe: a street person, a member of the lowest class of urban society.
  This epithet occurs often in the spirited exchanges

between Henry Higgins and Eliza Doolittle in Shaw's *Pygmalion*. See *mudsill* below.

harridan: a worn-out whore; also, a disreputable, violent woman.

jade: a sexually promiscuous woman. Also called a *biffer*.

lickspittle: a creature so wretched and servile that to gain favor he is willing to lick the spittle of his master.

mackabroin: a hideous old woman.

mudsill: a coarse, ignorant person from the lowest stratum of society. The mudsill, from Southern dialect, is the rural equivalent of the urban guttersnipe (see above).

pilgarlic: a bald-headed sad sack.

poltroon: (pahl-TROON) a cowardly, sneaky wretch.

pornogenitone: (POR-noh-JEN-i-tohn) the son of a prostitute.

quakebuttock: a quivering coward, pusillanimous wretch.

rantallion: a man whose scrotum is so relaxed that it hangs lower than his penis.

rixatrix: (rik-SAY-triks) a quarrelsome, brawling woman.

    Why the dictionaries don't contain an entry for *rixator*, the male counterpart, is mysterious indeed.

rudas: a repugnant, foulmouthed old hag.

slumgullion: a weak, insignificant, worthless person.

smellfungus: a captious person, one who complains about or finds fault with everything.

smellsmock: a licentious man.

    This word was once used as a derogatory term for a prurient priest.

snarge: a person no one likes, a total jerk.

swelp: a miserable wretch who constantly complains or protests.

    The word is a corruption of "so help me [God]."

termagant: (TUR-muh-gint) a violent, brawling woman.

trull: a deliciously obscure synonym for *prostitute*.

uzzard: a third-generation bastard.

virago: (vi-RAY-goh) a scolding, loudmouthed, overbearing woman.

wanker: literally, a masturbator; figuratively, a man who is weak, ineffectual, craven, untrustworthy, smug, undeserving of whatever he enjoys, or otherwise contemptible.

Wanker is a contemporary slang import from Britain, where saucy Brits also promiscuously employ the verb to *wank*, to masturbate, and the corresponding noun *wanking*. Robert Barltrop, coauthor of *The Muvver Tongue*, a 1980 treatise on the Cockney dialect, calls *wanker* "*the* great working-class swear word of today [in England]."

yazzihamper: a disliked or dislikable person.

zob: a worthless person, a nobody, a zero.

SOME CRUMMY KIDS

We tend to think of children as sweet, innocent, joyful creatures, brimming with energy, curiosity, and good humor—and many of them are just that. But let's face it: Some kids are flat-out rude, nasty, spoiled, whiny, or otherwise hateful little monsters. The next time you're faced with one of these intolerable tykes, here are a few words that may help:

awp or **azzard** (AZ-urd): a wayward or mischievous child.

bantling: a little bastard (figuratively or literally).

birsie: (BUR-see) an impertinent child, cheeky kid.

cade (rhymes with *made*) or **gobbin:** a spoiled brat.

carker: a whining, peevish, troublesome child.

diggot: a cruel or malicious young person.

lolaby: (LAH-luh-bee) a child who constantly cries or screams.

mammothrept: (MAM-uh-thrept) a spoiled child raised by its grandmother.

rantipole: (RAN-ti-pohl) a wild, unruly young person.

smatchet or **bratchet:** an impudent, contemptible child.

WHERE DO YOU LIVE?

If you want your insults to hit home, try hitting your opponents where they live. If the loser you loathe is **lapidicolous** (LAP-i-DIK-uh-lus), she lives underneath rocks, like certain beetles and grubs. If the odious creature thrives in mud or slime, he's **limicolous** (ly-MIK-uh-lus). If she inhabits a musty cave, she's **troglodytic** (TRAHG-luh-**DIT**-ik). If he calls a dung heap home, he's **fimicolous** (fi-MIK-uh-lus) or **fimetarious** (FIM-i-**TAIR**-ee-us). And for those folks most foul who reside in rotting waste or decaying matter, there's the especially putrid word **saprophilous** (sa-PRAHF-uh-lus).

WHAT DO YOU EAT?

Does your nemesis like to nibble on spiders? If so, he's **arachnivorous** (AR-ak-**NIV**-ur-us). If she likes to gobble lice, she's **phthirophagous** (thy-RAHF-uh-gus). How about feasting on a few juicy frogs? The word for that prince of a guy is **batrachophagous** (BA-truh-**KAHF**-uh-gus). And if she enjoys scarfing down snakes, call her **ophiophagous** (AHF-ee-**AHF**-uh-gus).

Don't slither away—there's more on the menu! If your slimy foe fancies worms, she's **scolecophagous** (SKAHL-i-**KAHF**-uh-gus). If he prefers to gnaw on wood rather than knock on it, he's **xylophagous** (zy-LAHF-uh-gus). If she has a penchant for ingesting mud, she's **limivorous** (ly-MIV-ur-us). And if your ugsome antagonist wants to suck your blood, he's **hematophagous** or **sanguivorous**.

Can you stomach a few more delectable epithets for the person you despise? For your excrement-eating enemies, there are three words you may employ: **scatophagous** (ska-TAHF-uh-gus); **coprophagous** (kuh-PRAHF-uh-gus); and **merdivorous** (mur-DIV-ur-us). Or try the sickening **saprophagous** (sa-PRAHF-uh-gus), which means feeding on dead or decaying animal matter.

ARE YOU AN AI?

Does the person you abhor remind you of some repulsive zoological specimen, but you just don't know what it is? Perhaps you'll find the appropriate creature in the list below:

ai: (AH-ee) a South American three-toed sloth.

anableps tetraophthalmus: (AN-uh-bleps TE-truh-ahf-**THAL**-m<u>u</u>s) a four-eyed fish that swims on the surface of the water with one pair of eyes trained above to watch for predators and the other pair focused below to search for food.

bandicoot: a humongous rat.

bonobo: (buh-NOH-boh) the pygmy chimpanzee.

coprophagan: (kuh-PRAHF-uh-g<u>i</u>n) a beetle that lives in dung.

dziggetai: (DZIG-guh-ty) an ass-horse.

> "The wild ass of Asia, *Equus hemionus*," says the *Century Dictionary.* "It is intermediate in appearance and character between the horse and the ass (hence the specific name *hemionus*, half-ass)."

emgalla: a South African warthog.

geep: the offspring of a sheep and a goat. Also called a **shoat.**

gruntling: a young pig. Also called a **grice.**

hippobosca: (HIP-oh-**BAHS**-kuh) a bloodsucking fly.

kiyoodle: (ky-YOOD'l) a mangy, worthless dog.

morwong: the Australian spiny-finned jackass fish.

nauplius: the larval form of a crustacean.

pollard: (PAHL-urd) a hornless animal.

quadrumane: (KWAH-druh-mayn) a four-handed animal, such as a monkey or ape, whose feet can function as hands.

tampan: a vicious South African tick with a venomous bite.

tuatara: (TOO-uh-**TAH**-rah) a two-and-a-half-foot-long, spiny-backed, iguanalike reptile.

wallydrag: a weak, undersized animal; the runt of the litter.

wanderoo: a purple-faced monkey.

zedonk: the offspring of a donkey and a zebra.

To round out our section on bestial billingsgate, here is a collection of adjectives for the repugnant creatures you know:

anserine: (AN-suh-ryn or rin) like a goose.

batrachoid: (BA-truh-koyd) like a frog.

blattoid: (BLAT-oyd) like a cockroach.

bovine: (BOH-vyn) resembling a cow or an ox.

bufoniform: (byoo-FAHN-i-form) like a toad.

chelonian: (ke-LOH-nee-in) like a turtle.

crotaline: (KRAH- or KROH-tuh-lin) resembling a rattlesnake.

cynocephalous: (SY-nuh-SEF-uh-lus) having a head or face like a dog.

discophoran: (dis-KAHF-ur-in) like a jellyfish.

echinoproctous: (e-KY-nuh-PRAHK-tus) having a spiny or prickly rump, like a porcupine.

gliriform: (GLY-ri-form) resembling a rodent.

herpetiform: (hur-PET-i-form) formed like a reptile, or having the character of a reptile. Also, **herpetoid** (HUR-pe-toyd).

hircine: (like *her sign*) goatlike, or smelling like a goat. Also, **hircinous** (HUR-si-nus).

hirudinoid: (hi-ROO-di-noyd) like a leech.

leporine: (LEP-uh-ryn- or -rin) resembling a rabbit.

limacine: (LIM-uh-syn) sluglike.

   Limaciform (ly-MAS-i-form) means shaped like a slug.

lupine: (LOO-pyn) like a wolf.

muriform: (MYUR-i-form) resembling a rat or mouse. Also, **myomorphic** (MY-uh-MORF-ik).

ophidian: (oh-FID-ee-in) snakelike.

ovine: (OH-vyn) like a sheep.

pelargic: (pe-LAR-jik) storklike.

porcine: (POR-syn) resembling a pig or swine.

rhinocerotic: (ry-NAHS-uh-RAHT-ik) like a rhinoceros.

saurian: (SOR-ee-in) like a lizard. Also, **lacertilian** (LAS-ur-TIL-ee-in).

selachian: (suh-LAY-kee-in) like a shark.

simian: (SIM-ee-in) apelike.

struthious: (STROO-thee-us) like an ostrich.

suoid: (SOO-oyd) like a hog.

theroid: (THEER-oyd) like a wild beast.

vermiform: (VUR-mi-form) like a worm.

vespine: (VES-pyn or -pin) wasplike.

xenarthral: (ze-NAR-thrul) resembling a sloth, anteater, or armadillo.

SOME OTHER DISGUSTING STUFF

Have you ever heard of **ambeer** (AM-beer)? It has nothing to do with beer, but it is a liquid, and a disgusting one at that, for ambeer is the spittle produced in the act of chewing tobacco. Tobacco-chewing etiquette (from which baseball players and certain other slubberdegullions are exempt) requires that you expectorate your ambeer into a **spittoon** or **cuspidor.** Remember the famous march in Bizet's opera *Carmen?* There's an old jocular lyric to the tune that goes like this:

> *Tor-ree-a-dor,*
> *Don't spit on the floor!*
> *Use the cuspidor,*
> *That'sa what it's for!*

In the spirit of that ditty, I shall now lead you to the cuspidor of language and show you a spittoonful of words for revolting qualities and things. I hope you will find many memorable ways to use them in grandiloquent bad taste.

bathybius: (ba-THIB-ee-us) a gelatinous, protoplasmic substance found in mud on the ocean floor.
codgel: the fat on the underjaw of a hog.
culch: rubbish or refuse of every variety.
curpin: a bird's behind.
fearns: (FAIRNZ) sheep intestines.
frass: the excrement of insect larvae, or "the refuse left behind by boring insects" *(OED).*
furfuraceous: (FUR-fur-RAY-shus) covered with dandruff flakes or scales. Cf. **scurfy** below.
gleet: slime; sludge; greasy filth.
graveolent: (gra-VEE-uh-lint) exuding a rank, repulsive odor.
helminthous: (hel-MIN-thus) infested with intestinal worms.
jumentous: (joo-MEN-tus) smelling like horse urine.

I once knew a blacksmith's apprentice
Who clearly was *non compos mentis*.
    He ate in a stable,
    And slept on a table,
And his essence was downright *jumentous*.
—WILLIAM COWPIE

keech: a large lump of fat.

merdurinous: (mur-DYUR-i-nus) composed of dung and urine.

metapneustic: (MET-ap-**N(Y)OOS**-tik) having the respiratory apparatus in the anal orifice; i.e., breathing through the butt.

mucopurulent: (MYOO-koh-**PYOOR**-uh-lint) consisting of mucus and pus.

pulicose: (PYOO-li-kohs) infested with fleas.

quisquilian: (kwis-KWIL-ee-in) consisting of trash or rubbish. Variants: **quisquilious, quisquiliary.**

saprogenic: (SAP-ruh-**JEN**-ik) causing rot or decay.

scurfy: having a bad case of dandruff.

sterquilinous: (stur-kwi-LY-nus) pertaining to a dung hill.

LAST LICKS

The verb to **crugset,** says Wright's *English Dialect Dictionary,* means "to drive an animal into such a situation as to prevent its escape." Figuratively, it means "to drive a person into a corner in an argument."

    Crugsetting may be achieved indirectly by deft use of the **charientism** (KAR-ee-in-tiz'm), which Grambs's *Endangered English Dictionary* defines as "an artfully veiled insult." In all-out fliting, however, as in boxing, once you have successfully crugset your opponent—when you have him on the ropes and you're ready to wrap up the match—you must proceed with all alacrity to **squabash** the poor kiyoodle mercilessly. Then, when his defenses collapse, you deliver the **sockdologer.**

To *squabash* (skwuh-BASH) is to defeat with cutting criticism, crush a person's spirits by pointing out his or her faults. The *sockdologer* (sahk-DAHL-uh-jur, also spelled *sockdolager*) is the decisive blow or sizzling retort that settles the dispute. An even more grandiloquent term for this is **recumbentibus** (REK-um-BEN-ti-bus), a knockout punch, a literal or figurative blow that makes you recumbent (flat on your back).

My vote for the best sockdologer or recumbentibus of all time is the brilliant rejoinder of John Wilkes, the rabble-rousing and infamously dissolute 18th-century English politician, to an insult from the Earl of Sandwich.

"I am convinced, Mr. Wilkes," Sandwich said, "that you will die either of a pox or on the gallows."

Without any hesitation, Wilkes replied, "That depends, my lord, whether I embrace your mistress or your principles."

And with that bit of debilitating derision, we come to the end of Billingsgate 101. You have passed this course in outrageous obloquy with fliting colors. Never again will you have to put up with the pulicose swelps, saprophilous pantanencephaliacs, and graveolent zobs of this wretched world, for now you can crugset any coof and squabash any sumph who dares cross your path. You are now certified in **nothosonomia**[*] (NOH-thoh-suh-NOH-mee-uh), and you are hereby licensed to **ballyrag**[†] with the best.

So go out and geck 'em, you snarge.

---

[*]Calling someone a bastard.
[†]To abuse violently with foul language.

❖

CHAPTER FIVE

PICK A PECK OF PEOPLE

> I've always been interested in people,
> but I've never liked them.
> —W. SOMERSET MAUGHAM

In the last three chapters you learned to eat and drink, make love, and hurl invective with the greatest of grandiloquent ease. Now let's take a look at some uncommon and uncommonly amusing words for people with whom you can do all those things and more.

If you're a **cacogen** (KAK-uh-jen), a **witling,** or a **fysigunkus** (FIZ-i-GUNGK-us), this chapter's not for you. On the other hand, if you're a **quidam** (KWY-dam) or a **dringle,** then what follows may help turn you into either a *bel-esprit* (bel-es-PREE) or a **morologist.**

Translation:

If you're an antisocial person *(cacogen)*, a person who tries to be funny but isn't *(witling)*, or someone totally devoid of curiosity *(fysigunkus)*, go read something else. However, if you're just an obscure somebody somewhere *(quidam)* or someone who likes to waste time *(dringle)*, then this chapter may help you become either a person of refined intellect and graceful wit *(bel-esprit)*, or a boring fool who speaks utter nonsensical garbage *(morologist)*.

SOME LOVING AND UNLOVING FOLKS

How are you *phil*-ing today? Are you all *mis*-ed up?

The prefix *philo-*, often shortened to *phil-*, means "loving," as in *philanthropist*, a lover of humankind, and **philodemic** (FIL-uh-DEM-ik), people-loving. Butting linguistic heads with *philo-* is the prefix *miso-*, often shortened to *mis-*, which means hate, as in **misandrist** (mis-AN-drist or MIS-andrist), someone who hates men, the opposite of the familiar *misogynist*, someone who hates women. Consult any respectably rotund English dictionary and you'll see that the language has some fascinating words for lovers and haters that incorporate the prefixes *phil(o)-* and *mis(o)-*.

For example, have you ever met a **philodox** (FIL-uh-dahks), a person in love with his own opinions, someone who loves to hear herself talk? I'm sure you've had the distinct displeasure of listening to one of those self-reverential bores. And how about a **philogynist** (fi-LAHJ-i-nist), a lover of women, or a **philandrist** (fi-LAN-drist), a lover of men? You may well be one or the other yourself. And have you ever known a **philogeant** (FIL-uh-JEE-int)? This word, formed from *philo-* and the Greek *ge*, earth, means literally "a lover of earth"; hence, someone who appreciates the good things of the world. Now that's the kind of lover we should all aspire to be!

Here are some more *philo-* folks, not all of them so lovable:

philalethist: (FIL-uh-LEE-thist) a lover of truth.

philocalist: (fi-LAHK-uh-list) a lover of beauty.

philocubist: (fi-LAHK-yuh-bist) a lover of dice games.

philodespot: (FIL-uh-DES-put) a lover of tyranny.

philologist: (fi-LAHL-uh-jist) a lover of literature and language.

philomath: (FIL-uh-math) a lover of learning; specifically, a devotee of mathematics and science.

philomythist: (fi-LAH-mi-thist) a person who loves myths, symbols, and legends.

philoneist: (FIL-uh-**NEE**-ist) a lover or obsessive follower of trends and fads.

philopolemicist: (FIL-uh-puh-**LEM**-i-sist) a person who loves to argue or debate.

philopornist: (FIL-uh-**POR**-nist) a lover of prostitutes. Also called a **cypripareuniaphile** (SIP-ri-puh-**ROO**-nee-uh-fyl).

philotherian: (FIL-uh-**THEER**-ee-in) an animal lover.

philoxenist: (fil-**AHK**-suh-nist) a person who loves to entertain strangers.

One *philo-* type to watch out for is the **philosophaster** (fi-**LAHS**-uh-**FAS**-tur), also known as a **philosophunculist** (fi-**LAHS**-uh-**FUNGK**-yuh-list). This is the intellectual lightweight or dabbler, the person who pretends to know more about something than he does as a way of impressing or manipulating others.

Now let's look at *miso-* words. The next time you're assaulted by someone who oozes aversion, perhaps you can retaliate with one of the following terms for hateful folks:

misandronist: (mis-**AN**-druh-nist) a fanatical *misandrist*, a person consumed with hatred for men and driven by the belief that men are the source of all the world's problems.

misarchist: (**MIS**-ahr-kist) a hater of government or authority.

misocapnist: (MIS-oh-**KAP**-nist) a person who hates smoking or the smell of tobacco smoke.

misodoctakleidist: (MIS-oh-**DAHK**-tuh-**KLY**-dist) someone who hates practicing the piano.

misogamist: (mi-**SAHG**-uh-mist) someone who hates marriage.

misologist: (mi-**SAHL**-uh-jist) a hater of reason or enlightenment.

misomath: (**MIS**-oh-math) one who detests mathematics or science.

misoneist: (MIS-oh-**NEE**-ist) a person who hates innovation.

misopedist: (MIS-oh-**PEE**-dist) a hater of children.

misopolemiac: (MIS-oh-puh-**LEM**-ee-ak) a hater of war or strife.

misoscopist: (mi-SAHS-kuh-pist) a person who hates to look.

misosophist: (mi-SAH-suh-fist) one who hates wisdom or learning.

Another word for this intransigently unlettered person is **misogrammatist** (MIS-oh-**GRAM**-uh-tist).

misotramontanist: (MIS-oh-truh-**MAHN**-tuh-nist) one who is averse to anything foreign or to the unknown, literally "one who hates what is beyond the mountains."

misotyrannist: (MIS-oh-**TIR**-uh-nist) a hater of tyranny.

misoxene: (mis-AHK-seen) a person who hates strangers.

Do you know someone who's impossible to please? He or she may be a **misomaniac,** a person who hates everything.

Some Well-Named Folks

What do Franklin Delano Roosevelt, Gabriel García Márquez, Mary Higgins Clark, George Washington Carver, Isaac Bashevis Singer, Joyce Carol Oates, Frank Lloyd Wright, Martin Luther King, Jr., Sandra Day O'Connor, and your grandiloquent guide, Charles Harrington Elster, all have in common?

Gee, was it obvious? Yes, we are all **trinomials,** people with three-part names. Trinomials are not as fashionable as they once were, and today most of us are **binomials,** people with two names. There are, however, a few odd folks who are **mononomials** (e.g., Moses, Sophocles, Liberace, God). Can you think of any **quadrinomials?** Let's see, there's George Herbert Walker Bush, Titus Flavius Sabinus Vespasianus, John Jacob Jingleheimer Schmidt. . . .

Before your brain cells overload trying to tackle that one, let's consider another question: Have you ever heard an **aptronym** (AP-truh-nym)? Derived from *apt* and the suffix *-onym*, name, an aptronym is literally "an apt name," one that is especially (and often humorously) suited to a person's profession or temperament: John Dough for a baker; Dr. DiMento for a psychiatrist; Professor Quirk for an eccentric professor.

Two other words for this quirky coincidence of name and fate are **euonym** (YOO-uh-nym), literally "a good name," and **ipsonym** (IP-suh-nym), coined by editor and author James Atlas from the Latin *ipso*, the thing itself.

SOME EPONYMOUS FOLKS

We've all known one or two Einsteins, Sherlocks, and Scrooges—geniuses, brilliant investigators, and mean-spirited misers, respectively. And surely you've known a few Sarah Bernhardts, overly dramatic people, and probably a few mavericks, people who stand apart from the herd (so-called after the Texas lawyer, rancher, and trinomial Samuel Augustus Maverick, who neglected to brand his cattle). These are examples of **eponyms** (EP-uh-nimz), names that have become words.

There are hundreds of **eponymous** (e-PAHN-i-mus) words in the English language. Common ones include *silhouette*, from Etienne Silhouette, a parsimonious French minister of finance who imposed heavy taxes and austerity measures that infuriated the people; *sideburns*, from Ambrose Burnside, a hirsute major general in the Civil War; and *Adam's apple*, from the biblical first fellow's bite of forbidden fruit.

Let's take a look at a few **eximious** (ek-SIM-ee-us, choice, select, excellent) eponyms that may apply to people you know. (You will find others scattered elsewhere throughout this book.)

Boswell: a biographer who idolizes his subject, or a person who writes a meticulous but wholly uncritical historical record.

    The word comes from James Boswell, the adulatory biographer of English lexicographer and essayist Dr. Samuel Johnson. To *Boswellize* is to write a faithful but overly flattering account; the adjective is *Boswellian*.

gradgrind: a dispassionate, inflexible, overly pragmatic person who deals with people as though they were items in a spreadsheet, and who has no sympathy for their needs or foibles: "The management's number-crunching gradgrinds treated the employees like machines, to be inspected and cleaned when necessary but otherwise ignored."

Gradgrind comes from the unfeeling, utilitarian merchant in Dickens's *Hard Times*.

Luddite: (LUH-dyt) someone fanatically opposed to technological innovation, especially to any machine or labor-saving device perceived to replace workers.

Luddite comes from Ned Ludd, a **misoneistic** (MIS-oh-nee-**IS**-tik, innovation-hating) nutcase and rabble-rouser in eighteenth-century England who went around smashing up stocking frames (mechanized looms). Examples of modern Luddites would include people who refuse to leave a message on your answering machine, who believe that microwave ovens destroy the nutrients in food (a widely held myth, by the way), and who are afraid that computers are taking over the world. (They are!)

myrmidon: (MUR-mi-dahn) a devoted follower or servant who obeys commands without question or scruple.

The Myrmidons were a bellicose people of ancient Thessaly who accompanied the Greek warrior Achilles to Troy and fought under his command. Because of their reputation for truculence and unquestioning obedience, *myrmidon* came to designate an unscrupulous follower, especially a roughneck or goon.

Pyrrhonist: (PIR-uh-nist) an absolute skeptic, one who takes nothing for granted and accepts nothing at face value.

Pyrrho was one of the great Greek skeptic philosophers. His doctrine *(pyrrhonism)*, the *Century Dictionary* explains, "was that there is just as much to be said for as against any opinion whatever; that neither the senses nor the reason are to be trusted in the least; and that when we are once convinced we can know nothing, we cease to care, and in this way alone can attain happiness. It is said that Pyrrho would take no ordinary practical precautions, such as getting out of the way of vehicles."

quisling: (KWIZ-ling) a traitor who acts as a puppet of the enemy.

Vidkun Quisling, a Norwegian leader who collaborated with the Nazis, is the source of this word.

Xanthippe: (zan-TIP-ee) an ill-tempered, browbeating woman.

Xanthippe was the wife of Socrates, a brilliant philosopher and teacher and also a repugnant runt who was hardly God's gift to woman. Xanthippe may have been a henpecking shrew, but then who wouldn't be when faced with a man of such hellacious ugliness and arrogance? "Various historians," notes Robert Hendrickson in his *Dictionary of Eponyms,* "argue that [Xanthippe] has been much maligned, that Socrates was so unconventional as to tax the patience of any woman, as indeed would any man convinced that he has a religious mission on earth."

SOME WORKING FOLKS

You've probably dealt with plenty of hucksters, but have you ever cut a deal with a **huckstress?** And while we're at it, have you ever bargained with a **chafferer** or haggled with a **higgler?** Of course you have, because although these words seem uncommon, the people they describe are not: A **huckstress** is a female huckster, a **chafferer** is a vendor who enjoys bantering while making a sale, and a **higgler** is a salesperson who is a stickler about price.

The world may have many wonders, but it also has a heck of a lot of vendors. Among the more colorful merchants you may meet in the grandiloquent marketplace are the **costermonger,** a vendor of fruits, vegetables, fish, or other edible goods, especially one who sells them in the street from a stand or cart; the **kurveyor** (kur-VAY-ur), a traveling merchant who sells dry goods from a large cart or wagon; the **kalewife,** a female greengrocer; the **jowter** (rhymes with *shouter*), a fish peddler; the **tranter,** a person who does odd jobs hauling or delivering; the **xylopolist** (zy-LAHP-uh-list), a vendor of wood products; and the

colporteur (KAHL-por-tur), a book peddler, especially an itinerant seller of Bibles or other religious materials.

Unless you're a **lychnobite** (LIK-nuh-byt), a person who works at night and sleeps during the day, when you're out scouring those commodity-laden streets for bargains you're bound to come across another type of vendor hawking a less tangible product: entertainment. In this ephemeral class we find the **cantabank,** a second-rate street singer; the **tregetour** (TREJ-i-tur), a street magician or juggler; and the **busker,** a street musician or balladeer—a word that today could apply to any street musician from a down-and-out harmonica player huddling in a doorway to a highbrow string quartet entertaining passersby in a park.

Finally, when something goes on the blink and you need a Mr. or Ms. Fixit fast, don't call Janie- or Johnny-on-the-spot; call a **fettler**! This fine old word (from the noun *fettle,* order, condition, state) means "one who puts things in order," a person skilled at cleaning and repairing tools, equipment, or machinery.

Some Curious "Collectics"

A stamp collector is a **philatelist** (fi-LAT-uh-list), a coin collector is a **numismatist** (n(y)oo-MIZ-muh-tist), a collector of picture postcards is a **deltiologist** (DEL-tee-AHL-uh-jist), and a collector of objets d'art is a **curioso.** But what do you call someone who collects matchbooks, teddy bears, flags, goofy names, beer coasters, or anything relating to the billionaire Howard Hughes? An eclectic? A "collectic"? Very curioso, indeed.

If you collect something odd, or if you know some oddball who does, here are some curious words for collectors and what they amass:

arctophilist: (ark-TAHF-uh-list) teddy bears.
brandophilist: (bran-DAHF-uh-list) cigar bands.
cagophilist: (ka-GAHF-uh-list) keys.

cartomaniac: (KAHR-tuh-**MAY**-nee-ak) maps.

comiconomenclaturist: (KAH-mi-koh-NOH-men-**KLAY**-chur-ist) funny names (coined by Peter Bowler).

conchologist: (kahng-KAHL-uh-jist) shells.

discophilist: (dis-KAHF-uh-list) originally, a collector of record albums; by technological extension, a collector of compact discs.

entredentolignumologist: (EN-truh-DEN-tuh-LIG-n(y)oo-**MAHL**-uh-jist) toothpick boxes and toothpick ephemera (coined by Paul Dickson).

ferroequinologist: (FER-oh-EE-kwi-**NAHL**-uh-jist) a railroad enthusiast.

Hughesianist: (HYOO-zee-uh-nist) items pertaining to Howard Hughes.

labeorphilist: (LAY-bee-**OR**-fuh-list) beer bottle labels.

lexiconophilist: (LEX-i-kuh-**NAHF**-uh-list) dictionaries and word books.

oologist: (oh-AHL-uh-jist) birds' eggs.

peristerophilist: (puh-RIS-tur-**AHF**-uh-list) pigeons.

phillumenist: (fi-LOO-mi-nist) matchbooks and matchboxes.

philographer: (fi-LAHG-ruh-fur) autographs.

plangonologist: (PLAN-juh-**NAHL**-uh-jist) dolls.

tegestologist: (TEJ-es-**TAHL**-uh-jist) beer coasters and bar mats.

timbromaniac: (TIM-bruh-**MAY**-nee-ak) another term for an avid stamp collector. It quickly got licked by the common term, *philatest* (fi-LAT'l-ist).

vexillologist: (VEKS-i-**LAHL**-uh-jist) flags.

Would you like a word for someone who collects all these words for collectors? Try **philophilist** (fi-LAHF-uh-list), another coinage by the inveterate wordcatcher Paul Dickson.

A GABBLE OF GROUP NOUNS

When birds of a feather flock together, the birdwise know there's a specific word for it, depending on the type of bird.

For example, surely you've seen a gaggle of geese, but have you ever seen a siege of herons, a rafter of turkeys, a murder of crows, or a murmuration of starlings? Such "group nouns," as linguists call these terms, exist for all sorts of human congregations as well. Most people have never heard them, however, and so they find themselves wordless when confronted with the problem of what to call a gathering of doctors, lawyers, plumbers, priests, waiters, clowns, or used-car dealers.

So you'll always get along in a throng and never be cowed by a crowd, here's an amusing gabble of nouns for various human groups:

> a *dash* of commuters
> a *drove* of cabdrivers
> a *blarney* of bartenders
> a *mess* of officers
> a *column* of accountants
> a *sample* of salespeople
> a *portfolio* of stockbrokers
> a *horde* of misers
> a *recession* of economists
> a *ring* of jewelers
> a *flush* of plumbers
> an *ohm* of electricians
> a *sprinkling* of gardeners
> a *lot* of used-car dealers
> an *indifference* of waiters
> a *sneer* of butlers
> an *unction* of undertakers (for a large group, an *extreme unction*)
> a *wince* of dentists
> a *rash* of dermatologists
> a *void* of urologists
> a *host* of epidemiologists
> a *pile* of proctologists
> a *smear* of gynecologists

an *eloquence* (or an *escheat*) of lawyers
a *sentence* of judges
an *odium* of politicians
a *slant* of journalists
a *scoop* of reporters
a *brow* of scholars
a *brood* of researchers
a *drift* of lecturers
an *entrenchment* of full professors
a *family* of biologists
a *nucleus* of physicists
a *galaxy* of astronomers
a *string* of violinists
an *illusion* of painters
a *plot* of playwrights
an *erudition* of editors
a *condescension* of actors
a *pan* of reviewers
a *shrivel* of critics
a *conjunction* of grammarians
a *wrangle* of philosophers
a *pontificality* (or a *mass*) of priests
a *superfluity* of nuns
an *abominable sight* of monks
a *riot* of comedians
a *pratfall* of clowns
a *skulk* of thieves
a *wheeze* of joggers
a *score* of bachelors
a *descent* of relatives
a *mutter* of mothers-in-law
an *ingratitude* of children

For the last word on these delightful group nouns, I refer you to the *locus classicus* on the subject, *An Exaltation of Larks*, by James Lipton.

Some Mismatched Folks

All right, it's time to play "Be All That You Can't Be." Tell me, would you rather be . . .

> an *eminento* or a *criddow?*
> an *agathist* or a *futilitarian?*
> a *bellibone* or an *objurgatrix?*
> an *Übermensch* or a *goobermensch?*
> a *crawk* or a *stalko?*

Except for the last pair, where I was sneaky and made both options undesirable, you did right by yourself if you picked the first word in each case. Here's why:

Given a choice (which I just gave you), anyone would rather be an **eminento,** a distinguished or famous person, than a **criddow** (KRID-oh), someone who is broken or bowed down from age, sickness, poverty, or grief.

Why is being an **agathist** (AG-uh-thist) better than being a **futilitarian?** It all comes down to their difference in **weltanschauung** (VEL-tahn-showng), a worldview or concept of humanity's function in the universe. The agathist is like an optimist, but more rational and profound. Like the inane "happy face" we see everywhere today, the optimist sports an unflappable smile and blithely believes things will work out or that good will triumph over evil. The agathist, on the other hand, accepts evil and misfortune but believes that it is the ultimate nature of things to tend toward the good and improve.

Now let's give the worldview coin a flip and compare the pessimist with the futilitarian. Though the pessimist may have no hope for today or tomorrow, or even for Tuesday, and little faith in people's ability to be good or do right, the futilitarian accepts the absolute futility of life and human aspiration, believing that it is pointless to strive for anything and foolish to have hope. Unlike the pessimist, who always expects the worst but somehow glumly manages to go on, the futilitarian has no intellectual survival mechanisms and is but a bottle of booze and a crafty syllogism away from suicide. To paraphrase an old joke: The pessimist is someone who predicts that we're all going to have to eat poop next year, to which the futilitarian responds that there won't be enough to go around.

If you're a woman, you want people to call you a **bellibone** (BEL-i̱-bohn), not an **objurgatrix** (AHB-jur-GAY-triks). *Objurgatrix* comes from the verb *objurgate*, to chide or rebuke harshly, and means a scolding, sharp-tongued, shrewish woman, a Xanthippe. *Bellibone*, an old word that comes through the French *belle et bonne* from the Latin *bellum*, beautiful, and *bonus*, good, means literally "a woman both beautiful and good."

> For the woman of my dreams
> A pedestal's too low, it seems.
> She deserves a gilded throne
> Because she is a *bellibone*.
> —R. E. SPECTER

If you're a man, I hope you aspire to be an *Übermensch* and not a **goobermensch.** *Übermensch* comes from German and means literally "over-man"; in the philosophy of Nietzsche it denotes an ideal man or superman who is a powerful creator and controller of his destiny. A *goobermensch*, on the other hand, is a man who thinks he's super but isn't, who believes he's a leader even though he lacks followers. The word is a combination of *goober*, a peanut or pimple, and *mensch*, man, and is the jocular coinage of molecular biologist Hiroshi Akashi.

Finally we have the choice, which I've already admitted was crooked, between a **crawk** and a **stalko** (STAW-koh). You will recognize both types, but I trust, dear reader, that you're not one of them. *Crawk*, a slang term from the radio industry, is a radio announcer who imitates animals; if you do your animal imitations without a microphone, you're a **theriomime** (THEER-ee-uh-mym). *Stalko*, which hails from Anglo-Irish dialect, is one of the most delightful words I stumbled across while writing this book. A stalko is a poor person who puts on airs or pretends to be rich—or, as the exquisitely genteel *Webster 2* puts it, "an impecunious idler posing as a gentleman."

A GRANDILOQUENT GATHERING

Are you still looking for the precise word for a particular peculiar person? If I've neglected thus far to cite a word for someone you know, I trust you will find the appropriate term in the following "word horde" or *horde oeuvre:*

agelast: (AJ-uh-last) a person who never laughs.

> There is a fine Jewish proverb: Man thinks, God laughs. Inspired by that adage, I like to imagine that François Rabelais heard God's laughter one day, and thus was born the idea of the first great European novel. . . . Rabelais invented a number of neologisms that have since entered the French and other languages, but one of his words has been forgotten, and this is regrettable. It is the word *agélaste;* it comes from the Greek and it means a man who does not laugh, who has no sense of humor. . . . Never having heard God's laughter, the *agélastes* are convinced that the truth is obvious, that all men necessarily think the same thing, and that they themselves are exactly what they think they are. But it is precisely in losing the certainty of truth and the unanimous agreement of others that man becomes an individual.
>
> —MILAN KUNDERA, *The Art of the Novel*

aeolist: (EE-uh-list) a pompous, windy bore who pretends to have inspiration.

alopecist: (uh-LAHP-i-sist) a person who claims to prevent or cure baldness.

analysand: (uh-NAL-i-sand) a person in psychoanalysis; the patient of a psychiatrist.

anonymuncule: (uh-NAHN-i-**MUHNG**-kyool) a petty anonymous writer.

An insignificant writer who publishes under a pseudonym is a **pseudonymuncle** or **pseudonymuncule**.

antiscian: (an-TISH-in) a person who lives on the opposite side of the earth from you.

ascian: (ASH-ee-in) a person without a shadow.

Ascian applies to those living on or near the equator, who cast a shadow only for a brief period during the day.

autodidact: (AW-toh-**DY**-dakt) a self-taught person.

The adjective is *autodidactic* (AW-toh-dy-**DAK**-tik).

autohagiographer: (AW-toh-**HAG**-ee- or AW-toh-HAY-jee-**AHG**-ruh-fur) someone who speaks or writes in a smug or self-aggrandizing way about his life or accomplishments (coined by Bernard Lewis, professor emeritus at Princeton).

autotonsorialist: (AW-toh-tahn-**SOR**-ee-uh-list) a person who cuts his own hair, or who looks as if he cuts his own hair (coined by writer Christopher Corbett).

bibliothecary: a keeper of a library.

blatherskite: an obnoxious, loudmouthed braggart.

blatteroon: a person who won't shut up; a constant talker.

cockalorum: a little man who thinks he's big; a bantam who struts like a heavyweight.

cogger: (KAHG-ur) a false flatterer, charming trickster.

Historically, a *cogger* was a person adept at "cogging the dice," cheating at dice-throwing games. The word later came to mean someone who offers compliments to mask a deception.

copulative: a person about to be married.

criticaster: a third-rate, mean-spirited, contemptible critic.

If male, the criticaster usually is also a cockalorum.

cruciverbalist: a devotee of crossword puzzles, or an expert at solving them.

dimbox: someone who settles a controversy or dispute.

doppelgänger: (**DAHP**-ul-GANG-ur) a person's double, especially a ghostly or sinister one that haunts its counterpart (as in Edgar Allan Poe's story "William Wilson").

eccedentesiast: (EK-si-den-**TEE**-zee-ast) a person who fakes a smile, especially on TV (coined by writer Florence King).

ecodoomster: a person who predicts environmental catastrophe.

famulus: (FAM-yuh-l<u>u</u>s) an assistant to a scholar or magician.

fashimite: (FASH-i-myt) a slave to fashion (coined by philosopher Michael Lockwood).

fewterer: a keeper of dogs or a manager of a dog kennel.

fidimplicitary: (FY-dim-**PLIS**-i-ter-ee) a person who has implicit faith.

> *Fidimplicitary* may be used positively or negatively. It may denote a steadfast spouse or a person with unshakable confidence in you, or it may refer to someone who swallows whole whatever foolishness he or she is fed. An unusual synonym for the latter sense is **gobemouche** (gawb-MOOSH), which means literally a "fly swallower."

franion: (FRAN-y<u>u</u>n) a pleasure seeker, hedonist; colloquially, a party slut or barfly. A *franion* may be male or female.

funambulist: (fyoo-NAM-by<u>u</u>-list) a tightrope walker, also called a **schoenobatist** (skee-NAHB-uh-tist).

> For those tricky life situations when you feel as if you're walking a tightrope, it may help to hang on to the adjectives *funambulatory* (fyoo-NAM-by<u>u</u>-luh-tor-ee) and *schoenobatic* (SKEE-nuh-**BAT**-ik), which mean performing on a tightrope or pertaining to tightrope walking.

gaffoon: a person who creates sound effects in a broadcast.

gammer: an old woman, the counterpart to a *gaffer*.

gork: (medical slang) a patient with unknown ailments, an acronymic word formed from "*G*od *o*nly *r*eally *k*nows."

heliolater: (HEE-lee-**AHL**-uh-tur) a sun worshiper.

hobbledehoy: someone who is not a boy but not yet a man, especially an awkward, gawky teenager.

hominist: (HAHM-i-nist) someone who advocates equal rights for men (the opposite of *feminist*).

> Though it's clearly a useful word, *hominist* is so rare that it appears only in the comprehensive second edition of the *OED*, which traces it to the preface to *Man and Superman* (1903) by G. B. Shaw, who apparently coined it. Well-known hominists today include the drum-beating

poet Robert Bly, the antifeminist media demagogue Rush Limbaugh, and the male-liberationist psychologist and author Warren Farrell. (Before Farrell became a hominist, he was a member of NOW and an ardent **femmenist,** a man who advocates feminism.)

infracaninophile: (IN-fruh-kuh-**NYN**-uh-fyl) someone who defends or champions the underdog (coined in 1930 by Christopher Morley in the preface to *The Complete Sherlock Holmes*).

macrologist: (ma̱-KRAHL-uh-jist) a boring conversationalist that you meet at a social event and that you evade by deftly passing on to someone else.

After attending an American Booksellers Association convention (an annual event that attracts almost every card-carrying bore in the world of books), mystery novelist Carolyn G. Hart and literary agent Deborah Schneider (both decidedly unboring) wondered if there was a word for the tiresome person that you pass on to an unsuspecting victim or to another certified bore by saying something like, "Jill, I'd like you to meet Jack. I think you guys will find you have a lot in common: Jill's a heliolater and expert eccedentesiast, and Jack's a prominent hominist and autohagiographer. Oh, was that my pager? My goodness, I have to meet a criticaster at the Fashimite Books booth in two minutes. See you later!"

Artful buck passers that they are, Ms. Hart and Ms. Schneider passed their query on to your grandiloquent guide, and I'm happy to report that the bombastic buck stops here. From the word *macrology,* which means redundancy or longwindedness, comes the word *macrologist,* the dull chatterer that you'll do almost anything to get rid of.

makebate: someone who stirs up trouble or strife between others. Synonyms include *breedbate* (a word you met in the beginning of chapter 3) and *chop-straw.*

marshaller: a person who signals with batons to direct taxiing airplanes.

microlipet: (MY-kroh-**LIP**-it) someone who gets all worked up about trivial things.

milver: a person who chatters incessantly during movies (coined by columnist Joel Achenbach).

momist: a faultfinder, captious critic.

monomath: a person who knows everything about one thing and nothing about anything else (coined by journalist L. J. Davis).

mumpsimus: (MUHMP-si-mus) someone who obstinately clings to an error, bad habit, or prejudice, even after the foible has been exposed and the person humiliated; also, any error, bad habit, or prejudice clung to in this fashion.

Mumpsimus has its obstinate roots in "the story of an ignorant priest," says the *Century Dictionary,* "who in saying his mass had long said *mumpsimus* for *sumpsimus,* and who, when his error was pointed out, replied, 'I am not going to change my old *mumpsimus* for your new *sumpsimus.*'"

mythomane: (MITH-uh-mayn) someone abnormally prone to lie, exaggerate, or believe something is true when it is not.

nacket: a person who picks up stray balls during a tennis match.

nullipara: (nuh-**LIP**-uh-ruh) a childless woman.

In medical parlance, a woman who has had one child is a **primipara** (pry-**MIP**-uh-ruh or prim-**IP**-uh-ruh), and a woman who has had two or more is a **multipara** (muhl-**TIP**-uh-ruh). A pregnant woman is called a **gravida** (**GRAV**-i-duh), and if a woman is pregnant for the first time, she's a **primigravida** (PRY-mi-**GRAV**-i-duh or PRIM-i-). When pregnant a second time, she's a **secundigravida** (suh-**KUHN**-duh-**GRAV**-i-duh). At three or more pregnancies, she's a **multigravida** (MUHL-ti-**GRAV**-i-duh).

omphalopsychite: (AHM-fuh-**LAHP**-si-kyt) a contemplator of the navel, bellybutton meditator; hence, a completely self-absorbed person (from the Greek *omphalos,* navel, umbilicus).

oneirocritic: (oh-NY-ruh-**KRIT**-ik) an interpreter of dreams.

onwaiter: a person who waits patiently.

opsimath: (AHP-si-math) a late-learner; one who acquires knowledge late in life.

pangrammatist: someone who composes sentences that contain all the letters of the alphabet: *pack my box with five dozen liquor jugs.*

pantomancer: (PAN-tuh-MAN-sur) a person who sees omens in all events or a lesson lurking in every experience.

philonoist: (fi-LAHN-oh-ist) a seeker of knowledge.

pithecanthrope: (PITH-i-KAN-throhp) a prehistoric ancestor of *Homo sapiens* who resembled a cross between an anthropoid ape and a Neanderthal—in short, the legendary missing link. Also called **anthropopithecus** (AN-thruh-poh-pi-THEE-kus).

polymath: a person of superior, wide-ranging knowledge.

polyphage: (PAHL-i-fayj) a person who eats all kinds of food, especially in great quantities.

   The adjective **polyphagous** (pah-LIF-uh-gus), a synonym of *omnivorous*, means eating many different kinds of food.

pseudapostle: a person who falsely claims to be an apostle.

quidnunc: (KWID-nuhngk) someone who always wants to know what's going on (from Latin *quid nunc,* what now?).

   The verbivoracious English language contains several interesting words for busybodies and other officious folks. Here's a sample: **numquid,** an obnoxiously inquisitive person; **polypragmon** (PAHL-ee-PRAG-mun), a compulsive meddler; **yenta,** from Yiddish, and **badaud** (ba-DOH), from French, which denote gossiping fools or blabbermouths; and the freshly minted **scuttlebutthead** (coined by journalist Paul Tough), which denotes a person whose chief pleasure in life is being the first to tell everyone the latest news, whether it's a breaking story in the media or a broken heart in the office.

sarcast: a person with a quick, cutting wit; an expert in sarcasm.

screever: a person who draws pictures or scrawls begging messages on the sidewalk to elicit money from passersby.

shaconian: (shay-KOH-nee-in) a person who believes that Sir Francis Bacon was the author of Shakespeare's works.

siffleur: (see-FLUR) a professional whistler. The term for a woman in this profession is *siffleuse* (see-FLUUZ).

silentiary: (sy-LEN-shee-er-ee) a person whose job is to keep people quiet; also, one who has taken a vow of silence.

snool: a cringing, craven person; one who meanly submits to authority.

snoutfair: a person with a handsome face.

swoophead: a balding man who lets the hair on one side of his head grow long and then swoops it over the top of his head in a futile and ridiculous attempt to cover his bald spot (coined by filmmaker Michael Holman).

thaumaturge: (THAW-muh-turj) someone who performs wondrous things, a miracle worker. The corresponding noun is *thaumaturgy* (THAW-muh-TUR-jee), the working of miracles.

theologaster: (thee-AHL-uh-GAS-tur) a religious quack or phony.

theriolater: (THEER-ee-AHL-uh-tur) a person who worships animals.

troglodyte: (TRAHG-luh-dyt) someone who lives in a cave.

> *Troglodyte* need not apply only to prehistoric cave dwellers. You may use it to describe someone who lives in a dingy domicile, or people who are so socially inept or culturally benighted that they seem to have just emerged from a cave into the blinding light of civilization.

tummler: (TUUM-lur) a merrymaker, the life of the party.

> In *The Joys of Yinglish,* Leo Rosten explains that a *tummler* is "the paid nonstop social director, entertainer and 'fun-maker' in those Catskill resorts that constitute the 'Borscht Belt.'. . . It is the *tummler*'s job to guarantee to the patrons of a summer resort that most dubious of vacation boons: 'Never a dull moment.' "

visagiste: a makeup artist.

whiffler: a person who clears the way for a procession or who keeps order on a march.

wowser: a persnickety, puritanical, self-righteous snob.
zouch: a slovenly, ungenteel man; also, a bookseller.

Now you have a word for almost anyone you happen to meet, except for one—the **exoduster,** a person who beats a hasty retreat.

❖

CHAPTER SIX

FRIGHTFUL WORDS

*The World's Greatest Gathering
of Phobias*

> It is a miserable state of mind to have few things to
> desire and many things to fear.
> —FRANCIS BACON

Everyone fears something, and for whatever you dread, there
is, or can be, a phobia. At least so say the phobiologists, who
specialize not in *faux biology* but in **phobiology** (FOH-bee-
AHL-uh-jee), the study of phobias. As Normas W. Schur has
noted, "It does seem that -*phobia* can be attached to every
noun in the dictionary."

Garden-variety phobias include **claustrophobia**, fear of
enclosed spaces; **acrophobia,** fear of heights; and **agoraphobia,**
fear of open spaces, public places, or crowds. More esoteric
phobias include **sophophobia**, fear of learning; **allodoxaphobia,** fear of others' opinions; **ataxiophobia,** fear of disorder;
and **neophobia,** fear of anything new.

There are also plenty of outrageous and bizarre phobias.
For example, phobiologists have identified **dishabillophobia,**
fear of disrobing in front of someone; **dermatophobia,** fear of
skin (don't say "gimme skin" to a dermatophobe); and Drac-
ula's hang-up, **staurophobia,** fear of crucifixes.

Though such fears may seem ludicrous, it's no joke that
modern life is so stressful and frightening that phobias have

become rampant. As a result, phobiology has made the leap from the analyst's couch to the angst-filled arena of popular culture, where guts are gleefully spilled on talk shows and newspapers dolefully serve up the dread *du jour,* fueling our **pananxiety,** mass hysteria (a blend of the Greek *pan,* all, *panic,* and *anxiety*—my coinage).

One choice example should serve to illustrate the point. Some time ago, my four-year-old daughter watched a **kidvid** (a video for kids) called "A Charlie Brown Christmas" (vol. 2), based on Charles M. Schultz's comic strip "Peanuts." In one scene, a dejected Charlie Brown approaches Lucy at her counseling booth, and the following exchange takes place:

Lucy: As they say on TV, the mere fact that you realize you need help indicates that you are not too far gone. I think we'd better pinpoint your fears. If we can find out what you're afraid of, we can label it. Are you afraid of responsibility? If you are, then you have *hypengyophobia.*
Charlie Brown: I don't think that's quite it . . .
Lucy: Are you afraid of staircases? If you are, then you have *climacophobia.* Maybe you have *thallassophobia.* This is fear of the ocean. Or *gephyrophobia,* which is the fear of crossing bridges. Or maybe you have *pantophobia.* Do you think you have *pantophobia?*
Charlie Brown: What's *pantophobia?*
Lucy: The fear of everything.
Charlie Brown: That's it!

If you suffer from **counterphobia,** the compulsion to seek out that which you fear, this chapter will help you label your phobia before you can **horripilate** (hahr-**RIP**-uh-layt), get goose bumps. If you've ever had a hair-raising experience, you have known the flesh-crawling feeling of horripilation.

Below you will find over six hundred words for every fear under the sun. Well, almost—there's always room for a few more. For example, though I have searched high and low, I haven't yet been able to locate a word for one of the more common fears: riding in an elevator. You'd think there'd be a word for that—*elevaphobia, goingupordownaphobia,* or in Britain, *liftaphobia*—but apparently not. Maybe the phobiologists consider the disorder simply a form of claustrophobia.

To locate a particular phobia, simply look up the object of the aversion. Pronunciations (for the prefixes) are supplied in those instances where analogy may not suffice.

May Phobos, deity of panic and fear, be your guide!

Fear . . .

of accidents: dystychiphobia (dis-TY-ki-).

of air (and drafts): aerophobia, airphobia, pneumatophobia. See **of wind.**

of airplanes or airsickness: aeronausiphobia (AIR-oh-NAW-si-).

of (drinking) alcohol: dipsophobia, alcoholophobia, methyphobia, potophobia (POH-tuh-), dipsomanophobia, rum phobia. See **of wine.**

of alcoholic beggars: winophobia (my coinage).

of amnesia: amnesiophobia (am-NEE-zhee-uh-).

of animals: zoophobia (ZOH-uh-); **of wild animals:** agrizoophobia (AG-ri-ZOH-uh-).

of ants: myrmecophobia (MUR-muh-kuh-).

of atomic energy or nuclear weapons: nucleomitophobia.

of automobiles: motorphobia; **of riding in automobiles:** amaxophobia (uh-MAX-uh-), ochophobia; **of making love in an automobile:** amomaxiaphobia (AM-oh-MAX-ee-uh-, my coinage).

of bad words: maledictaphobia.

This word, coined by Reinhold Aman, editor and publisher of *Maledicta: The International Journal of Verbal Aggression,* refers especially to a prudish, excessive, or immature fear of hearing vulgarity and profanity or seeing it in print.

of baldness or going bald: phalacrophobia (FAL-uh-kruh-);

alopeciaphobia (AL-oh-**PEE**-shee-uh-); **of bald people:**
   peladophobia (puh-LAD-uh-).

of bathing: ablutophobia (uh-BLOO-tuh-).

of beards: pogonophobia (POH-guh-nuh-).

of becoming, or not becoming, pregnant: pregnaphobia.

   Pregnaphobia, coined by journalist Robin M. Kovat,
   denotes either of two different fears common today
   among women aged twenty to forty-five: (1) that they
   will become pregnant before they want to or feel ready to
   have a baby; or (2) that they will be unable to conceive
   once they decide to have a baby. See **of staying single.**

of bedtime or going to bed: clinophobia (KLY-nuh-).

of bees: api(o)phobia, melissophobia.

of being alone: autophobia, eremophobia (ER-uh-muh-), isolo-
   phobia (EYE-suh-luh-), monophobia, solophobia.

of being bound or tied: merinthophobia (muh-RIN-thuh-).

of being buried alive: taphephobia (TAF-uh-).

of being corrected: rectiphobia. See **of being right.**

of being dirty: automysophobia (AW-toh-**MY**-suh-). See **of
   dirt** and **of contamination.**

of being left out: see **of staying single.**

of being misunderstood: ambiguphobia (am-BIG-yoo-).

of being right: rectiphobia. See **of being corrected.**

of being scratched: amychophobia, amyctophobia (uh-MIK-
   tuh-).

of being seen: see **of stares.**

of being shot (or of guns or missiles): ballistophobia.

of the belly button (navel): omphalophobia (AHM-fuh-luh-).

of (bi)cycles, (bi)cycling, or (bi)cyclists: cyclophobia.

of birds: ornithophobia.

of black people: negrophobia.

of blame: see **of ridicule** and **of sin.**

of (the sight of) blood: hematophobia, hemophobia, hema-
   phobia.

of blushing, or the color red: erythrophobia (e̱-RITH-ruh-),
   ereuthrophobia (e̱-ROO-thruh-).

of body odor (or sweat): bromidrosiphobia (BROH-mi̱-**DROH**-si̱-), osmidrosiphobia (AHZ-mi-**DROH**-si-), kakidrosiphobia; **of one's own body odor (being repugnant):** autodysomophobia (AW-toh-DIS-uh-muh-).

One of the many wonderful things about grandiloquent words is that they have a way of popping up in unexpected places. For example, while waiting to give blood one day (I'm no hematophobe), I was browsing through a copy of *Better Homes and Gardens* (August 1994), and I came across this sentence: "There is a condition called bromidrosiphobia—an unreasonable fear of foul-smelling sweat."

By the way, it occurs to me that if we need *four* words for the fear of funk, there must be an awful lot of people out there holding on to their noses for dear life.

of Bolshevism: Bolshephobia.
of books (or simply dislike of books): bibliophobia.
of the (female) breasts: mastophobia (my coinage).

HOW TO MURDER A MASTOPHOBE

The mastophobe becomes distressed
When you say, "Can you keep abreast?"
The merest glimpse of a brassiere
Induces paralyzing fear.

The cover of a *Cosmo* mag
Will surely make this creature gag.
Sports Illustrated's swimsuit shots
Will twist a mastophobe in knots.
And photos of those *Penthouse* pets
Will bring on panic and cold sweats.

If these techniques don't do the trick
There is one more that works real quick:
Dolly Parton's awesome chest
Should cause a cardiac arrest.
—MELANIE DISHE

of (crossing) bridges: gephyrophobia (juh-FY-ruh-).
of (passing) tall buildings: batophobia (BAT-uh-).

of bulls: taurophobia (TAW-ruh-).

of burglars or muggers: see under **of men.**

of butterflies: lepidophobia (LEP-i-duh-).

of cancer: see under **of disease.**

of cars: see **of automobiles.**

of cats: ailurophobia, aelurophobia, felinophobia (fuh-LY-nuh-), galeophobia, gatophobia, elurophobia.

of Celts: Celtophobia.

of cemeteries: koimetrophobia (koy-MEE-truh-), also spelled coimetrophobia, from the Greek *koimesis,* sleep, death, and *metropolis,* city.

   Necropoliphobia (ne-KRAHP-uh-li-), my coinage, is based on the unusual English word *necropolis,* literally "a city of the dead" (from the Greek *nekros,* a dead person, corpse, and *metropolis*). See **of being buried alive** and **of tombstones.**

of change (or making changes): tropophobia. See **of novelty.**

of chickens: alektorophobia.

of childbirth: tocophobia, maieuticophobia (may-YOO-ti-kuh-), maieusiophobia (may-YOO-see-uh-).

of children or infants: p(a)edophobia, p(a)ediophobia; **of having to care for children:** pediatricophobia (my coinage).

of China or the Chinese: Sinophobia (SY-nuh-).

of chins: geniophobia (ji-NY-uh-).

of choking or suffocation: pnigophobia (NY-guh-), pnigerophobia, anginophobia.

of cholera: see under **of disease.**

of (the) church: ecclesiophobia.

of the clergy: (see **of holy persons or things**) hierophobia.

of cliffs or precipices: cremnophobia.

of close(d) places: see **of enclosed spaces.**

of closeness or of being too close: propinquiphobia (proh-PING-kwi-), proximaphobia (PRAHKS-i-muh-). Both words are my intimate inventions. See **of marriage.**

of clothing: vestiphobia.

of clouds: nephophobia, nephelophobia, nebulaphobia.

of clowns: coulrophobia, bozophobia (my coinage).

of cold: cheima(to)phobia (KY-muh-), psychrophobia, frigo-
phobia. See **of ice.**

of colors: chromophobia, chromatophobia (KROH-muh-tuh-).

of comets: cometophobia.

of computers or high technology: technophobia, cyberpho-
bia, compuphobia.

of a condom's breaking or failing during sexual intercourse:
prophylacticofrangiphobia (my nonce-word, from *pro-
phylactic* and Latin *frangere,* to break).

of constipation: coprostasiphobia (KAHP-roh-STAY-si-),
coprostasophobia.

of contamination: mysophobia (MY-suh-), molys(o)mopho-
bia (MAH-lis-muh-), misophobia.

of corpses: necrophobia. See **of death.**

of correctness (or propriety): orthophobia; **of political correctness:** orthopolitiphobia (my coinage).

PC or not PC? They say that is the question.
Hey, orthophiles and orthophobes, may I make a suggestion?
Give it a rest, you guys. You give me indigestion.
                                        —CORY JENDA, *Ad Nauseam*

of criticism: see **of ridicule.**

of crosses: see **of crucifixes.**

of crowds: ochlophobia (AHK-luh-), demophobia (DEM-uh-),
enochlophobia. See **of other people.**

of crucifixes: staurophobia (STAW-ruh-).
          This is Dracula's hang-up. See **of the sun or sunlight.**

of curses: see **of bad words.**

of dampness: hygrophobia.

of dancing: chorophobia (KOR-uh-).

of darkness or night: nyctophobia, noctiphobia, lygophobia
(LY-guh-), scotophobia, achluophobia, myctophobia.

of dawn: eosophobia (ee-OH-suh-).

of daylight: see **of the sun or sunlight.**

of death or the dead: thanatophobia (THAN-uh-tuh-), necrophobia.

of decay or decaying matter: septophobia.

of (making) decisions: decidophobia.

of defecation (painful): defecalgesiophobia (DEF-uh-kal-JEE-
zee-uh-).

of deformed people: teratophobia (TER-uh-tuh-); **of defor-
mity in oneself:** dysmorphophobia (dis-MORF-uh-). See
of monsters.

of demons (goblins, etc.): d(a)emonophobia, bogyphobia.

of dentists or dental work: dentophobia, odontophobia.

of depth: bathophobia.

of deserts or sands: eremikophobia (e-REE-mi-kuh-).

of dining or dinner conversation: deipnophobia (DYP-nuh-).

of dinosaurs: dinosauriaphobia (DY-nuh-**SOR**-ee-uh-) or
ornithoscelidaphobia (OR-ni-thoh-**SEL**-i-duh-).

Phobias must keep up with the times, so I have coined
these two words in answer to the current craze—greatly
exacerbated by the success of Steven Spielberg's movie
Jurassic Park and by that miracle of toddler TV marketing, Barney—for everything dinosaurian. They are
formed from the paleontological group names *Dino-
sauria* and its obscure synonym *Ornithoscelida.* If you
or your children love dinosaurs, substitute the suffix
-philia; substitute the suffix *-mania* for an obsession with
them.

of dirt: mysophobia (MY-suh-), dustophobia, rupophobia,
rhypophobia, molysmophobia (MAH-lis-muh-). See **of
contamination, of being dirty,** and **of dust.**

of disease or of becoming ill: pathophobia, nosophobia
(NAHS-uh-).

There are numerous pathological (disease-related) phobias. Fear **of cancer**—practically an epidemic these days—
leads the pack with carcinophobia, carcinomatophobia,
and cancer(o)phobia. Fear **of a specific disease** is
monopathophobia; fear **of cholera** is cholerophobia; fear **of
diabetes** is diabetophobia; fear **of diphtheria** (first syllable

pronounced DIF-, not DIP-) is diphtheriophobia; fear of
epilepsy is hylephobia (also see of materialism); fear of
hereditary disease is patroiophobia (pa-TROY-uh-);
fear of hair disease is trichopathophobia (TRIK-uh-
PATH-uh-); fear of heart disease is cardiophobia; fear of
kidney disease is albuminuriaphobia (al-BYOO-mi-
NYOOR-ee-uh-) or alubuminurophobia; fear of leprosy is
lepraphobia or leprophobia; fear of pellagra is pellagra-
phobia (puh-LAY-gruh-); fear of scotoma, or blind spots in
one's vision, is scotomaphobia (skuh-TOH-muh-); fear of
skin disease is dermatopathophobia (DUR-muh-tuh-PATH-
uh-); fear of venereal disease is venereophobia or cypridophobia (SIP-rid-uh-); and fear of rectal disease is
proctophobia or rectophobia (pick your preferred pain in
the butt).

   One could coin a phobia word for almost any disease or
illness, but I'll spare you that dreadful exercise and instead
leave you with two of my own monopathophobic neologisms: *nosomaniaphobia* (NAH-suh-MAY-nee-uh-), fear of
suffering from an imaginary disease; and *cerebropathopho-
bia* (SER-uh-bruh-PATH-uh-), fear of going insane from
disease. See of health.

of disorder: atax(i)ophobia.

of dizziness (spinning, whirlpools, etc.): dinophobia (DIN-
   uh-), from the Greek *dinos*, a whirling, vertigo, the source
   also of the medical word *dinical* (DIN-i-kul), pertaining
   to dizziness. See of vertigo.

of (going to) the doctor: iatrophobia (eye-AT-truh-); **of foreign doctors:** xeniatrophobia (ZEN-eye-AT-truh-).

of dogs: cynophobia (SY-nuh-), kynophobia (KY-nuh-).

of dolls or dummies: see of children or infants.

of double vision: diplopiaphobia (dip-LOH-pee-uh-).

of drafts: see of air and of wind.

of dreams or dreaming: oneirophobia (oh-NY-ruh-); **of wet
   dreams:** oneirogmophobia (OH-ny-RAHG-muh-).

of drink or drinking: potophobia (POH-tuh-). See of (drinking) alcohol and of wine.

of drugs: see **of medicine.**

of dryness or dry places: xerophobia (ZEER-uh-).

of ducks, geese, swans, mergansers: anatidaephobia (uh-NAT-i-dee-).

of dust: koniophobia (KOH-nee-uh-), amathophobia (AM-uh-thuh-). See **of dirt.**

of eating (or swallowing): phagophobia (FAG-uh-). See **of food.**

of editing or editors: redactophobia (my coinage, from *redact*, to prepare for publication).

of electricity: electrophobia.

of (riding in) elevators: elevaphobia, goinguopordownaphobia, liftaphobia (all my nonce-words).

of emotion: see **of jealousy.**

of empty spaces: see **of the void.**

of enclosed spaces or of being shut in: claustrophobia.

There are two obscure variants: cleisiophobia and cl(e)ithrophobia.

of England or the English: Anglophobia.

of (losing an) erection during sexual intercourse: medomalacophobia (MED-oh-MAL-uh-kuh-).

of error or imperfection: atelophobia. See **of sin.**

of everything: pantophobia, pan(o)phobia; **of many things:** polyphobia; **of one thing:** monophobia.

of excrement: coprophobia (KAHP-ruh-), scatophobia (SCAT-uh-).

of exhaustion (mental or physical): kopophobia (KAHP-uh-), ponophobia (PAHN-uh-).

of (one's) eyeglasses falling into a sewer: spectocloacaphobia (SPEK-toh-cloh-AY-kuh).

This jocular coinage by journalist L. J. Davis combines *spectacles* with the Latin *cloaca*, a sewer or drain, and *phobia*, to designate the fear, specifically in a man, that while he is urinating in a public restroom or portable outdoor toilet, his eyeglasses will slip from his nose and into the stink.

of eyes: ommatophobia, ommetaphobia; **of opening one's eyes:** optophobia.

of (certain) fabrics: textophobia.
of failure: kakorr(h)aphiophobia (KAK-or-uh-FEE-uh-), aty-chiphobia (uh-TY-kuh-).
of fainting: see **of weakness.**
of fatigue: see **of exhaustion.**
of fear (itself) or of being afraid: phobophobia.

> Let me assert my firm belief that the only
> thing we have to fear is *phobophobia.*
> —From a discarded draft of FDR's
> 1933 inaugural address

of feathers: pteronophobia (TER-uh-nuh-).
of feeling: see **of jealousy.**
of fever: febriphobia (FEB-ri-), fibriophobia, pyrexiophobia, pyrexeophobia.
of fire: pyrophobia, arson(o)phobia.
of fish: icthyophobia (IK-thee-uh-).
of flogging: see **of whipping.**
of floods: antlophobia.
of flowers: anthophobia (see **of plants**).
of flutes: aulophobia (AW-luh-).
of flying: aviatophobia (AY-vee-AT-uh-), aerophobia, aeroacro-phobia.
of fog or humidity: nebulaphobia, hygrophobia, homichlo-phobia (HAHM-ik-luh-).
of food: sitiophobia (SIT-ee-uh-), sitophobia (SY-tuh-), cibo-phobia (SY-buh-).
of foreigners or anything foreign: xenophobia (ZEN-uh-).
of foreign hospitality or hotels: xenodochiophobia (ZEN-uh-DOH-kee-uh-).
of forests or woods: hylophobia, xylophobia (ZY-luh-).
of forgetting: obliviophobia (my coinage). See **of amnesia.**
    In his *Word Treasury,* Paul Dickson cites *friendorphobia* for the fear of forgetting a password.
of France or the French: Francophobia, Gallophobia.
of freedom: eleutherophobia (i-LOO-thur-uh-).

of friendship: see **of society.**
of frogs and toads: batrachophobia (BA-truh-kuh-).

> A princess who fell in a well,
> Met a frog-prince who thought she was swell.
>   When he asked for a kiss
>   She said, "Frog nemesis,
> I'm your *batrachophobia* belle."
>   —HELENA CROKE

of fur (or animal skins): doraphobia.
of garlic: alliumphobia (AL-ee-um-).
     This word could also be construed to mean fear of other bulbous herbs that the genus *Allium* comprises, such as onions, chives, leeks, and shallots.
of genitals: genitophobia; (female) colpophobia, kolpophobia, eurotophobia; (male) phallophobia.
of Germany or the Germans: Germanophobia, Teutophobia, Teutonophobia.
of germs: bacteriophobia, bacillophobia, microbiophobia.
of ghosts: phasmophobia.
of girls: see **of women.**
of glass: crystallophobia, hyalophobia (HY-uh-luh-), nelophobia.
of globalization: globaphobia.
of God, the gods, or the wrath of God: theophobia.
of gold: aurophobia, chrysophobia (KRIS-uh-).
of good news: euphobia.
of government: see **of politics (or government).**
of grammar or of making grammatical errors: grammarphobia.
of graves: taphephobia.
of gravity: barophobia.
of Greece, Greeks, or Greek culture: Grecophobia (GREK-uh-), Hellenophobia (HEL-uh-nuh-); **of Greek terms or complex terminology:** Hellenologophobia.
of gringos: gringophobia.
of guns or missiles: see **of being shot.**

of **hair:** trichophobia (TRIK-uh-), chaetophobia (KEE-tuh-). See also **of baldness** and under **disease.**

of **happiness:** see **of merriment or gaiety.**

of **health or of being healthy:** sanitaphobia, the affliction of hypochondriacs (coined by Norman W. Schur).

of **heart attack:** anginophobia (an-JY-nuh-).

of **heart disease:** cardiophobia.

of **heat:** thermophobia.

of **heaven:** uranophobia (YUUR-uh-nuh-), after the Latin for heaven, *uranus;* ouranophobia (UUR-uh-nuh-), after the Greek for heaven, *ouranós.*

of **heights or high places:** acrophobia, bataphobia (BAT-uh-), hypsiphobia, hypsophobia, altophobia.
      Fear of looking up at high places is called *anablepophobia* (AN-uh-BLEP-uh-).

of **hell:** Hadephobia (HAY-di-), stygiophobia (STIJ-ee-uh-).

of **heresy:** heresyphobia (pronounced like *heresy + phobia*).

of **holy persons or things:** hagiophobia (HAY-jee- or HAG-ee-uh-), hierophobia (like *hire a phobia*). See **of the clergy.**

of **home:** ecophobia, oikophobia (see **of houses**); **of returning home:** nostophobia.

of **homosexuals or homosexuality:** homophobia. See **of monotony.**

of **horses:** hippophobia, equinophobia.

of **hospitality, or of unfamiliar accommodations:** xenodo-chiophobia (ZEN-uh-DOH-kee-uh-).

of **hospitals:** nosocomephobia (NAHS-uh-KOH-muh-).

of **(being in or stuck in) houses:** domatophobia (see **of home**).

of **hurricanes, tornadoes, cyclones, etc.:** lilapsophobia (ly-LAP-suh-). See **of wind.**

of **hypnosis:** see **of sleep.**

of **ice (or frost):** cryophobia, pagophobia.

of **ideas:** ideophobia (ID-ee-uh-), ideaphobia.

of **illness:** see **of disease.**

of **(joint) immobility:** ankylophobia (ANGK-uh-luh-).

of **infection:** see **of contamination, of disease.**

of **infinity:** apeirophobia (uh-PY-ruh-).

of injections or inoculation: trypanophobia (TRIP-uh-nuh-).

of injury: traumatophobia (TRAW-muh-tuh-). See **of war.**

of in-laws: see **of parents-in-law.**

of insanity or of going insane: maniaphobia, lyssophobia, dementophobia.

of insects: entomophobia (EN-tuh-muh-), acarophobia; **of insect stings:** cnidophobia (NY-duh-).

of intimacy: see **of marriage** and **of closeness.**

of Iraq or Iraqis: Iraqnophobia.

During the months of tension leading up to the outbreak of the Persian Gulf War in January 1991, various wags and at least one cartoonist promulgated the word *Iraqnophobia* to describe America's growing aversion to Iraq. It was a clever coinage because of its similarity in sound to *arachnophobia,* which happened to be the title of a lightweight horror picture that at the time was scaring the hairy legs off the millions of Americans who have a morbid dread of spiders.

of itching: urticariaphobia (UR-ti-KAIR-ee-uh-), uredophobia (yuu-REE-duh-), cnidosiphobia (ny-DOH-si-). See **of mites.**

> An *urticariaphobe* we'll call Mitch
> Said, "I'm afraid that I'll die if I itch.
>   Of mosquitoes I'm wary,
>   And bedbugs are scary,
> But those hives—now they're a real bitch!"
> —HAVALICE DAY

of Japan or the Japanese: Japanophobia.

of jealousy (or intense emotion): zelophobia (ZEL-uh-).

of Jews: Judophobia, Jud(a)eophobia.

of jumping (from a high or low place): catapedaphobia (KAT-uh-PED-uh-).

of justice: dikephobia (DY-kuh-).

of a king or kings: regiphobia (REJ-uh-).

of kissing: philemaphobia (fi-LEE-muh-), philematophobia, osculaphobia (my coinage).

of knees: genuphobia (JEN-yuh-).

of knives: see **of pointed or sharp objects.**

of knowledge (or learning): sophophobia, from the Greek *sophos,* wise, and *sophia,* knowledge; scientiphobia, from the Latin *scientia,* wisdom (coined by Norman W. Schur).

My unlearned offering in this category is *opsimathiphobia,* the fear of learning something too late (from *opsimathy,* knowledge acquired late in life).

of lack of fear: hypophobia, pantaphobia.

of lakes: limnophobia.

of large things: megalophobia.

of laughter: gelophobia (JEL-).

of learning: see **of knowledge.**

of leeches or of being leeched: bdellophobia (DEL-uh-).

of (things to) the left: levophobia, sinistrophobia. See **of (things to) the right.**

The November 1994 elections, which ushered in the first Republican-controlled U.S. Congress in thirty years, confirmed that American voters had become levophobic.

of lice: pediculophobia (pe-DIK-yuh-luh-), phthiriophobia (thy-RY-uh-). See **of itching.**

of light: photophobia; **of flashing lights:** selaphobia; **of glaring lights** (or of being in the spotlight): photoaugiaphobia.

of lightning: see **of thunder.**

of liquids: hygrophobia. See **of water.**

of litigation or lawsuits: litigaphobia.

of loneliness: see **of being alone.**

of (falling in) love: philophobia (FIL-uh-).

of love-play: sarmassophobia (sahr-MAS-uh-), malaxophobia (MAY-laks-uh-).

My sources indicate that both these words apply only to a woman's fear of love-play. It's curious that there doesn't seem to be a word for this phobia among men.

of lying: see **of myths or lying.**

of machinery: mechanophobia.

of madness or going mad: see **of insanity.**

of magic: rhabdophobia (RAB-duh-). See **of (being beaten by) rods or sticks** and **of whipping.**

of marriage: gam(et)ophobia, commitment phobia.

of materialism: hylephobia.

of meat: carnophobia.

of medicine or drugs: pharmacophobia; **of new medicine or drugs:** neopharmaphobia; **of mercurial medicines:** hydrargyophobia.

of memories: mnemophobia (NEE-muh-).

of men: androphobia.

      Fear of bad or evil men (burglars, muggers, etc.) is *scelerophobia* (SEL-uh-ruh-), from the Latin *scelerosus*, guilty, wicked, accursed. Fear of male offspring is *arrhenophobia* (AR-en-uh-).

of meningitis: meningitophobia.

of menstruation: menophobia.

of merriment or gaiety: cherophobia (KEER-uh-).

of metals: metallophobia (me-TAL-uh-).

of meteors and meteorites: meteor(o)phobia.

of mice or rats: muriphobia (MYUR-i-), musophobia, suriphobia.

of the mind: psychophobia. See **of the shower.**

of mirrors: catoptrophobia (kuh-TAHP-truh-), spectrophobia, enoptrophobia (ee-NAHP-truh-), eisoptrophobia (eye-SAHP-truh).

of mites: acarophobia (AK-uh-ruh).

of mobs: see **of crowds.**

of moisture: see **of fog or humidity.**

of money: chrematophobia (KREE-muh-tuh-).

of monotony or sameness: homophobia. See **of homosexuals.**

of monsters (or of giving birth to a deformed child): teratophobia (TER-uh-tuh-). See **of childbirth, of deformed people.**

of the moon: selenophobia (suh-LEE-nuh-).

of mother(s)-in-law: pentheraphobia (PEN-thur-uh-).

of motion or movement: kinesophobia (ki-NEE-suh-), kinetophobia (ki-NET-uh-).

of music: musicophobia, melophobia.

of myths or lying: mythophobia.

of nakedness: see **of nudity.**

of a name: onomatophobia (AHN-uh-MAT-uh-), nomatophobia. See **of words.**

of narrow places: stenophobia (STEN-uh-).

of needles: see **of pins and needles, of pointed or sharp objects.**

of neighbors or a neighborhood: viciniphobia (vi-SIN-i-, my coinage, derived from the Latin *vicinus*, neighbor, the source of *vicinity*).

of night: see **of darkness.**

of noise: acousticophobia; **of loud noises:** ligyrophobia (LIJ-ur-uh-).

of northern lights: auroraphobia.

of nosebleeds: epistaxiophobia.

of nothing: see **lack of fear.**

of novelty or something new: neophobia, kaino(to)phobia, caino(to)phobia, centophobia. See **of change.**

of nuclear weapons: see **of atomic energy.**

of nudity: gymnophobia, nudiphobia. See **of undressing.**

of numbers: arithmophobia, numerophobia; **of number 13:** triskaidekaphobia (TRIS-ky-DEK-uh-).

of the ocean: see **of the sea or ocean.**

of odors: olfactphobia (ahl-FAK-tuh-), osmophobia (AHS- or AHZ-), osphresiophobia (ahs-FREE-zhee-uh-). See also **of body odor.**

of old age, or of growing old: gerontophobia (juh-RAHN-tuh-), geras(c)ophobia.

of open spaces, public places, or the outdoors: agoraphobia (AG-uh-ruh-), cenophobia, kenophobia.

of the opposite sex: sexophobia.

of others' opinions: allodoxaphobia.

of outer space: spacephobia.

> Some words and phrases to avoid when speaking to a spacephobic person: *vacuum; atmosphere; universal; shuttle; starry-eyed; Astroturf; space cadet; the Moonies; once in a blue moon; Planet X; heavens to Betsy; beam me up, Scotty.*

of pain: algophobia, odynophobia (oh-DIN-uh-).

of palindromes: aibohphobia.

of paper: papyrophobia (puh-PY-ruh-).

of parasites: parasitophobia (PAR-uh-SY-tuh-).

of parents: see **of relatives.**

of parents-in-law: soceraphobia (SOH-sur-uh-).

of peace: paxophobia.

of peanut butter sticking to the roof of the mouth: arachibu-
tyrophobia (uh-RAK-i-BYOO-ti-roh-).
>   *Warning:* Do not attempt to pronounce this word with
>   peanut butter in your mouth.

of the (erect) penis: ithyphallophobia (ITH-i-FAL-uh-), me-
dorthophobia (me-DOR-thuh-).
>   The fear that the shape or contour of one's penis is vis-
>   ible through one's clothes is known as *medectophobia*
>   (me-DEK-tuh-). The fear that the penis will fail to per-
>   form satisfactorily during sexual intercourse—a fear not
>   confined to men—is called *medomalacophobia* (MED-oh-
>   MAL-uh-kuh-). The Chinese word *koro* (KOR-oh), which
>   appears in Howard Rheingold's *They Have a Word for It,*
>   is the fear that one's penis is shrinking.

of (other) people: anthro(po)phobia, apanthropia, apanthropy,
phobanthropy, demophobia; **of a room full of people:**
koinoniphobia (KOY-nah-ni-).

of performing: topophobia (TAHP-uh-). See **of a place.**

of philosophy or philosophers: philosophobia.

of phobia words: See **of words.**

of pickpockets (foreign variety): xenonosocomiophobia (ZEN-
oh-NAHS-uh-KOH-mee-uh-).

of pigeons: peristerophobia (puh-RIS-tur-uh-).

of pigs or swine: swinophobia.

of pins and needles: belonephobia, enetophobia. See **of
pointed or sharp objects.**

of a place, especially a particular place: topophobia (TAHP-
uh-). See **of performing.**

of plans: teleophobia. See **of religious ceremonies.**

of plants: botanophobia. See **of flowers.**

of pleasure: hedonophobia (hi-DAHN-uh-). See **of unhappiness.**

of poetry: metrophobia.

of pointed or sharp objects: aichmophobia (*aich-* like *Ike*), aichurophobia (eye-KYUUR-uh-). See **of pins and needles.**

of poison or being poisoned: toxiphobia, toxicophobia, toxophobia, iophobia.

of politicians: politicophobia. See **of (things to) the right.**

of politics (or government): politiphobia (coined by Benjamin Barber, professor of political science at Rutgers).

of the pope or the papacy: papaphobia.

of poverty: peniaphobia (PEE-nee-uh-).

of pregnancy: see **of becoming, or not becoming, pregnant** and **of childbirth.**

of prices (high): hypselotimophobia (HIP-suh-LAHT-uh-muh-), coined by Louis Jay Herman from the Greek *hypselos,* high, and *timos,* price.

of profanity: see **of bad words.**

of progress: prosophobia (PROH-suh-).

of propriety: see **of correctness.**

of prostitutes: cypri(a)nophobia, cypridophobia (SIP-ri-).

of protein (foods): proteinphobia.

of punishment: poinephobia. See **of whipping.**

of purple: porphyrophobia (por-FEER-uh-).

> Don't give a copy of Alice Walker's novel *The Color Purple* to a porphyrophobe.

of rabies: lyssophobia (LIS-uh-), hydrophobophobia, cynophobia (SY-nuh-), kynophobia (KY-nuh-). See **of insanity** and **of dogs.**

of railroads or train travel: siderodromophobia (SID-ur-oh-DROH-muh-).

> If you find siderodromophobia too cumbersome to pronounce, try my facetious coinage: *allaboardaphobia.* See **of subways.**

of rain: ombrophobia, pluviophobia, hyetophobia (HY-uh-tuh-).

of rape: virgivitiphobia (VUR-ji-VIT-i-).

of recycling: recyclophobia (my coinage).

of red: see **of blushing.**

of relatives: syngenesophobia (SIN-juh-NES-uh-).
>   A relatively common phobia.

of religion: see **of God** and **of theology.**

of religious ceremonies: teleophobia.

of reptiles: herpetophobia. See **of snakes.**

of responsibility: hypengyophobia (hy-PEN-jee-uh-), hypegia-
>   phobia (hy-PEE-jee-uh-), paralipophobia (PAR-uh-LY-puh-).

of ridicule: catagelophobia, katagelophobia (KAT-uh-JEL-uh-).

of (things to) the right: dextrophobia.
>   Liberals suffer from *dextrophobia;* conservatives suffer
>   from *levophobia* or *sinistrophobia* (fear of the left).

of rivers: potamophobia.

of robbers: see **of thieves** and under **of men.**

of rodents: muriphobia, musophobia, suriphobia.

of (being beaten by) rods or sticks: rhabdophobia (RAB-duh-).
>   See **of whipping** and **of magic.**

of ruin: atephobia (AT-uh-).

of Russia or Russians: Russophobia.

of rust: iophobia (EYE-uh-). See **of poison.**

of saints: see **of holy persons or things.**

of Satan (or the devil): Satanophobia (SAY-tin-uh-).

of scabies: scabiophobia. See **of itching.**

of school: schoolphobia, scolionophobia, didaskaleinophobia.

of the sea or ocean: thalassophobia (thuh-LAS-uh-).

of semen: spermatophobia, spermophobia.

of sermons: homilophobia.

of sewers: seweraphobia.

of sex, anything having to do with: genophobia (JEN-uh-).

of sexual abuse: agraphobia, contrectophobia.

of sexual feelings or sexual love: erotophobia.
>   The term applies to men and women.

of sexual intercourse: coitophobia, esodophobia (i-SAHD-uh-);
>   **of the first act of:** prime(i)sodophobia; **of (causing) painful
>   sexual intercourse:** anophelophobia (an-AHF-uh-luh-).
>   In his *Lecher's Lexicon,* J. E. Schmidt notes that *coito-
>   phobia* usually refers to women and *esodophobia* (literally,
>   "a fear of a coming into") refers to women exclusively.

The presumption here seems to be that men rarely suffer from hang-ups or hesitation about having sex. But wait a minute—*anophelophobia,* says Schmidt, is indeed a male problem, one "frequently the cause of sexual impotence, especially during the first months of married life."

Schmidt wrote his book in the 1960s, and the world has changed some since then. Today it seems reasonable to suppose that either a man or a woman could develop anophelophobia, fear of painful sexual intercourse, simply as the result of having *anophelot* of it. There is also no doubt that prime(i)sodophobia has afflicted many young males, and I'm sure that coitophobia among men has already been the subject of many a TV talk show. See **of love-play, of sexual feelings.**

of sexual perversion: paraphobia, paraphiliaphobia (from *paraphilia,* a preoccupation with unusual or abnormal sexual practices).

of shadows: sciaphobia (SY-uh-), sciophobia, or skiaphobia (SKY-uh-), from the Greek *skia,* shadow.

This is the perennial phobia of the groundhog.

of sharks: galeophobia (GAY-lee-uh-), selacophobia (SEL-uh-kuh-).

of shellfish: ostreophobia (esp. oysters); ostraconophobia.

of shock: hormephobia.

of the shower, being attacked in: psychophobia.

This anonymous coinage, inspired by Alfred Hitchcock's movie *Psycho,* logically could be applied to the fear of being attacked by a psychopath *anywhere.* See **of the mind.**

of sickness: see **of disease.**

of sin or sinning: hamartophobia (huh-MAHR-tuh-), peccatiphobia (puh-KAY-ti-).

The fear of having already committed an unpardonable sin is *enosiophobia* (e-NOH-see-uh-) or *enissophobia.*

of a single thing: monophobia.

of sitting: cathisophobia, thaasophobia, kathisophobia.

of skin: dermatophobia. See also under **disease.**

of sleep: hypnophobia.

of slime: blennophobia, myxophobia.

of smells: see **of odors.**

of small things: microphobia, tapinophobia, acarophobia.

of smoking: see **of tobacco.**

of smothering: see **of choking.**

of snakes: ophidiophobia (oh-FID-ee-uh-), ophiophobia (AHF-ee-uh-), snakephobia, herpetophobia (HUR-pe-tuh-).

of snow: chionophobia (KY-ahn-uh-), hyetophobia (HY-uh-tuh).

of society (or friendship): sociophobia. See **of other people.**

of solitude: see **of being alone.**

of sound: phonophobia. See **of speaking, of noise.**

of sourness: acerophobia, acerbophobia.

of speaking: lalophobia (LAL-uh-), laliophobia (LAY-lee-uh-), glossophobia, phonophobia.

of speaking straightforwardly: simphobia.

> *Simphobia* was coined by writer Will Stanton to refer specifically to "the fear among radio and TV broadcasters of saying anything in a straightforward, unequivocal manner," and to the accompanying proclivity for vague, ambivalent, or evasive locutions.

of speed: tachophobia.

of spiders: arachnophobia (uh-RAK-nuh-), arachneophobia.

of squeezing or being squeezed: charminophobia (from the ad campaign for toilet paper featuring the slogan, "Please don't squeeze the Charmin").

of stairs (climbing or falling down): climacophobia.

of standing (for fear of falling): stasiphobia (STAS-i-); **of standing and walking:** stasibasiphobia (STAS-i-BAY-suh-), basistasiphobia (BAY-suh-STAS-uh-).

of stares or being stared at: ophthalmophobia (ahf-THAL-muh-), scop(t)ophobia.

of stars: astrophobia, siderophobia (SID-uh-ruh-).

of staying single: anuptaphobia (an-UHP-tuh-).

> Another word for this phobia that is on the verge of entering English is the German *torschlüsspanik* (TOR-shloos-PAHN-ik), cited in Howard Rheingold's *They Have a Word for It.* Literally translated as "door-shutting

panic," the word refers to a young woman's fear of not being able to find a suitable husband before she loses the race against the biological clock and grows too old to have children. Rheingold muses that it also could be applied to the fear of competing in "the mating marketplace," a sense that these days would seem applicable to both sexes. See **of becoming, or not becoming, pregnant.**

of stealing: see **of thieves.**

of (one's) stepfather: vitricophobia (VI-tri-kuh-).

of (one's) stepmother: novercaphobia (noh-VUR-kuh-).

of stillness: eremophobia. See **of being alone.**

of stooping: kyphophobia (KY-fuh-).

of storms: see **of hurricanes** and **of thunder.**

of strangers or anything strange: xenophobia (ZEN-uh-).

of streets or crossing the street: agyiophobia (AJ-ee-uh-), dromophobia. See **of subways.**

of string: linonophobia (li̱-NAHN-uh-).

of stuttering: psellismophobia (suh-LIZ-muh- or SEL-iz-muh-).

> *Psellism* (SEL-iz'm) is the technical term for a speech defect such as stuttering, stammering, or lisping.

of Styrofoam: polystyrophobia.

> I have taken the liberty of coining this word because I needed a name for my lifelong morbid dread of handling, or of hearing others handle, that awful squeaky expanded plastic made from polystyrene known by the trade name Styrofoam. As you can imagine, a bad case of polystyrophobia can turn the simple act of opening packages or Christmas gifts into a gruesome ordeal.

of subways or underground trains: bathysiderodromophobia (BATH-ee-SID-ur-oh-DROH-muh-).

> This marvelous mouthful of a word is composed of four combining forms from Greek: *bathy,* deep; *sidero,* iron; *dromo,* a course or track; and *phobia,* fear.

of suffering: see **of pain** and **of disease.**

of suffocation: see **of choking.**

of the sun or sunlight: heliophobia, phengophobia (FEN-juh-).

> This is Dracula's other hang-up. See **of crucifixes.**

of supernatural powers: deisidaimonia (DY-si-dy-**MOH**-nee-uh-).
of surgery: tomophobia.
of sweat: see **of body odor.**
of symbolism: symbolophobia.
of symmetry: symmetrophobia.
of syphilis: syphilophobia. See also under **of disease.**
of talking: see **of speaking.**
of tapeworms: t(a)eniophobia (TEE-nee-uh-).
of taste: geumaphobia, geumophobia, geumatophobia (GYOO-).
of taxes: taxophobia.

> These days it seems there's nothing like the specter of new taxes to inspire fear in the electorate or make a politician run scared. Such rampant fear requires an appropriately dreadful new word: "The ads, which chastised [Sen. Robert] Dole for refusing to sign a pledge not to raise taxes, arguably cost him the primary in the taxophobic state" (*The New York Times Magazine,* March 5, 1995).

of technology: technophobia.
of teeth: odontophobia. See **of dentists.**
of (using) the telephone: telephonophobia.

> Thankfully, modern technology has provided a simple cure for those afflicted with telephonophobia:

> This telephonophobe once groaned
> Whenever someone telephoned;
> I'd panic, then have an attack,
> And yank the wire from the jack.
> A dial tone would make me queasy—
> I'm telling you, life wasn't easy.

> Today I do not fear a ring,
> Nor do I climb the walls;
> But you won't catch me blathering—
> My machine takes all my calls.
> —HUBIE TOLFREY

of termites: isopterophobia.

of tests or taking a test: testophobia.

of tetanus (or lockjaw): tetanophobia. See **of disease.**

of theater(s): theatrophobia.

of theology: theologicophobia.

of thieves, or of becoming a thief: kleptophobia, cleptophobia, harpaxophobia.

of thinking: phronemophobia (fruh-NEE-muh-).

of (the number) thirteen: triskaidekaphobia (TRIS-ky-DEK-uh-).

Triskaidekaphobia is also often used to mean fear of Friday the 13th. Apparently, however, there's another way to skin a Friday-the-13th fraidy-cat. Recently I saw an ad for a book on conquering fear by a certain Dr. Donald Dossey, who specializes in treating phobias, anxiety, and stress. The headline screamed, "PARASKEVIDEKATRIAPHOBIA: Do You Fear Friday the 13th?"

Dr. Dossey, who makes frequent appearances on radio and TV talk shows to discuss "fascinating facts about Friday the 13th," is the author of *Holiday Folklore, Phobias, and Fun.* In that book, which I dug out of the public library, I discovered why I hadn't found *paraskevidekatriaphobia* in any dictionary or reference book I'd consulted.

"'Triskaidekaphobia,'" writes the fearless doctor, "means only 'the fear of the number 13.' 'Friday' is not even in the word. The term 'paraskevidekatriaphobia,' which I coined circa 1982, is the true word for the combined fear of the day Friday and the number 13."

I'm afraid even to hazard a guess on how to pronounce *paraskevidekatriaphobia.* "When you learn to pronounce it," says Dr. Dossey in his ad, "you are cured." Oh, well. Back to the dreading board.

The humorous nonce-word *triskaidekaphobiaphobia,* invented by writer and editor Mark J. Estren, means a morbid dread of the simpleminded stories on triskaidekaphobia that saturate the media every Friday the 13th.

Variants for the thirteen-phobia include *tridecaphobia,* *tredecaphobia,* and *triskadekaphobia,* all of which lack the pedigree of *triskaidekaphobia.*

of thunder: brontephobia, brontophobia, tonitruphobia (toh-NI-truh-); **of thunder and lightning:** astrapophobia (AS-truh-puh-) or astraphobia; keraunophobia (ke-RAW-nuh-), from the Greek *keraunos,* thunderbolt, may be used of a fear of thunder and lightning or of lightning alone.

of time: chronophobia (KRAHN-uh-).

of tobacco or smoking: tobaccophobia.

of tombstones: placophobia. See **of cemeteries**.

of touching or being touched: (h)aphephobia, haptephobia, haptophobia, thixophobia.

of travel: hodophobia, turistaphobia. See **of hospitality**.

of trees: dendrophobia.

of trembling: tremophobia.

of trichinosis: trichinophobia (see **of disease**).

of tuberculosis: tuberculophobia, phthis(i)ophobia. See **of disease**.

of (finding) typographical errors: typophobia.

Richard Dowis, a fellow logophile and president of the Society for the Preservation of English Language and Literature (SPELL), coined this word in a letter to me. I'm sure that Dowis, a confessed typophobe, would agree that *typophobia* could be construed to mean either the fear of discovering a typographical error in one's published work or an aversion to typos in general.

of tyrants: tyrannophobia.

of uncleanliness: mysophobia (MY-suh-).

of undressing (in front of someone): dishabillophobia (DIS-uh-BIL-uh-), from *dishabille* (DIS-uh-**BEEL**), the state of being incompletely or carelessly clothed.

Dishabillophobia applies not only to the fear of taking one's clothes off in another's presence but also to the fear that someone will surprise you in a state of undress. Another word for this phobia, coined by Philip Howard of the London *Times,* is *misapodysis* (MIS-ap-uh-**DY**-sis), built from *mis-*, aversion (pinch-hitting for *-phobia*), and *apod-ysis,* from the Greek *apodyesthai,* to undress.

of unhappiness: anhedoniphobia (an-hi-DOH-nuh-).

of urinating: urophobia.

of vaccination: vaccinophobia.

of vegetables: lachanophobia (luh-KAN-uh-).

of vehicles: see of automobiles.

of vertigo: dinophobia (DIN-uh-), illyngophobia (il-LINJ-uh-). See **of dizziness.**

of (losing one's) virginity: see under of sexual intercourse.

of virgins: parthenophobia (PAHR-thuh-nuh-).

of voices: see of speaking.

of the void: kenophobia (KEN-uh-).

of vomiting: emetophobia (EM-uh-tuh-).

of waiting (a long while): macrophobia.

of walking: ambulophobia, basiphobia, basophobia (BAY-suh-).

of war: machiaphobia (MAK-ee-uh-, my coinage, from the Greek *mache,* battle). See **of injury** and **of atomic energy.**

of washing: see of bathing.

of wasps: spheksophobia (SFEK-suh-).

of water: hydrophobia, aquaphobia; **of bad or contaminated water:** cacohydrophobia, malaquaterror, turistaphobia (all coined by Louis Jay Herman for one of the greatest fears of travelers).

of waves: cymophobia (SY-muh-), kymophobia (KY-muh-).

of weakness: asthenophobia (as-THEE-nuh-).

of wealth: chrematophobia (KREE-muh-tuh-), from the Greek *chremata,* goods, money; divitiphobia (di-VIT-i-), from the Latin *divitiae,* wealth (coined by Norman W. Schur).

of (gaining) weight: obesophobia, procrescophobia.

of whipping or being whipped: mastigophobia (MAS-ti-guh-).

    Mastigophobia, from the Greek *mastigos,* a whip, means fear of being whipped; *rhabdophobia* (RAB-duh-), from the Greek *rhabdos,* a rod or stick, means fear of being caned or flogged with a stick. Both words may also be used to mean fear of punishment or castigation.

of whirlpools: see **of dizziness.**

of white people: albophobia, Anglophobia; **of the color white:** leukophobia.

of wind: anemophobia (AN-uh-muh-), from the Greek *anemos,* wind. See **of hurricanes.**

of wine: oenophobia (EE-nuh-), oinophobia (OY-nuh-). See **of drink or drinking.**

of wisdom: see **of knowledge.**

of women: gynephobia, gynophobia, feminophobia; **of beautiful women:** venustaphobia (vi-NUHST-uh-), calligynia-phobia (KAL-i-JIN-ee-uh-); **of lewd women or prostitutes:** cypri(a)nophobia or cypridophobia; **of young girls or virgins:** parthenophobia (PAHR-thuh-nuh-).

For the fear that women will subvert men and run the show, I offer *lysistrataphobia* (LIS-is-TRAHT-uh-), after the comedy by Aristophanes in which the women of Athens lock their husbands out of the city and refuse to have intercourse of any kind with them until they promise not to make war.

If the antifeminist broadcaster Rush Limbaugh ever sees this book, he'll probably propose his own female-phobia based on his favorite word: *feminaziphobia,* a morbid dread of ardent feminists or of strong-willed, independent women.

of wood: xylophobia (ZY-luh-), hylophobia (HY-luh-).

of words: verbophobia, logophobia; **of a certain word or name:** onomatophobia (AH-nuh-MAT-uh-); **of words about phobias:** phobologophobia (coined by Paul Hellweg); **of long words:** sesquipedaliaphobia; **of repeating the same word:** monologophobia (coined by Theodore Bernstein).

of work: ergophobia, ergas(i)ophobia; **of overworking:** pono-phobia (PAHN-uh-).

of worms: vermiphobia, scoleciphobia (sko-LES-uh-); **of being infested with worms:** helminthophobia (hel-MIN-thuh-).

of (getting) wrinkles: rhytiphobia (RIT-i-).

of the act of writing, or of the written word: graphophobia, pen-
  phobia, scriptophobia; **of writing love letters, or of erotic
  writing:** erotographophobia (i-RAH-tuh-GRAF-uh-).

of X-rays or radiation: radiophobia.

of youth or young people: hebephobia (HEE-buh-), from the
  Greek *Hebe*, goddess of youth (my coinage).

❖

CHAPTER SEVEN

RELIGIOVERBOSITY*

An Arkful of Words About Religion, Belief, and the Prescient Art

Have you ever looked at a painting or sculpture of Christ on the cross and wondered if there was a word for the little block of wood under his feet? If you're anything like me—and you must be since you're still reading this nutty book—no doubt you've been plagued by that question for years and have searched in vain for an answer. Your search, I'm happy to say, is at an end; you may rest in peace. The block of wood that supports the feet of a crucified person is called a **suppedaneum** (SUHP-uh-**DAY**-nee-<u>um</u>). Isn't it a relief to have that stupendous word under your feet?

Before we begin our exploration of esoteric ecclesiastical English, I should note that the vast majority of religious terms residing in our dictionaries pertain to Christianity. Long-winded analysis of the complex reasons for that state of affairs is beyond the scope of this grandiloquent guide. I make the point simply to alert you that in this chapter I have made every effort to be catholic in my selection (with a lowercase *c*, *catholic* means universal, wide-ranging, of interest to all), but most of the polysyllabic verbal relics I dug up in my pilgrimage to the sanctum sanctorum of language have their roots in the classical Latin and Greek of Christian tradition. Nevertheless, whatever your faith, I have faith that you will find these heav-

*My nonce-word for "a running off at the mouth about religion."

enly words sometimes reverent, sometimes irreverent, sometimes holy, and wholly irresistible.

Now, with that disclaimer out of the way, let's get back to cross-purposes. Another of my religioverbal vexations was the meaning of the four letters often depicted on a plaque affixed to Christ's cross: I.N.R.I. It turns out this is an abbreviation of the Latin *Iesus Nazarenus, Rex Iudaeorum* (the Latin *I* being equivalent to the English *J*), which means "Jesus of Nazareth, King of the Jews." The New Testament (John 19:19ff) shows that Pontius Pilate ordered these words placed on Christ's cross.

The night before the crucifixion, Jesus and the apostles shared the Last Supper. Did you know there's a special word for the room in which the meal took place? The "large upper room furnished and prepared," described in Mark 14:15 as the site of the Last Supper, is called the **cenacle** (SEN-uh-kul).

During the Last Supper, Jesus led the apostles in Holy Communion, also known as the Eucharist. Those who wish to disparage Holy Communion refer to it as **theophagy** (thee-AHF-uh-jee), which means literally "god-eating." The word is more generally used to describe the practice, among certain primitive tribes, of eating some symbol of a god. When the Eucharist is given to a dying person, it is called a **viaticum** (vy-AT-i-kum), a word used by the ancient Romans to mean money and supplies given to someone going on a journey—in today's lingo, an expense account.

In depictions of the resurrected Christ we often see the terrible scars of crucifixion on His hands and feet. These wounds, or any marks resembling them that are said to have appeared supernaturally on someone's body (such as St. Francis of Assisi's), are known as **stigmata** (STIG-muh-tuh or stig-MAH-tuh). This is the plural of *stigma*, which today may refer to a physical defect, such as a blemish or lesion, or to a figurative defect, a mark of infamy or stain on one's reputation.

An appearance of the resurrected Christ (with or without stigmata) is called **Christophany** (kri-STAHF-uh-nee). From Hindu mythology we inherit the word **avatar** (AV-uh-tahr), which refers to the incarnation of a deity (especially Vishnu) as a human being or animal. The general terms for a manifestation of a deity on earth are **theophany** (thee-AHF-uh-nee) and **epiphany** (e-PIF-uh-nee). The reverse phenomenon, when a person becomes a god or is elevated to godlike stature, is called **apotheosis** (uh-PAH-thee-OH-sis).

> In churches everywhere we see
> The faithful praying for *theophany*.
> But if God is Man, and Man is God,
> Then my religion's not so odd:
> What I've always prayed for most is
> Personal *apotheosis*.
> —WILLIAM FLAKE

Here are a few more **crucificial** words—ones pertaining to the cross. **Cruciferous** (kroo-SIF-ur-us) means bearing or carrying a cross. Worship of the cross, or of the figure of Christ on the cross, is called **staurolatry** (staw-RAHL-uh-tree). Historically it is not a complimentary term. According to *Webster 2*, the word was originally used opprobriously by Protestants to denigrate Roman Catholic veneration of the cross. **Mariolatry** (MAIR-ee-AHL-uh-tree) means worship of the Virgin Mary, and is equally uncomplimentary. Two inoffensive synonyms of *Mariolatry* are **hyperdulia** (HY-pur-du-LY-uh) and **parthenolatry** (PAHR-thuh-NAHL-uh-tree), which also means worship of a virgin or virgins. The latter term comes from the same Greek source as *Parthenon*, the famous Doric temple built on the Acropolis at Athens for Athena, the virgin goddess of wisdom.

Although I occasionally feel cruciferous (that I'm bearing my cross), staurolatry and Mariolatry were not part of my religious upbringing. (As a teenager, however, I once had a mild case of parthenolatry.) I was brought up in two faiths: in the good-natured, meditative fellowship of the Society of Friends, or Quakers, and in the New England–grown, vaguely transcendental, "liberal theology" of Unitarian-Universalism, a Protestant sect perhaps best known for planting its faithful feet firmly in midair. The traditional doctrine of Unitarian-Universalism (if there actually is one) is anti-Trinitarian; that is, U-U folks reject the Trinity and instead worship a single God (the *unit* in Unitarian) and embrace the notion of universal salvation (Universalism). Therefore, as a youngster in Sunday school I was inculcated with **psilanthropy** (sy-LAN-thruh-pee) or **psilanthropism** (sy-LAN-thruh-piz'm), the belief that Jesus was not divine but merely a man (albeit divinely inspired).

Those who believe in the divinity of Christ adhere, of course, to the opposite doctrine: **theanthropy** (thee-AN-thruh-pee) or **theanthropism** (thee-AN-thruh-piz'm), which means belief in the union of the divine and human. The adjectives *theanthropic* (THEE-an-THRAHP-ik) and *theandric* (thee-AN-drik) mean combining the human and divine, or pertaining to a person who is both a god and human.

A **theanthropist** (thee-AN-thruh-pist) believes that the divine can manifest itself in mortal form, or that mortals can be divine. (Watching Sophia Loren in a movie is enough to make me a theanthropist.) If you're into **anthropolatry** (AN-thruh-PAHL-uh-tree), you worship a human being as a god. ("Beatlemania" was one salient example of anthropolatry.) And if you're the awesome object of such worship, then you are either a **theanthropos** (THEE-an-THROH-pahs), a godlike person, or Elvis Presley.

NEARER MY THEO- TO THEE

To find out all you want to know about God or the gods, you need to get acquainted with the combining form *theo-*, "god," which comes from the Greek *theos*, god. A peep into any unabridged dictionary reveals a host of *theo-* words, many of them languishing in lexical purgatory awaiting resurrection.

Here is a selection of my favorites:

theochristic: (THEE-oh-KRIS-tik) anointed by God.
theocracy: (thee-AHK-ruh-see) government by persons who claim to represent God.

theocrasy: (thee-AHK-ruh-see) the worship of different gods.

theogamy: (thee-AHG-uh-mee) a marriage between gods.

> *Theogamy* could also apply to a marriage between two pop idols—for example, Michael Jackson and Lisa Marie Presley. The word for their breakup is *theomachy* (see below).

theoktony: (thee-AHK-tuh-nee) the death of God or the gods.

theologoumenon: (THEE-uh-lah-GOO-muh-nahn) individual opinion on God or divinity, as distinguished from doctrine.

theomachy: (thee-AHM-uh-kee) a battle among gods, or a battle against God or the gods.

> A *theomachist* is a person who fights God or the gods.

theomania: (THEE-oh-MAY-nee-uh) religious madness, specifically that sort in which someone believes he or she is God or has been chosen by God to carry out some divine mission.

> *Theomaniacs* tend to lead religious cults, often destructive ones. Memorable theomaniacs of our time include Jim Jones, of the People's Temple mass suicide in Guyana; David Koresh, of the Branch Davidian or Koreshian holocaust in Waco, Texas; and Charles Manson, of the Sharon Tate or Helter-Skelter murders.

theomastix: (THEE-oh-MAS-tiks) When a deity or the deities are thoroughly fed up with humankind, the result is a theomastix. Loosely, the word is a synonym of plague, but *Webster 2* offers this more illustrative definition: "a divinely constituted or designated scourge of mortals." The biblical flood is the classic example of a theomastix.

theomicrist: (thee-AHM-uh-krist) a person who mocks God or divinity.

theomorphic: (THEE-oh-MOR-fik) having a godlike form or aspect.

> When someone says, "Darling, you look divine tonight," then you are theomorphic.

theonomy: (thee-AHN-uh-mee) government by God, or the state of being under the rule of God.

theophobia: the fear of God.

theophilanthropist: (THEE-oh-fi-LAN-thruh-pist) someone who loves both God and humankind.

The adjective is *theophilanthropic* (THEE-oh-FIL-an-THRAHP-ik).

theopneusty: (THEE-ahp-NYOOS-tee) divine inspiration, especially that which enables a person to receive and reveal divine truth.

The adjective is *theopneustic* (THEE-ahp-N(Y)OOS-tik), divinely inspired.

The Belief Beef

Are you a good believer or have you strayed from the flock? People who strictly adhere to the doctrine of their chosen faith engage in **orthopraxy** (OR-thuh-PRAK-see), while those who don't are guilty of **heteropraxy** (HET-uh-roh-PRAK-see).

Are you hoping for salvation? If so, you should get acquainted with the word **soterial** (soh-TEER-ee-'l), of or pertaining to salvation. Although *soterial* may be used generally, the related noun **soteriology** (soh-TEER-ee-AHL-uh-jee) refers specifically to the doctrine that salvation is obtained only through Jesus Christ.

If you think soteriology is a tad restrictive, then you certainly won't want to adopt the Calvinist doctrine of **preterition** (PRET-ur-ISH-in), which espouses the "done-deal" philosophy of salvation—namely that God, after deciding whom to save, simply passed over everyone else. On the sunny side of Salvation Street is **apocatastasis** (AP-oh-kuh-TAS-tuh-sis), which maintains that when it comes to God's grace, all souls get to play and everyone will eventually be saved.

Here are some more exceptionally grandiloquent words pertaining to religious belief:

allotheism: (AL-oh-thee-iz'm) the worship of strange gods.
anthropotheism: (AN-thruh-puh-THEE-iz'm) the belief that

the gods originated from human beings and are essentially human in nature.

apikoros: (AP-i-**KOR**-us) a Jewish person who either does not believe in Judaism or who is lax in observing Jewish law.

Curiously, the words *apikoros* and *epicure* come from the same Greek root. The plural is *apikorsim*. For the Christian counterpart, see **Laodicean** below.

autolatry: (aw-**TAHL**-uh-tree) self-worship; the cult of looking out for number one (the number-one faith in America).

bitheism: (BY-thee-iz'm) belief in two gods, also called **ditheism** (DY-thee-iz'm).

Belief in three gods is **tritheism,** but note that this word has an especially refined meaning: belief that the Trinity—the Father, Son, and Holy Ghost—comprises three distinct gods. After tritheism we stop counting and settle for the general term **polytheism,** belief in many gods.

chiliasm: (KIL-ee-az'm) the doctrine that, in accordance with biblical prophecy, Jesus Christ will return to earth and reign for one thousand years (also called *millenarianism* or *millennialism*). *Chiliast* (KIL-ee-ast) is the noun.

ecclesiolatry: (e-KLEE-zee-**AHL**-uh-tree) excessive devotion to the church.

eidolism: (eye-DOH-liz'm) belief in ghosts and spirits.

fideism: (FY-dee-iz'm) reliance upon faith, rather than reason, as the foundation of belief and the source of truth.

hecastotheism: (he-**KAS**-tuh-**THEE**-iz'm) the practice of investing all sorts of objects with supernatural powers.

hylotheism: (HY-luh-**THEE**-iz'm) the doctrine that God and matter are the same.

Hylozoism (HY-luh-**ZOH**-iz'm) is the belief that matter has life, or that life is a property of matter.

Laodicean: (lay-AHD-uh-**SEE**-in) lukewarm or indifferent in one's religious beliefs.

The early Christians of Laodicea, a city in Greater Phrygia, were infamous for their ho-hum attitude toward their faith. As affluent and complacent ECUMPs (Early Christian Upwardly Mobile Persons), their most fervent response to religion was a yawn or a shrug—about the level of excitement a modern teenager displays when a parent is talking. St. John the Divine, however, was not about to let the Laodiceans get away with paying lip service to the Lord, and he read them the riot act in Revelation 3:14–17:

> I know thy works, that thou art neither cold nor hot: I would thou wert cold or hot. So then because thou art lukewarm, and neither cold nor hot, I will spew thee out of my mouth. Because thou sayest, I am rich, and increased with goods, and have need of nothing; and knowest not that thou art wretched, and miserable, and poor, and blind, and naked. . . .

Today *Laodicean* is used as an adjective to mean lukewarm or indifferent toward religion, or as a noun to mean anyone who is spiritually lukewarm or lackadaisical.

latitudinarian: (LAT-i-T(Y)OO-di-**NAIR**-ee-in) a broad-minded person who is tolerant of others' religious views; as an adjective, broadly tolerant of different religious beliefs.

minimifidian: (MIN-i-mi-**FID**-ee-in) having the least faith possible, being but a hairsbreadth away from faithlessness.

This word may also be used as a noun: a *minimifidian* has almost no faith—in anything.

monogenism: (muh-NAHJ-uh-niz'm) the belief that the human race is descended from two people—Adam and Eve, for example.

parousiamania: (puh-ROO-z(h)ee-uh-**MAY**-nee-uh) obsession with the Second Coming of Christ.

Parousiamaniaphobia (my nonce-word) is a morbid dread of proselytizers who come to your door every week to remind you that the Second Coming is at hand and ask for a handout.

physitism: (FIZ-i-tiz'm) worship of nature, also called **cosmolatry** (kahz-MAHL-uh-tree).

theriolatry: (THEER-ee-**AHL**-uh-tree) worship of animals as gods—a common practice among avid football fans.

ACCOUTERMENTS AND OTHER DOODADS

Here are a few words for religious accouterments that you've probably seen but didn't know what they were called:

aspergillum: (AS-pur-JIL-<u>um</u>) an instrument for sprinkling holy water, typically a short-handled brush or perforated globe.

aspersorium: (AS-pur-SOR-ee-<u>um</u>) a basin for holy water, usually placed at the entrance to or in the vestibule of a church. It is more commonly known as a **stoup** (STOOP).

crosier: (KROH-zhur) the ceremonial pastoral staff of a bishop, abbot, or abbess. It has a hook at the top like a shepherd's crook.

miter: (MY-tur) the tall ceremonial headdress resembling a pointed arch traditionally worn by bishops and abbots (and, of course, the bishop of Rome, otherwise known as the Roman Catholic pope)—"that conehead hat," as my wife described it when recommending that I include the word in this book.

   The two strips of cloth that hang from the back of the miter are called **lappets** (LAP-its) or **infulae** (IN-fyoo-lee).

payess: (PAY-<u>es</u>) In *The Joys of Yinglish*, Leo Rosten defines *payess* as "the unshorn ear-ringlet hair and sideburn-locks worn by Orthodox Jewish males, especially Hasidim."

   According to Rosten, "the custom among Orthodox Jews of letting their ear curls grow long and wearing a full beard comes from an instruction in Leviticus 19:27: 'Ye shall not round the corners of your heads, neither shalt thou mar the corners of thy beard.' (*Payess* are regarded as symbolizing the uncut corners of a field at harvest time, which were by tradition left to be gleaned by the widow, the orphan, the stranger.)"

phylactery: (fi-LAK-tur-ee) one of the two small, square, black leather boxes containing slips of parchment on which are written certain biblical verses pertaining to Jewish law and the proper worship of God. Each phylactery is connected to a slender leather strap. During weekday morning prayers, one is worn on the head and the other is attached to the left arm, with the strap wound around the forearm.

pyx: (PIKS) a vessel or container for the Eucharistic wafer, also called *tabernacle* or *ciborium* (si-BOR-ee-<u>u</u>m).

tallith: (TAH-lis or tah-LEET) the traditional prayer shawl worn by Jewish men. The fringes at the corners of the tallith are called **zizith** (tsee-TSEET or TSI-tsis).

thurible: (THOOR-<u>i</u>-buul) the incense holder used in religious ceremonies, also called *censer* (SEN-sur). It is "usually cup-shaped, has a cover pierced with holes, and is suspended by chains," says *Webster 2.*

You've probably seen a **thurifer** (THOOR-<u>i</u>-fur), the person who carries the thurible, swinging the vessel and leaving a trail of perfumed smoke. The swinging is practical, not ritualistic; it quickens combustion.

wimple: (WIM-p'l) the traditional headgear of a nun—a cloth draped around the head, chin, neck, and shoulders.

zucchetto: (zoo-KET-oh) a skullcap worn by Roman Catholic clerics—the cousin, you might say, of the Jewish yarmulke. What color zucchettos do the following clerics wear?

1. priests	a. red
2. bishops	b. white
3. cardinals	c. black
4. the pope	d. violet (or purple)

(Answers appear at the end of the chapter.)

THE LEXICAL COLLECT FOR THE DAY

The sermon is over. All the prayers have been muttered and all the hymns sung. Now it's time to pass the plate, but this time instead of money we're collecting glorious, grandiloquent words, and you get to keep them all.

Below, rescued from the linguistic Styx, is a selection of the most recondite bits of religioverbosity I could conjure. These words may not save your soul, but they may inspire it.

Adamitism: nakedness, in imitation of the biblical Adam, for religious reasons.

As the story goes, in the fifteenth and sixteenth centuries, the Adamites, an obscure sect of religious fanatics, would gather secretly and perform occult rituals *sans* antipudic attire (i.e., fig leaves).

"One Picard, of Bohemia, was the founder in 1400, and styled himself 'Adam, son of God,' " explains Brewer's *Dictionary of Phrase and Fable*. "He professed to recall his followers to the state of primitive innocence. No clothes were worn, wives were in common, and there was no such thing as good and evil, but all actions were indifferent."

I tried, but I couldn't find hide nor hair of any "Eveism" or "Evites."

agathocacological: (AG-uh-thoh-KAK-uh-**LAH**-jik-'l) composed of good and evil; pertaining to both good and evil.

> Before the serpent, and that forbidden bite,
> Eve and Adam knew not wrong from right.
> Tempted to sin, they bit and fell,
> And now we're all *agathocacological*.
> —JOHN MILTOWN,
> *Pair of Dice Tossed*

altitonant: (al-TIT-uh-nint) thundering from above or on high.

amrita: (uhm-REE-tuh) a beverage imparting immortality, the elixir of the gods.

Amrita is Hinduism's equivalent to the nectar imbibed by the Greek gods. The food of the Greek gods is called *ambrosia*.

anthropopathy: (AN-thruh-**PAHP**-uh-thee) ascribing human feelings and passions to God or to the gods.

The related word **anthropophuism** (AN-thruh-**PAHF**-yoo-iz'm) means ascribing human nature or human traits to God or to the gods.

bulla: the seal affixed to an authoritative decree (called a *bull*) issued by the Roman Catholic pope.

conventicle: (kuhn-**VEN**-tik-'l) a secret or unlawful religious assembly, especially one conducted by those at odds with the established church.

deiparous: (dee-**IP**-uh-rus) giving birth to a god or goddess.

This word denotes what all first-time parents feel in the brief period before they become sleep-deprived zombies.

ecclesioclastic: (e-**KLEE**-zee-oh-**KLAS**-tik) disruptive or destructive to the church.

eisegesis: (EYE-suh-**JEE**-sis) bad exegesis, or, as *Webster 2* puts it, "faulty interpretation of a text, as of the Bible, by reading into it one's own ideas."

entheate: (EN-thee-it) divinely inspired, possessed by a god.

exclaustration: (EKS-klaw-**STRAY**-shun) the act of leaving, or being expelled from, a religious retreat.

I found this rare specimen in Norman W. Schur's *1000 Most Obscure Words,* a book that is far more entertaining than its title. *Exclaustration* comes from the Latin *ex-*, out, and *claustrum,* enclosure, the source of the English *cloister;* by derivation it denotes the act of booting someone out of a religious retreat, or, as Schur puts it more diplomatically, the "resumption of secular life by one who has been released from his or her vows."

hagiolatry: (HAG-ee- or HAY-jee-**AHL**-uh-tree) worship of saints.

hajj: (HAHJ) a pilgrimage to Mecca.

A *hajji* (HAHJ-ee) is a person who has made a pilgrimage to Mecca.

hamartiologist: (huh-**MAHR**-tee-**AHL**-uh-jist) an expert on the subject of sin.

From Moses (the Ten Commandments) to Milton (*Paradise Lost*) to Madonna ("Like a Virgin"), our culture—high and low, from the sublime to the slime—is strewn with hamartiologists of every stripe. Perhaps Ogden Nash put it best when he wrote,

> The only people who should really sin
> Are the people who can sin with a grin.

hermeneutics: (HUR-muh-**N(Y)OO**-tiks) biblical interpretation.

hieromachy: (HY-ur-**AHM**-uh-kee) a dispute or conflict among members of the clergy.

ichor: (EYE-kor or EYE-kur) the ethereal fluid that flows in the veins of the gods instead of mortal blood.

jnana: (juh-NAH-nuh) in Hinduism, spiritual knowledge obtained through meditation and study.

The Hindu method of achieving salvation through rigorous study and self-discipline is called *jnana-marga*. When it is sought through good works, it is called *karma-marga*. When pursued through intense devotion to a deity, it is called *bhakti-marga* (BUHK-tee-MAHR-guh).

lustration: ceremonial purification, especially one performed before entering a holy place.

martext: a blundering preacher who stumbles through a sermon.

muezzin: (m(y)oo-EZ-in) the person who, five times a day, calls Muslims to prayer.

The muezzin traditionally makes his call—known as the **azan** (ah-ZAHN)—from atop a **minaret** (min-uh-RET), a slender tower or turret attached to a mosque.

physitheism: (FIZ-i-thee-iz'm) ascribing physical form (animal, vegetable, or mineral) to a deity.

When an ancient Greek or Roman god assumed the form of an animal, or when God spoke to Moses from the burning bush, that was physitheism in action.

pilpul: (PIL-puul) keen and subtle debate among rabbinical scholars regarding rules and principles in the Talmud.

The word for this kind of disputation among Christian scholars is **quodlibet** (KWAHD-li-bet), an elaborate, subtle argument over a theological (or scholarly) fine point.

ponerologist: (PAHN-ur-AHL-uh-jist) someone who expounds on the nature of evil.

prelapsarian: (PREE-lap-SAIR-ee-in) pertaining to the time or state before the biblical Fall; hence, innocent, carefree, insouciant. The antonym is **postlapsarian,** occurring after the Fall.

preterist: (PRET-ur-ist) a person who believes the prophecies of the Apocalypse have already been fulfilled.

In its nontheological sense, *preterist* denotes a person who lives in the past or derives pleasure from studying it.

scaldabanco: (SKAHL-duh-BAHNG-koh) a preacher who delivers a fiery sermon.

simony: (SIM-uh-nee or SY-muh-nee) a slimy deal made with the church; specifically, the buying or selling of an ecclesiastical preferment (promotion) or benefice (a job with perks you can't refuse).

Surely it was simony, among other things, that prompted French novelist and critic Émile Zola to write, "Civilization will take its first great step forward when the last stone from the last church falls on the head of the last priest."

tartarology: (TAHR-tur-AHL-uh-jee) instruction or doctrine concerning Hell.

trayf: (TRAYF) unclean or unfit according to religious law.

According to orthodox Jewish law, that which is fit to eat or use and has been ritually pronounced so by the proper authorities is called *kosher.* This Hebrew word is now so common in English that it has come to be used broadly to mean proper, legitimate, genuine, reliable, or approved. The antonym of *kosher,* less well known but just as useful, is *trayf,* unfit for consumption, not proper or approved.

vaticide: (VAT-i-syd) the murder of a prophet.

THE PRESCIENT ART,
OR ALL THINGS DIVINED

All you have to do is wear rags, pretend to be blind, go into a man's home, drink up his wine, play with his food, do outrageous things to his livestock, then mumble a few words to the skies. He'll eat it up. Guaranteed.

—D. CARNEGIUS (fl. 4th century B.C.),
How to Make Prophecies and Incense People

Once upon a time, prophets, oracles, and soothsayers held as respectable a position in society as doctors, lawyers, and clerics do today. (On second thought, maybe just the doctors and clerics. Or maybe just the clerics. Or maybe we should just skip the whole comparison.) At any rate, nobility sought their clairvoyant counsel, and common folk were cowed by their pompous presaging. Though the wizards and druids and sorcerers have long since surrendered to science and fled to the hills (or perhaps to the merry old land of Oz), the esoteric language of their profession survives. Consult your local unabridged dictionary and you will find it well stocked with words pertaining to the prescient art. (For **prescient,** having foresight or foreknowledge, my preferred pronunciation is PREE-shint.)

Most of these divine words contain the combining form -*mancy*, which means divination. This element comes through the Greek *manteia* from *mantis*, a prophet.

Perhaps the most common form of prophecy is **chiromancy** (**KY**-ruh-**MAN**-see), divination by examining the palm of the hand, also called **palmistry** or **chirognomy** (ky-**RAHG**-nuh-mee). Almost as common is **cartomancy,** divination with playing cards. (Tarot is one popular form of cartomancy.) Other forms of prophecy still widely practiced include **phyllomancy,** divination by observing leaves (especially tea leaves); **astragalomancy** (uh-**STRAG**-uh-luh-**MAN**-see), divination by means of dice; and **oneiromancy** (oh-**NY**-ruh-**MAN**-see), divination through dreams.

On the practical side of prophecy we have **rhabdomancy** (**RAB**-duh-MAN-see), using a switch or wand to locate water. The common term for this is *dowsing*. The dowser, or rhabdomancer—depending on what the person's business card says and whether he or she has a doctorate in divination—strolls over the land holding a divining rod. When it twitches or dips toward the earth, that's the spot where water (or in some cases, precious metals or minerals) will be found.

If you're sick, before you rack up those medical bills on a series of expensive diagnostic tests, you might want to consider undergoing **catoptromancy** (kuh-**TAHP**-truh-MAN-see), divination with a mirror. This ancient practice, says the *Century Dictionary*, was performed "by letting down a mirror into water for a sick person to look at his face in it. If the countenance appeared distorted and ghastly, it was an ill omen; if fresh and healthy, it was favorable." The question is, who decides whether you look good or bad? When submitting to **medicomancy** (my nonce-word for divination by doctors), I say get a second opinion—perhaps from a certified **scryer,** a fortune-teller who gazes into a crystal ball.

And with that prophetic preamble, let us now divine and conquer. For your soothsaying pleasure, and to help you get a leg up by looking ahead, I have compiled the following ominous (by derivation "containing an omen") and auspicious (by derivation "manifesting a favorable omen") list of various species of divination—both common and outlandish.

DIVINATION . . .

by air: aeromancy (the ancestor, notes the *OED*, of modern meteorology or weather forecasting). See **by wind.**
by (movements of) animals: theriomancy (THEER-ee-uh-), zoomancy (ZOH-uh-).
by (human) appearance or form: schematomancy (ski-MAT-uh-).
by ashes: spodomancy, ceneromancy (SEN-uh-ruh-).

by birds' flight: augury; **by the flight and cries of birds:** ornithomancy.

by black magic: necromancy.

by blood: hematomancy (HEEM-uh-tuh-); **by dripping blood:** dririmancy (DRIR-i-).

by boiling an ass's head: cephalomancy (SEF-uh-luh-).

The combining form *cephalo-* means "head"; thus by derivation *cephalomancy* does not specifically denote the head of an ass, although it stands to reason only an ass would submit to divination by this means.

by bones: osteomancy, ossomancy.

by books, or Bible verses: bibliomancy; **by lines or passages in books, picked at random:** stichomancy (STIK-uh-). See **by poetry.**

by cards: cartomancy.

by a cat's manner of jumping: ailuromancy (ay-LOOR-uh-).

by cheese: tyromancy.

by (burning) coals: anthracomancy.

by convulsions or twitches of the limbs: spasmatomancy.

by corn, grains of: alectryomancy (uh-LEK-tree-uh-).

Webster 2 explains this peculiar practice: "Divination by means of a cock encircled by grains of corn placed on the letters of the alphabet, the letters being then put together in the order in which the grains were eaten." The message thus revealed is the prophecy—which in most cases I imagine would be so inscrutable as to require the services of another professional unraveler, the **cryptanalyst.**

by communicating with the dead: necromancy, sciomancy (SY-uh-), psychomancy.

by counting: mathemancy.

by a crystal ball or sphere: scrying, spheromancy, gastromancy.

by demons: demonomancy (DEE-muhn-uh-).

Necyomancy (NES-ee-uh-) is divination by summoning Satan.

by dice or hucklebones: astragalomancy (uh-STRAG-uh-luh-), cleromancy (KLER-uh-).

by dreams: oneiromancy (oh-NY-ruh-).

by eggs: oömancy (OH-uh-).

by the embryonic sac: amniomancy.

> Frankly, I haven't the slightest idea how this bizarre mode of foretelling was performed, and I doubt there's a woman in the world who would want to know, anyway.

by entrails: hieromancy (HY-ur-uh-), hieroscopy, extispicy (eks-TIS-puh-see), haruspication, haruspicy (huh-RUS-puh-see), anthropomancy (AN-thruh-puh-).

> Judging by the number of words I was able to disembowel from the dictionaries, divination by innards apparently was a popular pastime.

> *Anthropomancy* applies specifically to divination from the entrails of sacrificed human beings; the other words may apply either to sacrificed animals or human beings.

> In ancient Roman culture, the person who did this sort of gutsy work was known as the **haruspex** (ha-RUHS-peks) or **extispex** (eks-TIS-peks).

by excrement or feces: scatomancy; **by animal droppings:** spatilomancy (SPAT-uh-luh-).

> The excremental mess of modern life requires one more term in this category: *splatomancy*, divination by the pattern of the bird droppings on a car.

by the face or countenance: physiognomancy (FIZ-ee-**AHG**-nuh-); **by the forehead or face:** metopomancy (MET-uh-puh-). See **by a mirror.**

false divination: pseudomancy.

by figs: sycomancy (SIK-uh-).

by the fingernails: onychomancy (AH-ni-kuh-), onimancy.

> *Onychophagists* (compulsive nail-biters) make poor subjects for this form of divination.

by fire: pyromancy.

by fish: ichthyomancy (IK-thee-uh-).

by flour or meal: aleuromancy (al-YUUR-uh-); **by barley meal:** alphitomancy (al-FIT-uh-); **by meal or dough strewn over sacrificed animals:** crithomancy (KRITH-uh-).

by flowers: anthomancy.

foolish divination: moromancy.

by footprints: ichnomancy (IK-nuh-).

by the (lines on the) hand: palmistry, chiromancy, chirognomy.

by handwriting: graptomancy.

by the heavens: uranomancy, ouranomancy.

by (the neighing of) horses: hippomancy.

by icons or idols: iconomancy, idolomancy.

by (burning) incense: knissomancy (NIS-uh-).

by a key: cleidomancy (KLY-duh-).

by (the shape of the) land: topomancy.

by laughter: geloscopy (je-LAHS-kuh-pee).

by leaves (especially tea leaves): phyllomancy (FIL-uh-).

by reading lips: labiomancy.

by lots: sortilege (SORT'l-ij).

by meteors: meteoromancy.

by (movements of) mice: myomancy.

by a mirror: enoptromancy (ee-NAHP-truh-); **by how the face appears in a mirror placed underwater:** catoptromancy.

by the moon: selenomancy (suh-LEE-nuh-).

by names, or the letters of a name: onomancy, nomancy.

by numbers: numerology, arith(o)mancy.

by an object: (largest nearby) macromancy; (smallest nearby) micromancy; **by excavated objects:** oryctomancy (or-IK-tuh-).

by onions: cromnyomancy (KRAHM-nee-uh-).

by oracles or gods: theomancy.

by pearls: margaritomancy (MAHR-guh-**RIT**-uh-).

by pebbles: thrioboly (thry-AHB-uh-lee), pessomancy.

by plants: botanomancy.

by poetry or verse (lines or passages picked at random): rhapsodomancy (RAP-suh-duh-).

by a (divining) rod or switch: rhabdomancy.

by sacrifices: see **by entrails.**

by salt: halomancy (HAL-uh-).

by shells: conchomancy (KAHNGK-uh-).

by the shoulder blades of animals: armomancy, spatulamancy; **by an animal's shoulder blade charred, blotched, or**

      cracked by fire: scapulimancy (SKAP-yuh-li-), omopla-
      toscopy (OH-moh-pluh-**TAHS**-kuh-pee).

by looking over one's shoulder: retromancy.

by sleep: meconomancy (MEK-uh-nuh-), hypnomancy, narco-
      mancy.

by smoke: capnomancy. See **by fire.**

by snakes or serpents: ophiomancy (AHF-ee-uh-).

by spots: maculomancy (MAK-yuh-luh-).

by the stars: astrology, astromancy, sideromancy (SID-ur-uh-),
      horoscopy (huh-RAHS-kuh-pee).

by stones: lithomancy; **by drawing marked stones from a ves-
      sel:** psephomancy (SEF-uh-).

by strangers (usually the first one to appear): xenomancy
      (ZEN-uh-).

by straws, burned on hot metal: sideromancy (SID-uh-ruh-).

by tea: see **by leaves.**

by teeth: odontomancy.

by thunder: brontomancy, keraunoscopia; **by thunderbolts:**
      ceraunomancy (si-RAW-nuh-).

by time (specifically by determining the most favorable time
      for action): chronomancy (KRAHN-uh-). Chronomancy
      is a popular practice among the Chinese.

by the umbilical cord (specifically by counting the knots in a
      firstborn child's umbilical cord to determine how many
      children the mother will have): omphalomancy (AHM-
      fuh-luh-). See **by the navel.**

by ventriloquism: gastromancy.

by walking: ambulomancy; **by walking in a circle until falling
      from dizziness:** gyromancy (JY-ruh-).

There once was a wizard named Nancy
Who specialized in gyromancy.
    When she fell on her head,
     She just shrugged and then said,
"This business is iffy and chancy."
                 —ANNE OMINUS

by water: hydromancy.
by wheel tracks: trochomancy.
by wind: austromancy.
by wine: oenomancy (EE-nuh-), oinomancy (OY-nuh-).
by (pieces of) wood: xylomancy (ZY-luh-).
by words or speech: logomancy.

And now your grandiloquent logomancer predicts that you are about to leave the celestial realm of religioverbosity and proceed to the next chapter for a look at some more down-to-earth words.

Answers to the Zucchetto Trivia Question

1. c.   2. d.   3. a.   4. b.

❖

CHAPTER EIGHT

SNOLLYGOSTERS
AND QUOMODOCUNQUIZERS

*A Grasp of Words About
Politics and Business*

Step this way, my **peripatetic*** reader, for a not-so-pedestrian peregrination through the mundane terrain of wealth and power. First we'll hit the campaign trail and look at some nifty (and a few shifty) words about politics and government. Then we'll run a rat race through the worldly words of money and business. I hope you will elect to join me, for I promise it will be a profitable excursion.

Are your lexical legs in shape? All right, let's go.

POLITICS AND PUBLIC LIFE

You don't have to be a political pundit, or be well-versed in **psephology** (sef-AHL-uh-jee), the study of elections, to know that the world of politics is far from squeaky clean. And thank goodness for that, for as a result of all the disreputable things that go on in the political arena, the English language has gained some downright dandy words.

In many countries, voters may chose which form of leadership they prefer—generally either **snobocracy,** rule by snobs,

---

**peripatetic:* (PER-i-puh-TET-ik) walking about, itinerant. Aristotle taught his "peripatetic school" of philosophy while strolling about the Lyceum of ancient Athens.

or **boobocracy,** rule by boobs. There is a perennial hope, played out every election day, that by casting our ballots we will bring about **meritocracy,** rule by the most talented; instead, we often wind up getting **kakistocracy** (KAK-i-**STAHK**-ruh-see), rule by the worst. And though our elected officials usually claim they are committed to **eunomy** (like *you know me*), the enactment of good laws that promote the welfare of the people, all the wheeling and dealing of government often results in **dysnomy** (DIS-noh-mee), the enactment of flawed legislation that generates further difficulties and discontent.

Open a newspaper on any given day and you can read about some new **malversation,** corruption or misconduct in public office. Somehow that doesn't stop us from continuing to elect more **snollygosters,** sleazy politicians (or lawyers) who are willing to discard their principles (if they have any) to do whatever will increase their power and prestige. Of course, every so often people become so outraged by these megalomaniacal misfits that they rise up and demand change. Guess what happens then? We rally behind whichever demogogue criticizes the snollygosters the loudest, and invariably that person turns out to be a **politicaster,** a second-rate, incompetent leader.

If you entertain notions of entering the electoral fray, bear in mind that there are two essential things you must do to become a **gubernator,** a powerful man in government, or a **gubernatrix,** a powerful woman in government.

First you'll need to develop a terminal case of **empleomania** (EM-plee-oh-**MAY**-nee-uh), an insatiable desire to run for or hold public office. Then you'll have to cultivate the exquisitely slimy art of **girouettism** (ZHEER-oo-**ET**-iz'm), altering your opinion or position to follow popular trends—otherwise known as flip-flopping. (The word comes from the French *girouette,* a weathercock—one of those weathervanes with a rooster on it.)

Once you're on the campaign trail, you will need to sharpen your ad hominem (character assassination) skills. To that end, it won't hurt (at least it won't hurt you) to know two especially underhanded words for dirty political tricks:

roorback, an ugly rumor or fabricated news story that discredits a political opponent; and **lolodacity** (loh-loh-DAS-i-tee), the tactic of hitting way, way below the belt (coined by writer Lewis Burke Frumkes). The corresponding adjective is *lolodacious*, hitting way below the belt.

> It takes no special erudition
> To be a winning politician:
> Among your friends, you must be gracious;
> Among your foes, be *lolodacious.*
> —RUTH LESLIE

Let us now rise like miasma from the political swamp of lolodacious politicasters and mudslinging, Machiavellian snollygosters and take a deep, rejuvenating breath of hot air from the glorious realm of governance.

What's your favorite, and least favorite, form of government? Thanks to the Baskin-Robbins Act of 1931, political leadership is now available in a wide variety of flavors.

If a woman ran for president, would you vote for her? If your answer is "No way!" then the government for you is **androcracy,** one consisting of men alone. For those who look forward to the day when women rule the roost, in addition to the familiar *matriarchy* there are four words for government by the kinder, gentler sex: **gynarchy, gynecocracy, gynocracy,** and **metrocracy** (from the Greek combining form *metro-,* mother, womb).

How much money do you think your elected representatives should make? For government by the wealthy elite, there's a mother lode of words to choose from: **plutocracy, moneyocracy, plutarchy, plousiocracy, millionocracy,** and **chrysocracy** (from the Greek *chrysos,* gold). If you prefer your leaders poor, then there's but one down-and-out word for you: **ptochocracy** (toh-KAHK-ruh-see). And if you think politicians should be comfortable but not *too* comfortable, chances are you'd be most comfortable in a **mesocracy,** government by the middle class.

If social classifications bore you and you yearn for spiritual leadership, you have your choice of numerous higher powers, including **theocracy, hierocracy,** and **parsonarchy,** all of which mean rule by priests or religious poobahs; **ecclesiarchy,** rule by a particular church; **paparchy,** rule by a pope; **hagiocracy** (or **hagiarchy**), rule by holy persons or saints; **angelocracy,** rule by angels; and **thearchy,** rule by God or a god. Frankly, I prefer a clear separation of church and state, but I'll take any of the afore-mentioned forms of government any day over **demonocracy,** rule by devils or by the Devil (also called **diabolarchy**).

Those who oppose term limits for elected officials fear **neocracy,** a government run by amateurs; those who favor them fear either **squirearchy** (or **squireocracy**), rule by the landed gentry, or **gerontocracy,** a government run by old fogies. For most people, however, any of those states of affairs would be preferable to suffering under **stratocracy,** rule by the military, or **ochlochracy** (ahk-LAHK-ruh-see), rule by the mob (also called **mobocracy** or **pollarchy**).

Other distinctly undesirable forms of government include **riotocracy,** violent or disorderly rule; **chirocracy,** rule by force (literally "by a strong hand"); **oligarchy,** government controlled by a few persons or a select group; **cryptarchy,** government conducted in secret; **slavocracy,** rule by slave owners; **beerocracy,** rule by brewing interests (along with their political consulting firm, Suds & Sons, and their unscrupulous advertising agency, Hops, Barley, and Malt); **oiligarchy** or **oilogarchy,** rule by slippery oil magnates; **paedarchy** (PEE-dar-kee) or **paedocracy,** rule by a child or children; **ethnocracy** or **chromotocracy,** government by a particular race; **pedantrocracy,** rule by pedants (this is common in the groves of academe, which we'll explore in the next chapter); **athletocracy,** rule by athletes (the worst form being **baseballocracy**); **narcokleptocracy,** rule by drug dealers in collusion with politicians and the military; and **strumpetocracy** (or **pornocracy**), government by prostitutes.

Some would argue that America is a strumpetocracy, but I think that judgment is too harsh. In my opinion, government in the United States is an unfathomably inert admixture of

adhocracy, rule by committees or task forces; **papyrocracy** (PAP-i-**RAHK**-ruh-see), rule by paperwork or by the press; and **technocracy,** rule by technicians or experts.

What can we do to avoid all these awful, unruly ocracies and "reinvent government"? The answer, I think, is threefold. First, we must put aside petty differences and work toward **shurocracy,** government by consensus. Then we must strive for **timocracy,** Plato's term for rule by honorable persons, or by a love of honor and glory. And finally, we must aspire to the most glorious form of governance: **logocracy,** rule by words.

All in favor, say "aye"! Or better yet, say **chirotony** (ky-RAH-tuh-nee), which means a vote taken by a show of hands.

A DIVINE DEMOCRACY

Would you care for a final piece of political word trivia? The United States was founded as a democracy—and, at least theoretically, as an **isocracy,** a government in which all share equal power. Some time ago, however, with little fanfare and without an amendment to the Constitution, America became a **theodemocracy,** a democracy under divine rule.

How is that, you ask?

In 1954, by an act of Congress, two words Abraham Lincoln had used in the Gettysburg Address were inserted into the Pledge of Allegiance, making the government "of the people, by the people, for the people" subject to divine will. Can you guess what those two words were?

Before the interpolation, the pledge had ended with the words "one Nation, indivisible, with liberty and justice for all." Afterward, it read "one Nation *under God. . . .*"

MONEY MAKES THE WORDS GO ROUND

Literary legend has it that someone once asked Dorothy Parker, one of the quickest wits of the famed Algonquin

Round Table, what she thought the two most beautiful words in the English language were. "Check enclosed," she said.

For as long as human beings have exchanged currency for goods and services, we have had a love-hate relationship with money. Even the admonitions of the Bible are paradoxical: Paul's first epistle to Timothy warns that "the love of money is the root of all evil," while the world-weary preacher of Ecclesiastes counsels that "money answereth all things."

Whether you believe that money is the source of all the world's troubles or the solution to them, whether you're **pecunious** (rolling in dough) or **impecunious** (strapped for cash), a **centimillionaire** (a person worth more than $100 million) or a person without one red cent, there's no denying that our daily lives are inextricably entwined with loot, lucre, and the pursuit of mammon. There's also no denying that the English language has profited enormously from our incessant getting and spending, as you will see from the grandiloquent gems I am about to display.

If you're interested in making moola (as most of us are) but you lack financial know-how, then the first two words you need to learn are **chrematistic** (KREE-muh-**TIS**-tik) and **quaestuary** (KWES-choo-er-ee).

Chrematistic means pertaining to business or moneymaking, or occupied in the pursuit of wealth. As an adjective, *quaestuary* means profit seeking, undertaken to make money; as a noun it means a profit seeker, one driven to make money. On any street corner you can find people willing to offer you their chrematistic counsel, but you have a long walk ahead if you want to find one without an ulterior, quaestuary motive.

Do you need a word to describe someone whose every waking hour is devoted to the hot pursuit of wealth? Try **nummamorous** (nuh-MAM-uh-rus), which combines the Latin *nummus,* coin, with *amorous.* Two other words for the money-loving include **plutolatry** (ploo-TAHL-uh-tree), the worship of wealth, and **plutomania**, obsession with money.

If you dream about joining the ranks of the rich and famous and becoming a **plutocrat,** a member of the affluent ruling class, then the word that may fulfill your dreams is **psa-phonic** (sa-FAHN-ik), which means preoccupied with plotting your ascent to wealth and renown.

If you are driven by a plutomaniacal desire to accumulate wealth by hook or by crook, then there's only one verb for you: **quomodocunquize** (KWOH-moh-doh-**KUHNG**-kwyz), to make money any way you can. "Those quomodocunquizing clusterfists and rapacious varlets," wrote Sir Thomas Urquhart in 1652, probably referring to unscrupulous hordarians who practice latrocination.

Did you grasp that last sentence, or did your brain go bankrupt on you?

Clusterfist practically gives its meaning away, but you won't get much else out of it, for a clusterfist is a miser, tightwad. Likewise with the **hordarian.** *Webster 2* defines this word as "the treasurer of a monastery"; in resurrecting it from that venerable tome I have taken the liberty of using it more literally to mean any "keeper of a hoard," such as a banker, moneylender, or asset manager. **Latrocination** (LA-truh-si-**NAY**-shin), which hails from the same Latin source as *larceny*, means highway robbery, stealing the shirt off someone's back.

Speaking of rip-offs, have you ever been burned by someone who borrowed money from you and never paid it back? If the scamp skipped out and left you with a megathirst for retribution, then before you ever lend money again you need to know the word **nexum.** In ancient Roman law, the nexum was a type of loan whose terms stipulated that the creditor could enslave and flog the debtor if he failed to make his payments. Now that's satisfaction!

By the way, there's also a word for the act of skipping out without settling your debts: **swedge,** to leave without paying. The classic example of swedging is the restaurant customer who eats and then sneaks out before the bill arrives.

In these financially fickle times we need a downwardly mobile locution for the opposite of the nouveau riche, the parvenu, and the arriviste. Can you think of one? Fresh from French, and still so wet behind the ears as to require italics, comes the down-and-out term *nouveau pauvre* (NOO-voh POH-vruh), which *Random House II* defines as "a newly poor person." (How about a reality TV show called *Lives of the* Nouveau Pauvre?)

There are many factors that can bring about the abject state of the *nouveau pauvre*. Two of the most common are a penchant for **larging** (LAHR-jing), prodigal spending, especially the wasteful spending of money received from someone else (an inheritance, a loan, an expense account, etc.), and ill-considered or unlucky **agiotage** (AJ-ee-uh-tij), speculation in the stock market.

Most of us can't expect to make big bucks if we aren't willing to put in an honest **darg**, a day's work. As anyone who is accustomed to a long, hard darg knows well, if you want to get ahead you have to pay your dues, which means that occasionally you will have to **glorg**, do dirty work.

If you're an extra-eager beaver—a real quomodocun-quizer who is willing to glorg—you can speed up your trip to the top with a **parergon** (par-UR-gahn), additional work such as freelancing or a second job. Factlet for word trivialists: *Webster 2* notes that *parergon* may also refer to "one of the exploits or deeds of Hercules not included among the generally accepted twelve labors."

Such herculean industriousness is indeed admirable, but as often as not in the indolent modern world, what's all in a darg is doing little or nothing. It seems that in every workplace there are always a few feckless folks who are **gnatling** (NAT-ling), busy doing nothing, engrossed in trifles. And I'll bet my bottom dollar you've known someone who's forever finding creative ways to **snurge**, shirk undesirable work, dodge an unpleasant duty.

Speaking of snurging, have you ever met a **quiddler**? That's the thumb-twiddling trifler who has perfected the art of loitering around the coffee machine or photocopier, sidetracking more industrious types with trivial conversation in an attempt to waste as much of the workday as possible. To **quiddle**, the verb, means to dawdle or procrastinate in carrying out one's duty. Dilly-dallying alongside *quiddle* are the lackadaisical twin verbs **perfunctorize** (pur-FUNGK-tuh-ryz) and **perfuncturate** (pur-FUNGK-chur-ayt), which mean to perform in a perfunctory manner, do something listlessly or carelessly.

> If your boss you do despise
> For stabbing backs and telling lies,
> You could stab back, but that's not wise.
> The best revenge? *Perfunctorize.*
> —Sybil Cervantes

> It is not a happy fate,
> To have employment that you hate.
> The best recourse when in that state?
> Make them pay: *perfuncturate.*
> —Shirley A. Slacker

After quomodocunquizing or perfuncturating for forty-odd hours a week, what do you like to do with that paltry paycheck? Those with disposable income, and those who are compelled to dispose of whatever income they have, share a popular pastime: shopping.

Two priceless words you should know about that all-American (or perhaps I should say "mall-American") activity are **oniomania** (OH-nee-uh-MAY-nee-uh), an uncontrollable desire to buy things, and **emacity** (ee-MAS-i-tee), an itch to buy or spend. There is a marked difference in intensity between the words. If, as the bumper stickers say, you'd rather be shopping, then you're experiencing emacity. If you want to shop till you drop, you've got oniomania.

Our workaday word sale is almost over, but there are still a few items left on the lexical rack. May I interest you in any of the following verbal fashion statements—at fifty percent off?

backspang: a tricky evasion in business; specifically, a retreat from a bargain.

Now that we've learned the seven habits of highly successful people and how to swim with the sharks, what today's ambitious businesspeople need is a no-holds-barred guide to mendacity and chicanery like *Mastering the Backspang and Passing the Buck: How to Succeed in Business by Accepting the Quiddling Clusterfist Within.* Alternative (more warm-and-fuzzy) title: *Chicken Soup for the Snarge.*

defalcation: (DEE-fal-**KAY**-shin) misappropriation of funds by the person or agency entrusted with them.

habbie-gabbie: to throw money into a crowd.

In Mexico there is a custom called *bolo,* in which a *padrino,* a godfather of a newly baptized child, tosses a handful of coins outside the church to the children who have attended the ceremony. It is supposed to bring good fortune to the baptized child.

intrapreneur: an employee in a large company who is not bound by corporate routines and regulations and who has considerable freedom to create or refine products, services, or procedures.

jeofail: (JEF-ayl) a costly mistake made by a lawyer in court.

You'd think that at some point during all the missteps and melodramatic bombast of the interminable O. J. Simpson trial we would have learned this unusually useful word—but *nooo.* No one from *Nightline* or *The Today Show* or CNN ever thought to call *this* grandiloquent guide for a jurisprudential word to the wise!

Suggestion for Scott Turow or John Grisham: Write a novel with a lawyer-protagonist named *Jeff Ayle.*

pismirism: (PIZ-mi-riz'm) "petty saving," says *Webster 2;* squirreling away one's nickels and dimes.

Pismirism has become an obsession for many of today's Baby Boomers, who see themselves retiring in an era of Social Insecurity.

redhibition: the act of taking back defective merchandise.

As every oniomaniac knows, it's a jungle out there in the world of retail; you have to be vigilant or you'll get fleeced. You know those "All Sales Final" signs at certain shady "discount" stores? Here's what they really mean:

> We thank you for your time today
> Shopping here at "Pay 'n' Pray."
> We take cash, or checks, or plastic.
> (Our profit margin is fantastic.)
> To rip you off, that is our mission—
> Sorry: No refunds on your *redhibition*.
> —MARK EDDING DODGE

rouleau: a cylinder of coins rolled up in paper.

sloyd: skilled manufacturing work requiring a dexterous use of tools.

snup: to snap up something of value that someone else has discarded or is selling for a bargain price.

sportulary: dependent on donations, subsisting on handouts.
    Remember the *shnorrer*, the clever, pushy panhandler or chiseler you met in chapter 4? He might also be called a "sportulary entrepreneur." Other sportulary enterprises include art, literature, politics, and organized religion.

trantlums or **trantles:** miscellaneous articles of little value, the sort of bric-a-brac one sees at swap meets and yard sales.

ultimogeniture: (UHL-ti-moh-JEN-i-chur) a system of inheritance in which an estate passes to the youngest child. It is the opposite of **primogeniture** (PRY-moh-JEN-i-chur), in which the estate passes to the oldest child.

I shall leave you, dear sportulary reader, with one last verbal trantlum to snup:

zeigarnik effect: an obsession with unfinished work or business; a tendency to focus on things left . . .

❖

CHAPTER NINE

OF ELOQUENCE AND EGGHEADS

Expressive Words and a Trip to the Ivory Tower

I would be remiss in my duty as your grandiloquent guide if I did not give you a glimpse of the lofty garden of eloquence and the eggheaded groves of academe.

TEST YOUR IQ

By now, my learned reader, if you've learned anything from this book, then you are well on your wordful way to becoming one of the most grandiloquent persons on the planet. However, before you can proudly don the laurels of loquacity you must become conversant with the many *-iloquent* varieties of **loquence** (LOH-kwe̱ns), speech, discourse.

English has at least thirty-seven words for ways of speaking that incorporate the element *-iloquent,* which hails from the Latin *loqui,* to speak. Let's test your IQ (*-Iloquent* Quotient) and see how many you know:

grandiloquent	pauciloquent
altiloquent	multiloquent
stultiloquent	magniloquent
planiloquent	alieniloquent
blandiloquent	tolutiloquent
longiloquent	inaniloquent

pleniloquent	doctiloquent
omniloquent	breviloquent
somniloquent	melliloquent
sanctiloquent	suaviloquent
veriloquent	dentiloquent
polyloquent	vaniloquent
flexiloquent	mendaciloquent
ambiloquent	anteloquent
dulciloquent	pectoriloquent
fatiloquent	turpiloquent
largiloquent	diversiloquent
fallaciloquent	tristiloquent

Altiloquent and **magniloquent** mean speaking pompously, in a high-flown, turgid manner; they are synonyms of *grandiloquent*.

Has your tongue tired of *garrulous, loquacious,* and *voluble* for folks fond of flapping their gums? Try these four grand *-iloquent* words: **pleniloquent**, full of talk; **multiloquent**, talking a great deal; **largiloquent**, full of words; and **longiloquent**, extremely long-winded.

Have you ever met a master of multiloquence who can talk all over the map? **Polyloquent** (stress on *-lyl-*) and **diversiloquent** (stress on *-sil-*) mean talking about many things, and **omniloquent** (from the Latin *omnis*, all) means talking about everything.

On the straight-talking side of loquence we have three straightforward words: **planiloquent**, speaking plainly; **breviloquent** (from the Latin *brevis*, short), speaking briefly; and **pauciloquent** (from the Latin *paucus*, few, the source of *paucity*), using the fewest possible words to make the point.

When you speak learnedly, as an expert on some subject, you are **doctiloquent**. If you like to make prefatory remarks, you are **anteloquent**. You are **sanctiloquent** when you speak solemnly of sacred things. When you speak nothing but the truth, you are **veriloquent**. And when you speak prophetically, you are **fatiloquent.**

Want some eloquent words for smooth talkers? A glib or fluent speaker may be described as **melliloquent** (literally "honey-tongued") or **tolutiloquent** (from the Latin *tolutim*, trotting along). A person who speaks softly and sweetly is **dulciloquent**; the flattering or mildly ingratiating speaker is **blandiloquent**; and the urbane, sophisticated speaker is **suaviloquent**.

Loquence also has its unflattering side: If your speech is gloomy or melancholy, you're **tristiloquent** (from the Latin *tristis*, sad); if you talk in your sleep, you're **somniloquent**; if you talk through your teeth, you're **dentiloquent**; and if your voice can be heard through your chest (a sign of serious lung problems), a doctor will pronounce you **pectoriloquent**.

If your speech is evasive, you're **flexiloquent**; if you speak ambiguously, you're **ambiloquent**; if you're misleading or deceptive, you're **fallaciloquent**; if you habitually stray from the point, you're **alieniloquent**; if you speak vainly or egotistically, you're **vaniloquent**; if you tell artful lies, you're **mendaciloquent**; and if your speech is foul or obscene, you are **turpiloquent**.

Finally, we have two *-iloquent* words for silly, senseless speech: **inaniloquent**, for someone who speaks foolishly, and **stultiloquent**, for the person who babbles idiotically.

Are you wondering, pleniloquent reader, about the thirty-seventh *-iloquent* word? (There were thirty-six in the list above.) Actually, it's a slight spelling variation: **sialoquent** (sy-AL-uh-kwint), spraying saliva when speaking.

This uncommon word for a common human malady appears in *Doggerel Days*, an expectorating collection of drivel compiled by Lotta Schpitt and April Drool:

> I once knew a fellow named Fritz,
> Who spoke with conspicuous spritz.
>   Whatever he'd say
>   Came out with a spray—
> His *sialoquent* spurts gave me fits!
>   —CHLOE S. YARMOUTH

By the way, should you wish to make a noun out of any of these *-iloquent* words, simply change *-iloquent* to *-iloquence.* (*Sialoquent*, of course, would become *sialoquence.*)

Logo- Lore

Engish has a number of suaviloquent words that incorporate the prefix *logo-*, which comes from the Greek *logos*, word. With that etymological clue, can you deduce the meanings of the following "word words"?

logophile	logorrhea
logomaniac	logodaedaly
logomachy	logolept
logographer	logogogue

A **logophile** (LAHG-uh-fyl) is a word lover, and a **logomaniac** (LAHG-uh-**MAY**-nee-ak) is someone who is nuts about words.

Logomachy (loh-GAHM-uh-kee) is a war of words or a battle about words (from the Greek *mache*, battle). Anyone who contends verbally—e.g., a lawyer, politician, or critic—is a *logomachist* or *logomacher* (stress the *-gom-*). To *logomachize* (loh-GAHM-uh-kyz) is to wage or engage in a war of or about words.

A **logographer** (loh-GAHG-ruh-fur), from the Greek *graphein*, to write, is a speechwriter, historian, or chronicler: Edward Gibbon was a longiloquent logographer of the Roman Empire.

Logorrhea (LAHG-uh-**REE**-uh) is excessive talkativeness, verbal diarrhea. A useful word, as one example will illustrate:

> The airwaves now are full of talk,
> With hosts who rant and guests who squawk.
> Have you ever heard one good idea
> In all that broadcast *logorrhea?*
> —Wynne D. Bagges

Webster 2 defines one of my all-time favorite words, **logo-daedaly** (LAHG-uh-**DED**-uh-lee), as "verbal legerdemain," using another one of my all-time favorite words, *legerdemain* (LEJ-ur-duh-**MAYN**), sleight of hand, artful trickery. If you suspected that the -*daedaly* half of *logodaedaly* might be related to Daedalus, the Athenian artificer of Greek mythology who designed the famed Labyrinth for the Minotaur of Crete, you're right. The unusual adjectives **daedal** (DEED'l) and **daedalian** (di-DAY-lee-in) both mean ingenious, intricate, cunningly contrived. *Logodaedaly* refers to an ingenious, intricate, or cunning use of words.

In **logolept** (LAHG-uh-lept), the -*lept* comes from the Greek suffix -*lepsia,* a seizure, paroxysm; thus, a *logolept* is someone who has seizures about words. The logoleptic person can lose verbal control in various ways—by going gaga over a pyrotechnic display of logodaedaly, by participating in a logomachy over some obscure point of grammar or etymology, or by being rendered senseless by a logographer's logorrhea.

Finally, a **logogogue** (LAHG-uh-gahg) is not someone agog about words but rather someone -*agogue* about them. What do I mean by that bit of logodaedaly? The suffix -*agogue* means leading, guiding, as in *demagogue,* a rabble-rouser (by derivation "a leader of the people," from the Greek *demos,* people). A *logogogue,* literally "leader or guider in words," is a language legislator or dictator, a person who lays down rules about words. The logogogue's despotic cousin is the **grammaticaster** (gruh-MAT-i-KAS-tur), a petty or pedantic grammarian.

Your grandiloquent guide pleads guilty on both counts.

Dirty Verbal Tics

Now let me tell you about three doctiloquent words for indelicate expression.

When you have a megacase of matutolypea (getting up on the wrong side of the bed), or when life's deck seems stacked against you, do you ever let off steam by howling outrageous oaths at the heavens? When you stub your toe, smash your finger, or bang your head, do you just groan and hop around or do you do what most folks do—swear profusely? If in such situations a few choice epithets escape your lips, then you are guilty of **lalochezia** (LAL-uh-**KEE**-zee-uh), the use of foul or abusive language to relieve stress, cursing for anxiolytic effect.

Are you a hell-raising person who is hell on wheels, who is hell to be around, who is hell-bent on doing everything like a bat out of hell, and who believes we'll all have hell to pay because we're all going to hell in a handbasket? If so, then—hell's bells!—do I have a helluva word for you: **hadeharia** (HAY-dị-**HAR**-ee-uh), the hellacious practice of constantly using the word "hell" in one's speech.

Behind door number three we have our final doctiloquent dirty word: **latrinalia** (LA-trị-**NAY**-lee-uh). Any idea what it means? (*Hint:* This indecent specimen comes straight from the linguistic toilet and it's always off the wall.)

If you guessed bathroom graffiti, you're right. *Latrinalia* was popularized by Alan Dundes, a professor at UC Berkeley who apparently has made an academic specialty out of *latrinology*, the study of restroom writings.

A TACHYDIDACTIC TOUR OF THE IVORY TOWER

Are you an **aristophren** (uh-RIS-tuh-fren), a person with a superior intellect? Do you have **scholaptitude**, a gift for scholarly achievement? Let's hope so, because our next lexical stopover is academia, and you'll need to be a quick study if you hope to keep up with my **tachydidaxy** (TAK-ị-dị-DAK-see), swift teaching, rapid instruction (formed from the Greek *tachy-*, quick, swift, and *didactic*, pertaining to instruction).

Under my inscrutable, tachydidactic tutelage, your excursion to the ivory tower should be nothing less than **chrestomathic** (KRES-tuh-**MATH**-ik), devoted to useful learning. Follow me now into the **phrontistery** (FRAHN-tis-TER-ee), a place for study and contemplation (colloquially known as a "think tank"), and I will unveil my esoteric collection of learned words, otherwise known as **scholasms** (SKOH-laz-<u>u</u>mz), locutions that smell of the lamp.

Scholasms, by the way, may be divided into two classes: aureate terms and inkhorn terms. In *The Treasure of Our Tongue,* Lincoln Barnett nicely elucidates the distinction between them. *Aureate* (AW-ree-it) refers to "fancy, florid words put forth by poets," says Barnett, and *inkhorn* to "pompous, ponderous words produced by pedants." (You see, I'm not the only grandiloquent logogogue with a penchant for alliteration.)

If you've ever traipsed through the groves of academe in pursuit of a degree, then you know that what goes on in those hallowed halls is not always **eupsychics** (yoo-SY-kiks), good education. In fact, academia is often a refuge for some of society's most peculiar folks, for within that eggheaded enclave you will find—along with the usual nitpickers, quibblers, and aeolists—a congrehooligation composed of the following types:*

- the **tanquam** (TAN-kwam)
  A person with enough education to attend college.
- the **philiater** (FIL-ee-AY-tur)
  A medical student.
- the **stagiary** (STAY-jee-ER-ee)
  A student of law.
- the **lucubrator** (LOO-kyoo-BRAY-tur)
  A person who studies at night. To *lucubrate* means to work by lamplight, burn the midnight oil. *Lucubration* is nocturnal study—which, if it persists all night, becomes **pernoctation**.
- the **sciolist** (SY-uh-list)
  An intellectual fake, a person who affects erudition.
- the **sophist** (SAHF-ist)
  An intellectual cheater who uses deceptive reasoning and specious or equivocal arguments to triumph in logomachy.

---

*Aeolist (EE-uh-list)—a word you met in chapter 5—is a pompous, windy bore who pretends to have inspiration. A **congrehooligation** (my joculism) is an assembly of hooligans, ne'er-do-wells, and other unsavory characters.

- the **casuist** (KAZH-oo-ist)
  A fiendishly subtle and dishonest sophist who specializes in splitting the thinnest of intellectual hairs.
- the **quodlibetarian** (KWAHD-li-be-**TAIR**-ee-in)
  A pedantic blowhard who engages in elaborate arguments about theoretical fine points.
- the **tomecide** (TOHM-i-syd)
  A person who murders books, such as a criticaster, deconstructionist, or Hollywood producer. A degree in English generally is enough to qualify one to become a successful tomecide in journalism or book publishing; in Hollywood, the prerequisite is illiteracy. *Tomecide* may also mean the killing of a book; it is the specialty of envious academics, sadistic editors, and oligophrenic (see chapter 4) reviewers.
- the **wegotists** (WEE-guh-tists)
  Pompous types who refer to themselves with the nominative plural "we." This pseudoroyal practice is called **nosism** (NOH-siz'm). Those who refer to themselves as "he" or "she," or by their name or title, are guilty of **illeism** (IL-ee-iz'm).
- the **anoegenetic** (AN-oh-uh-juh-**NET**-ik)
  Not producing knowledge, unable to generate new understanding, e.g., a well-endowed, anoegenetic think tank. You can't yet get a degree in anoegenetics, but published evidence of anoegenetic aptitude is a prerequisite for tenure at most universities.
- the **parisologist** (PAR-i-SAHL-uh-gist)
  A person who uses ambiguous or equivocal language (from the Greek *parisos*, almost equal, and *logos*, word). *Parisology* is ambiguous or evasive writing or speech, flexiloquence.
- the **bibliobibuli** (BIB-lee-oh-**BIB**-yoo-ly)
  People who read too much (coined by H. L. Mencken).
- and **bibliobesity** (BIB-lee-oh-**BEE**-si-tee)
  This word (coined by biographer and music critic Terry Teachout) means literally "book obesity," vast rolls of verbal flab squeezed between hard or soft covers. Bibliobesity is the result of **remplissage** (RAHM-plee-**SAZH**), literary (or musical) padding.

So that you will not depart the pleasure dome of duncery (i.e., the university) without being **omnierudite** (universally learned, educated in all things), I have compiled the following list of words for a variety of academic specialties and sciences, otherwise known as *ologies*, branches of knowledge. Like academia itself, they run the gamut from the obscure to the inane.

What's your outrageous expertise? . . .

algology: (al-GAHL-uh-jee) study of seaweed and marine algae.

autology: study of oneself.

> This is the primary academic pursuit. Students approach it haphazardly; professors engage in it earnestly.

biometeorology: study of the effect of weather on human beings.

campanology: study of bells.

chaology: study of chaos.

coprology: (kuh-PRAHL-uh-jee) study of pornography.

dactyliology: (dak-TIL-ee-AHL-uh-jee) study of finger rings.

dendrology: (den-DRAHL-uh-jee) study of trees.

dermatoglyphics: study of skin patterns (e.g., fingerprints).

enigmatology: study and construction of puzzles.

> Factlet for cruciverbalists (crossword puzzle fans): Will Shortz, crossword puzzle editor of *The New York Times*, is the world's only academically certified enigmatologist.

eremology: study of deserts.

ethnomethodology: study of social customs, rules, and rituals.

ethnomusicology: study of folk music.

eudemonics: study or science of happiness.

> The eudemonician's motto: "Have a nice day!"

ichnology: study of fossilized footprints.

irenology: study of peace.

kalology: study of beauty, more commonly called *aesthetics*.

latrinology: study of bathroom graffiti.

limnology: study of freshwater lakes and ponds.

melittology: (MEL-i-TAHL-uh-jee) study of bees.

momiology: (MOH-mee-AHL-uh-jee) study of mummies.

museology: (MYOO-zee-AHL-uh-jee) the science of museum

curatorship, covering the systematic collection, care, and arrangement of objects for museums.

nassology: science of stuffing and mounting animals; taxidermy.

neossology: (NEE-ahs-**AHL**-uh-jee) study of young birds.

noology: (noh-**AHL**-uh-jee) study of intuition and comprehension.

nosocomology: (NAHS-uh-kuh-**MAHL**-uh-jee) study of hospital management.

　　A related term is *stichemology* (my coinage), the study of how to surreptitiously stuff patients full of all sorts of drugs and then stick them with an exorbitant bill.

nostology: study of senility.

oikology: (oy-**KAHL**-uh-jee) science of housekeeping.

ontology: study of the nature of being.

orology: study of mountains.

osmology: (ahz-**MAHL**-uh-jee) study of odors.

paleography: study of ancient writings.

paleozoology: study of prehistoric animals.

pestology: study of pests, whether of the insect variety or of the human persuasion.

pharology: (fair-**AHL**-uh-jee) study of lighthouses and signaling devices.

phrenology: (fri-**NAHL**-uh-jee) study of the shape of the skull to determine mental ability and character traits. Phrenology was popular in the nineteenth and early twentieth centuries but is now a debunked science.

piscatology: science of fishing.

polemology: (POH-luh-**MAHL**-uh-jee) study of war.

pomology: (poh-**MAHL**-uh-jee) science of growing fruit.

proxemics: science of spatial organization and concepts of territoriality (coined by sociologist Edward T. Hall in 1963).

pteridology: (TER-i-**DAHL**-uh-jee) study of ferns.

pterylology: (TER-i-**LAHL**-uh-jee) study of the feather arrangements of birds.

pyrgology: (pur-**GAHL**-uh-jee) study of towers.

scarpology: a method of reading character (or assessing experience) by examining the heels and soles of shoes.

I'd go the extra mile any day to discover a word like *scarpology*. I stumbled across this rare beauty in the *Century Dictionary*, and I have yet to find it listed anywhere else.

Scarpology reminds me of an old high school pal of mine who used to take off his shoes every night and spend a minute scrutinizing their soles. If anyone asked what he was doing, he'd say he was gauging the "emotional mileage" he'd put on that day.

scatology: study of excrement, or an abnormal interest in feces.

somatology: the study of human physical characteristics as indicators of personality or character (like *phrenology*, also a debunked science).

stigmeology: (STIG-mee-**AHL**-uh-jee) the art of punctuation.

> *Punctuation:* A set of symbols that a writer uses to establish the rhythm of a piece, which an editor then uses to destroy it.
> —HEINUS BOMBASTICUS,
> *De Profundis Astigmaticus Editorialis*

storiology: study of folklore and popular legends.

telmatology: study of bogs and swamps.

thaumatology: (THAW-muh-**TAHL**-uh-jee) study of miracles.

toponymics: etymological study of place names.

trichology: (trik-**AHL**-uh-jee) science of hair and hair disease.

tropoclastics: (TROH-poh-**KLAS**-tiks) science of breaking habits.

typhlology: (tif-**LAHL**-uh-jee) study of blindness.

uredinology: (yuu-RED-i-**NAHL**-uh-jee) study of rust.

vexillology: study of flags.

xylology: (zy-**LAHL**-uh-jee) study of the structure of wood.

zymology: science or study of fermentation.

I leave you with the most whimsical intellectual pursuit, one whose practitioners will never win a Nobel Prize for their theories: **pataphysics** (PAT-uh-**FIZ**-iks). The brainchild of Alfred Jarry (1873–1907), a French absurdist, pataphysics is nonsensical philosophy, or as one of the citations in the *OED* puts it, "the science of imaginary solutions." If you're a fan of the Beatles, perhaps you'll remember these lines from John Lennon and Paul McCartney's "Maxwell's Silver Hammer": "Joan was quizzical / studied pataphysical / Science in the home ..."

　　And now it's time to graduate from all this doctiloquent logorrhea and receive your final word:

> *Sheepskin:* a rag presented to a dunce upon completing the fourth year of a fleecing.
> —R. W. JACKSON,
> 　*The Diabolical Dictionary*
> 　*of Modern English*

❖

CHAPTER TEN

SOUND AND FLURRY

Words for What We Hear and Do

Think of the many sounds you have heard in your life that you can describe but cannot name. What would you call the sound made by a galloping horse, the scratchy call of a cricket, or the noise made by a frightened pig? Did you know that there are words for the first wail of a newborn babe, for the crisp rustle of silk, for the sound of a sword being drawn from its sheath, and for the noise made by birds rising swiftly into flight?

The words for these and scores of other sounds, both ordinary and unusual, are rarely heard amid the incessant *tap, crash, plunk, boom, rattle, rasp,* and *squeak* of everyday noise. The dull roar of the daily grind has drowned them out. Nevertheless, these majestic locutions sit quietly in the cobwebbed corners of our dictionaries, mute and forlorn, like neglected musical instruments waiting to be dusted off, put in tune, and played again.

Here is a **multisonous** (muhl-TIS-uh-n<u>u</u>s, having many sounds) orchestra of resonant nouns, verbs, and adjectives that are worth rescuing and re-sounding:

FORTE AND FORTISSIMO (LOUD AND VERY LOUD)

bourdon: (BOORD'n) the bass drone of a bagpipe or a very low-pitched stop on a pipe organ.

> The dim roar of London was like the bourdon note of a distant organ.
>
> —OSCAR WILDE, *The Picture of Dorian Gray*

cachinnation: (KAK-i-NAY-shin) loud or hysterical laughter, or an outburst of immoderate laughter.

When you're "rolling in the aisles" or laughing so hard you get tears in your eyes, you're in the throes of a cachinnation. If, as they say, laughter is the best medicine, then a hearty cachinnation probably could cure just about anything. *Cachinnate* (KAK-i-nayt) is the verb.

callithumpian: (KAL-i-THUHMP-ee-in) having the sound of a *callithump*, a boisterous parade accompanied by the sound of tin horns and other raucous noises.

chavish: (CHAY-vish) the sound of many birds chirping and singing at once, or the sound of many people chattering at once.

chirr: the vibrating, high-pitched whirring or trilling sound made by grasshoppers, cicadas, and certain birds such as the partridge. The verb to *chirr* means to make such a sound. See **stridulate** below.

exsibilation: (ek-SIB-i-LAY-shin) the collective sound of hissing made by a disappointed or offended audience.

To *exsibilate* (ek-SIB-i-layt) is to reject or object to by hissing: Exsibilating the umpire is a baseball tradition.

feep: any of a variety of loud, obnoxious beeps or bleeps made by a computer, usually in response to the user's ineptitude. *Feep* may also be a verb. See **jargle** below.

fulmination: (FUHL-mi-NAY-shin) a loud, violent explosion, either a literal one (such as the detonation of a bomb) or a figurative one (a vehement denunciation, for example).

A fulmination of either kind that echoes or reverberates loudly is called a **reboation** (REB-oh-AY-shin).

grandisonant: (gran-DIS-uh-nint) great-sounding, grand in sound.

Grandisonant would seem to be a combination of *grand* and *dissonant*, but the word does not connote a harsh or strident sound. That which is grandisonant is like a symphony orchestra playing *fortemente* (strongly and loudly) or *appassionato* (with deep emotion). Grandiloquent words are often grandisonant. See **polyphloisboian** below.

gweek-gwak: the squeaking noise made by someone walking in leather boots or in shoes with rubber soles.

hirrient: (HIR-ee-int) a heavy trilling sound, like the audible purring of a cat or a strongly rolled *r* in speech.

The adjective *hirrient* means heavily trilled.

jargle: to make a sharp, shrill noise again and again in quick succession: the obnoxious jargling of car alarms; computers that feep and jargle when you type in the wrong command.

kinclunk: the sound of a car running over a manhole cover.

Kinclunk, coined by poet Alastair Reid, is a nifty addition to the underdeveloped vocabulary of automobile sounds, to which I humbly offer the following contributions: **chudduck,** the sound of a car running over a pothole; and **nogonition,** the sound of someone trying to start a recalcitrant engine.

plangent: (PLAN-jent, from Latin *plangere,* to beat) having a loud, deep, reverberating sound like bells clanging, thunder rumbling, or the roar of waves breaking on the shore.

pobble: the sound made by boiling water.

polyphloisboian: (PAHL-ee-floys-BOY-in) making an incredible racket. Also spelled *polyphloesbean* (PAHL-ee-fles-BEE-in).

This jocular mouthful of a word made its appearance in English in the early nineteenth century, but its origin can be traced all the way back to Homer, who used its Greek etymon (root word) to describe his turbulent "wine-dark sea."

In *1000 Most Obscure Words,* Norman W. Schur (who prefers the spelling *polyphloisbic*) suggests we use the word to modify "anything that makes a hell of a noise," such as "the rush of a New York subway express train" or the metallic fulminations of "a frantic rock group."

rataplan: (rat-uh-PLAN) a repetitive beating or rapping sound; specifically, the sound of a drum roll, the sound made by the hoofs of a galloping horse, or the sound of rain pounding on a roof.

rhinophonia: (RY-nuh-**FOH**-nee-uh) an extreme nasal sound in the voice.

rote: the roar of the surf crashing on the shore.

skirl: a shrill, piercing sound, such as that made by a high-pitched scream or the higher tones of a bagpipe.

    Skirl in the pan, notes *Webster 2*, is the "sizzling sound made by fat in a hot frying pan."

skirr: (rhymes with *sir*) the whirring sound of birds scurrying into flight. *Skirr* may also be used generally to mean the sound of any noisy scurrying.

stentorian: (sten-**TOR**-ee-in) very loud and resonant.

    In Homer's *Iliad*, Stentor was a herald with an extra-healthy set of pipes. From his name and vocal talent we inherit the noun *stentor*, a person with a powerful voice, along with the adjectives *stentorian* and *stentorophonic* (STEN-tuh-roh-**FAHN**-ik), having or making a loud, powerful sound, especially with the voice.

sternutation: (stur-nyoo-**TAY**-shin) the *kyerchoo!* sound of a sneeze, or the act of sneezing. The adjective *sternutatory* (stur-**NYOO**-tuh-tor-ee) means causing sneezing.

stertorous: (**STUR**-tur-us) having a deep, hoarse, rasping sound caused by obstruction of the air passages.

stridulation: (STRIJ-uh-**LAY**-shin) the shrill, grating, high-pitched sound made by the cricket and various other insects. The verb is *stridulate*.

    In James Thurber's story "Interview with a Lemming," a philosophical lemming tells an itinerant scientist that "there are many things animals can do that you cannot, such as stridulate, or chirr, to name just one. To stridulate, or chirr, one of the minor achievements of the cricket, your species is dependent on the intestines of the sheep and the hair of the horse." See **chirr** above.

tirl: (rhymes with *curl*) to make a rattling or clattering sound by spinning or moving rapidly up and down; also, to make a string vibrate by plucking it.

As a noun, *tirl* may mean either a rattling noise or a vibrating sound, as of a plucked string.

tonitruous: (toh-NI-troo-u̱s) reverberating with the sound of thunder.

The device used to create the sound of thunder in a musical or dramatic performance is called a **tonitruone** (toh-NI-troo-ohn) or **bronteum** (BRAHN-tee-u̱m). It is usually a large, thin sheet of metal that reverberates when shaken.

tubicination: (t(y)oo-BIS-i̱-NAY-shi̱n) the sound made by someone blowing a trumpet, horn, or any brass wind instrument; also, the act of blowing on a brass wind instrument.

ululation: (UL-yuh-**LAY**-shi̱n or YOOL-yuh-**LAY**-shi̱n) the plaintive howl of a dog or wolf, the screech of an owl, or any similar howl or wail (such as that made by a jilted lover or a person who has stubbed a toe).

vagitus: (vuh-JY-tu̱s) the first cry of a newborn child.

Vagitus may look as though it means the cry of a woman in labor, or the sigh she heaves upon delivering the child, but the word is not related to *vagina*, which comes directly from a Latin word meaning "sheath, scabbard." *Vagitus* comes from the Latin *vagire*, to cry.

wamble: (WAHM-bu̱l) the rumble, gurgle, or growl made by a distressed stomach on the verge of nausea. The adjective is *wambling*, making nauseated gurgling sounds.

Two related words, mentioned at the end of chapter 2, are **borborygmus** (BOR-bor-**RIG**-mu̱s) and **gurgulation**, which denote an audible (and embarrassing) exclamation emanating from the stomach or intestines.

> When *borborygmi*, or *gurgulations*,
> Interrupt my conversations,
> I simply shrug and say, "It's true—
> My belly has an opinion too."
> —WILLY BRAKEWYNDE

week: the squeal of a frightened pig or the squeak of a frightened mouse. Also spelled *weke*.

wheep: the sound of a sword or steel blade being drawn from its sheath.

wheeple: a poor attempt to whistle loudly; also, the weak, shrill whistle of a bird.

 Wheeples of the human variety are commonly heard at the ballpark, mixed in with the usual slobbering chorus of raspberries (also called Bronx cheers).

PIANO AND PIANISSIMO (SOFT AND VERY SOFT)

blodder: to flow with a gurgling sound out of a vessel with a narrow aperture. See **glink** below.

bombilate or **bombinate:** to hum or buzz, especially in a loud, continuous manner. The corresponding nouns are *bombilation* and *bombination*.

brontide: (BRAHN-tyd) a low, rumbling sound like distant thunder.

chuttering: the sound of subdued chirping. To *chutter* is to chirp quietly, or to converse quietly in chirping tones.

crepitation: (KREP-i-TAY-shin) a snap, crackle, and pop like burning leaves and twigs, or the sound allegedly produced by a certain rice cereal when mixed with milk. To *crepitate* means to snap, crackle, and pop. It's easy to imagine other figurative uses for these words:

> Youth is limber, youth is lithe,
> The body strong, the spirit blithe.
> Old age is such a sorry state—
> You ache, you groan, you *crepitate*.
>
>   —LORD BYGONE

croodle: to coo like a dove, or the cooing sound of a dove.

croosle: (KROOS'l) to make a low, whimpering noise, as an infant often does upon waking. Cf. **gruzzle** below.

drintling: clucking noises made by turkeys.

> *Drintling* might also be applied to the semiliterate drivel of athletes and sports commentators, the mind-numbing chatter on TV talk shows, and most political discourse.

fluctisonant: (fluk-TIS-uh-nint) having the sound of rolling waves. Also, *fluctisonous* (fluk-TIS-uh-nus).

fremescence: (fre-MES-ins) in a crowd or mob, the murmuring or grumbling sound of rising dissatisfaction or indignation. The adjective is *fremescent.*

fritinancy: (FRIT-i-nin-see) the twittering, chirping, or croaking of insects.

> *Fritinancy,* which dates back to Blount's *Glossographia* of 1656, could be applied quite nicely to insectile noises produced by human beings: the *fritinancy* of your in-laws.

glink: the sound of a liquid escaping from a narrow-mouthed vessel. Cf. **blodder** above.

gruzzle: to make a faint, inarticulate sound. Cf. **croosle** above.

gwick: the sound made in swallowing; also, to make a swallowing sound.

huam: (rhymes with *swam*) the moan of an owl on a summer night.

psellism: (SEL-iz'm) defective or indistinct pronunciation: e.g., stammering, lisping, mumbling, or garbling one's words.

psithurism: (SITH-yur-iz'm) the sound of wind whispering in the trees or the sound of rustling leaves.

purl: a gentle murmuring or bubbling sound like the water of a shallow stream flowing over stones.

scroop: the soft, crisp rustle of silk; also, a crunching or grating sound. The verb to *scroop* means either to rustle crisply or to crunch or grate harshly.

susurrus: (suu-SUR-us) a soft, subdued whispering, murmuring, rustling, or muttering sound. Also, **susurration.**

> The adjective is *susurrous* or *susurrant* (both stressed on the second syllable), softly whispering, rustling, or murmuring. The verb is *susurrate* (suu-SUR-ayt).

tirra-lirra: (TIR-uh-LIR-uh) the repetitive, melodic sound made by a songbird, such as a robin or a lark: "The lark, that *tirra-lirra* chants" (Shakespeare, *The Winter's Tale*).

If your brain is crepitating after that cavalcade of sounds, then you probably are **obmutescent** (AHB-myoo-TES-int), inclined to silence, taciturn. And if you're an obmutescent admirer of Simon and Garfunkel, you may be wondering if there are any grandiloquent words for the sounds of silence. Listen carefully to this quiescent pair: **silential** (sy-LEN-shul), pertaining to or performed in silence; and **silentium** (sy-LEN-shee-um), a place where silence is imposed, such as a library or religious retreat.

THE WORD IS THE DEED

Suit the action to the word,
the word to the action.

—SHAKESPEARE, *Hamlet*

Words are also actions,
and actions are a kind of words.

—RALPH WALDO EMERSON

One of the fundamental principles of grandiloquence is that things are easier said than done. If you accept that precept, then the corollary is this: Why bother to do anything when you can simply talk about it?

For centuries writers have realized the advantages of stringing words together as a way of shirking real work while appearing to do something worthwhile. The humorist Dave Barry once quipped, "As a professional journalist, I am always looking for new ways to get paid for being motionless."

What is the fourth estate, after all, but a bunch of overgrown children who (being slightly more clever and devious than their peers, and infinitely more lazy) realized that they could turn their penchant for pleniloquence into a decent living by yapping and scribbling about what others do? And then there are the poets, who are some of the most altiloquently indolent people on the planet.

Take Chaucer, for example. All he did was hang out at a tavern, eavesdrop on a lively conversation, and transcribe the anecdotes. Then there's Shakespeare. If you think he was a prolific worker, think again. He lifted his plots from popular legends or ripped them off other writers, and some say there's credible evidence that another person wrote all the plays while "the Bard" counted his guilders.

Do you think Samuel Taylor Coleridge made up "The Rime of the Ancient Mariner" all by himself? Likely as not he met some daffy old salt, plied him with grog, and stole his tale. And how do you think William Wordsworth came by his immortal intimations? He wandered lazy as a cloud around the English countryside, stopping every so often to recollect his emotions in tranquillity beside some blooming copse or crumbling abbey.

If you wish to live the grandiloquent life, clearly you must aspire to let others do the dirty work while you revel in the otiose luxury of language. As the Roman philosopher Pratus Pontificatus wrote in *Quid Faciendum?* ("What's to Be Done?"), "The social order is founded on a strict division of speech and labor: The slave must do everything and say nothing; the plebeian says you can't do something for nothing; and the patrician does nothing and says whatever he likes."

Only the ungrandiloquent embrace the worn-out notion that actions speak louder than words. The grandiloquent wisely know that words speak softly but carry a big stick. They also know that if you're stuck on your words and you want them to stick, then your words must be true in deed, and they must indeed be words.

And with that horbgorbling preamble, dear reader, let us proceed to haingle, feek, and dwale through the words you need for all your deeds. (We'll have definitions for those words, as they say on TV, after this break.)

For All You Do, There's a Word for You

It's been said that we spend a third of our lives sleeping, another third working, one-sixth eating, and one-sixth in the bathroom. I think something vital was overlooked in that assessment (sorry, not sex—that was probably factored in with sleep). In my learned estimation, I'd say most of us spend a significant portion of our precious time on earth **horbgorbling,** puttering around aimlessly.

Shuffling alongside *horbgorble* are the equally feckless words *haingle, feek,* and *dwale.* ("Haingle, Feek, and Dwale" sounds like the name of a pettifogging law firm in some Dickens novel, doesn't it?) To **haingle** is to amble about in a feeble or listless way; to **feek** is to wander around aimlessly; and to **dwale** means to wander about deliriously. Spend a day horbgorbling downtown in any metropolis and you are sure to see a few haingling oldsters, some feeking tourists and shoppers, and at least one major loon dwaling about the streets, ranting at imaginary enemies.

Shall we **oxter** (walk arm and arm) through my grandiloquent garden of handy-dandy words for human deeds? Here we go. . . .

When was the last time you took some well-deserved time off work? In Amspeak (the American language) they call it "going on vacation," in Britspeak they call it "going on holiday," but the grandiloquent call it **feriation** (FEER-ee-AY-shin). This word descends from the ancient Roman **feriae** (FEER-ee-ee), certain days during which all business and political activities were suspended and even slaves got a break from slaving.

Does your feriation involve a trip to the country? That's called **rustication;** the verb to *rusticate* means to spend time in the bucolic boonies. Do you like to rusticate in the summer? If so, then the word for that is **estivation;** to *estivate* means to go away for the summer. As you may have guessed, *estivation* and *estivate* are the opposites of *hibernation* and *hibernate,* to take a winter vacation (among bears and other animals, to take a long winter's nap). *Estival* (rhymes with *festival*) and *hibernal* (hy-BUR-nul) are the corresponding adjectives.

If going to the beach is your preferred estival activity, you probably love to **apricate** (AP-ri-kayt), bask in the sun, sunbathe. Just be careful that your **heliolatry** (HEE-lee-**AHL**-uh-tree), sun-worship, doesn't make your skin **coriaceous** (KOR-ee-**AY**-shus), tough and leathery. Another useful verb for absorbing warmth is **beek,** which means to bask either in the sun or before a fire. Thus, when you estivate, you can apricate, and when you hibernate, you can beek.

If you think the world is a menacing wilderness, unfit for benign recreation, then I have a few **feral** (FEER-ul, wild, savage) words that may help you navigate the jungle of life. First, do you know how to **brachiate** (BRAY-kee-ayt)? **Brachiation** is the act of swinging through the trees with the greatest of ease, the graceful mode of locomotion employed by apes and monkeys.

If you're a corporate animal, somewhere in your brachiation through the workplace jungle you will probably be challenged by another ambitious beast. In that situation it may help to know how to **latrate** (LAY-trayt), bark like a dog, and **kevel** (KEV'l), paw the ground or toss the head like a horse or bull.

If those tactics don't help get you out of trouble, you can always **spartle,** flounder, kick, or flail about. My advice, however, would be to **arsle** (AHRS'l), move backward, retreat— literally, "move one's *arse*"—as swiftly as possible. If you do happen to get into a dogfight, and you are **suggilated** (SUHG-ji-lay-tid), beaten black and blue, then you'll probably need to arsle off somewhere to lick your wounds and **foof,** howl or whine like a wounded, sick, or melancholy dog.

Foof reminds me that there's a lesson to be learned here, and it's not that dumb one about dogs who fight and run away. Rather, it's that grandiloquence is not always polysyllabic and **sesquipedalian** (SES-kwi-puh-**DAY**-lee-in), consisting of or pertaining to foot-and-a-half-long words. Quite often a well-chosen word of one or two syllables will do the grandiloquent trick. And, perhaps more than any other tongue on earth, English abounds with unusual monosyllabic verbs like *foof, feek,* and *dwale* that denote precise and vivid action.

Take, for example, one of my favorites: **fyerk,** to shoot away or flick off with the finger and thumb. Isn't it marvelous that there's such a short, forceful word for that common action? You can fyerk a crumb off a table, fyerk lint off your clothes, fyerk a marble, or fyerk a pesky mosquito. If you dare, you can even tell someone who's bothering you to go fyerk off. Perhaps we could even take the liberty of employing this serviceable word as a noun: "Frankly, my dear, I don't give a *fyerk!*"

Fyerk is dialectal and unfortunately obsolete. Unabridged dictionaries list the word *fillip* (probably a variation on *flip*) for the same action, but in my opinion *fillip* falls flat on its face compared with the monosyllabic zip of *fyerk*. ("I don't give a *fillip*" just doesn't cut it, don't you agree?)

Below I have assembled twelve more monosyllabic curiosities of the language. They may look like nonce-words, or "sniglets," but they are all real words that repose in the miry depths of our unabridged dictionaries. Take a **gliff** (a brief look, passing glance) and try to guess what they mean.

lirp	thrip	snurl	snurt
mimp	brump	fruzz	gaum
gaure	gooze	grouk	winx

Give up? Here are the definitions:

Lirp and **thrip** both mean to snap the fingers.

Snurl and **snurt**—like their cousins in sound, *snort, snout,* and *sniffle*—are nosy words. *Snurl* means to turn up the nose in scorn or repugnance; *snurt* means to expel mucus in sneezing. Surely you will snurl if someone snurts on your shirt.

You are also likely to snurl at a mimping wimp, for to **mimp** is to speak in a prissy or affected manner, with the lips pursed.

Brump means to collect twigs and sticks that have fallen from trees. Brumping is a favorite pastime of horbgorblers.

Fruzz means to rub the hair the wrong way, as when

you're scratching a dog's back, petting a cat, tousling a child's hair, or vacuuming a rug.

The next three specimens are lookers. **Gaure** (GOW-<u>ur</u>) means to stare at in astonishment; **gooze** means to stare aimlessly; and **gaum** (GAWM) may mean either to stare vacantly or handle in a clumsy or overly intimate manner: "That lascivious crambazzle was gauming my thigh under the table!" (A *crambazzle* is a dissipated old man.)

To **grouk** is to become gradually enlivened after waking up. Some people can't grouk until they've had a second cup of coffee.

Finally, to **winx** means to bray like a jackass. It's not polite to winx when you win a bet.

The long and the short of it is that the language is littered with spectacular words—short and sweet as well as sesquipedalian and grandisonant—for practically everything we do or can imagine doing. After many laborious hours **perquesting** (searching through) various dictionaries for exceptional words about human activity, I have compiled the following eclectic selection of noteworthy verbs, nouns, and adjectives. I think you will find them **eesome** (EE-s<u>um</u>), pleasant to look upon, and some may even make you **kink,** choke with laughter.

algerining: (AL-jur-EE-ning) prowling about with the intention of stealing or committing burglary.

ambisinister: awkward in using the hands; performed in a clumsy way, as if by a person with two left hands.

> The randy young bride of a minister
> Prayed that her man could administer.
>> When the time came to bless
>> Her sweet nakedness,
> She found he was quite *ambisinister.*
>   —ANITA RIELMAN

Ambisinister, the little-known antonym of *ambidextrous,* is the perfect grandiloquent replacement for the shopworn expression "he's all thumbs."

arefy: (AR-i-fy) to dry up.

>   Hot grandiloquent tip: The next time someone bothers you, try telling the importunate clodpate to *arefy.*

arietate: (AR-ee-uh-tayt) to butt like a ram or strike with a battering ram.

beaze: to dry in the sun (clothes *beazing* on the line).

blirt: to fire a gun aimlessly or carelessly: a pack of drunken hunters *blirting* through the woods.

charrette: (shuh-RET) an intensive, eleventh-hour effort to complete or accomplish something before a deadline.

chimble: to crumble or gnaw into small fragments.

claum: (KLAWM) 1. to handle with dirty fingers. 2. to paw with the hands in an intimate or fawning manner: lovers *clauming* each other; a star *claumed* by adoring fans.

climp: to touch a clean or shiny surface with dirty or greasy fingers and leave smudges on it. Children are especially adept at *climping.*

cloffin: to sit idly by a fire, or the act of doing so.

collifobble: to talk secretly.

couther: to comfort by giving refreshment and warmth; to cure by administering remedies.

cribble: to pass something through a sieve; colloquially, to put through the wringer.

crose: (rhymes with *hose*) to whine in sympathy with a person who is in pain or distress.

dactylonomy: (DAK-ti-LAHN-uh-mee) counting on one's fingers.

deasil: (DEEZ'l) to move in a clockwise direction.

defenestrate: to throw out of a window.

diurnation: (DY-ur-NAY-shin) sleeping during the day.

dollum: to spoil a thing with too much handling.

eggtaggle: to waste time in bad company.

explaterate: (eks-PLAT-ur-ayt) to run off at the mouth, have a bad case of verbal diarrhea.

festinate: to walk fast, move forward rapidly.

>   The noun is *festination,* hasty ambulation.

floccillation: (FLAHK-si-LAY-shin) delirious picking at the bedclothes by a sick person (also called *carphologia*).

forslug: to forfeit or ruin by sluggishness or indolence.

fossick: originally, to search for gold in abandoned claims; later, to rummage around looking for anything of value.

frustling: shaking out and exhibiting the feathers or plumage. The word may apply to a bird (such as a peacock) or to a person fond of strutting in fancy dress.

funkify: to run away in fright.

glink: to glance at slyly or sideways.

As noted earlier, *glink* may also mean the sound of liquid flowing from a narrow-necked bottle.

gorgonize: to stare at with a petrifying or mesmerizing look (like one of the Gorgons of Greek mythology).

greg: to tease or tantalize by offering something without intending to give it.

grimthorpe: to remodel a building badly, without regard for its original quality, character, or history.

"*Grimthorping* implies lavish expenditure without appropriate skill or decent taste," writes Norman W. Schur in *1000 Most Obscure Words.* This eponym comes from Sir Edmund Beckett, Baron Grimthorpe, a nineteenth-century English lawyer and (much-reviled) architect.

hatchetate: to chop something up, either literally or figuratively. The noun is *hatchetation*.

humicubate: (hyoo-MIK-yuh-bayt) to lie prostrate or prone, especially in penitence or prayer.

The noun is *humicubation*.

hypermimia: (HY-pur-MIM-ee-uh) waving or gesticulating with the hands while talking.

Here's a hypermimic riddle:

WHAT AM I?

I tawk wid an accent
Dat some would cawl crude.
Duh tings dat I say
Yuh might tink ah rude.

I like wavin' my hands
When makin' a point.
Gotta problem widdat?
Den get outta dis joint!

Answer: A New Yorker

ipsedixitism: (IP-si-**DIK**-si-tiz'm) "The practice of dogmatic assertion," says the *Century*. The word comes from the Latin *ipse dixit*, "he himself has said (it)."

My favorite example of ipsedixitism is a pronouncement my father once made during one of his tirades on the inequities of life. "I'm telling you," he bellowed, pounding the table with his fist, "it's the categorical people who are screwing up the world!"

jactitate: (JAK-ti-tayt) to toss and turn, or to toss to and fro or back and forth.

The noun is *jactitation:* the insomniac's fitful *jactitation;* the brisk *jactitation* of a tennis match.

jarble: to smear with grime or mud.

kaming: issuing forth in a stream, like bees leaving the hive.

lapidate: to stone a person to death.

Shirley Jackson's classic parable "The Lottery" climaxes in *lapidation*, the act of stoning someone to death.

noctivagant: (nahk-**TIV**-uh-gint) roving around at night; also, a person who wanders in the night.

pandiculation: (pan-DIK-yuh-**LAY**-shin) stretching and yawning upon waking up or before going to bed.

parapraxis: (PAR-uh-**PRAK**-sis) a blundering act, lapse of memory, or slip of the tongue, especially one that reveals a hidden motive—colloquially known as a *Freudian slip*. The plural is *parapraxes*.

parrhesiastic: (puh-REE-zhee-**AS**-tik) speaking freely or boldly.

patavinity: (PAT-uh-**VIN**-i-tee) the use of local or provincial words and expressions in one's writing and speech.

pedipulate: (pe-**DIP**-yuh-layt) to operate with the feet (as opposed to **manipulate,** to operate with the hands).

> Visit your local health club and you will see fitness freaks *pedipulating* the Exercycles and treadmills.

periclitate: (puh-RIK-li-tayt) to put in danger, expose to risk.

pernoctation: the act of staying up all night; "pulling an all-nighter" to work, study, or party.

polylogize: (puh-LIL-uh-jyz) to talk excessively.

pseudandry: (SOOD-an-dree) the use of a masculine pseudonym by a woman.

pseudogyny: (soo-DAHJ-uh-nee) the use of a feminine pseudonym by a man.

pysmatic: (piz-MAT-ik) always asking questions or inquiring.

> To children and philosophers
> The world is enigmatic.
> These young and old interpreters
> Must therefore be *pysmatic*.
> —Q. RIUS KATZ

quonking: (slang) noise from the sidelines that interrupts an athlete's (or a performer's) concentration.

The world of sports fandom desperately needs a verb to complement this noun, so I shall take the liberty of coining *quonk*, to make a noise that interrupts an athlete's or performer's concentration. (Linguists call this a "back formation.")

Quonking may include chatter among the spectators, catcalls or exsibilations from disgruntled fans, or simply an ill-timed cough or sneeze. Quonking (the noise itself or the act of making noise) is perceived differently depending on the sport. In baseball, for example, it is customary to quonk the visiting team's batters or outfielders. In sportspeak, this is known as "intentional quonking." At a tennis match or golf tournament, however, even the mildest disturbance is considered a gross breach of etiquette. Such interference is dubbed "unsportsmanlike quonking."

rasorial: habitually or compulsively scratching the ground in search of food, the way chickens and other fowl do.

> Of all the ways to eke out a living, writing is surely
> the most wretched and *rasorial.*
> —CACOËTHES SCRIBENDI

sarcle: to dig up weeds.

sciamachy: (sy-AM-uh-kee) fighting with a shadow or imaginary opponent; shadowboxing.

sclaff: in golf, to strike or scrape the ground with the club before hitting the ball.

siffilate: to speak in whispers.

smoodge (or **smooge**): to play the sycophant, curry favor, flatter with ulterior motives.

snarf: (prep school slang) to fall asleep with your clothes on; also, the act of falling asleep with your clothes on.

snoach: to speak through the nose.

snuzzle: to sniff or poke around with the nose, as dogs do.

sororize: (of women) to get together with other women, associate as sisters.

> *Sororize* (from Latin *soror,* a sister, female friend) is the grandiloquent sister of *fraternize* (from Latin *frater,* a brother, companion).

sparge: to make moist by sprinkling: The gentle rain sparged the parched fields. The noun is *spargefaction.*

spiculate: to sharpen to a point (to *spiculate* a pencil).

thanatopsis: (THAN-uh-**TAHP**-sis) contemplation of death.

> *Thanatopsize* (my coinage) means to think about death.

tootle: of an old person, to mutter incoherently or like a child.

> The adjective is *tootlish,* babbling unintelligibly.

triturate: (TRICH-ur-ayt) to grind up or crush into powder.

trullization: the act of laying on plaster with a trowel—or, figuratively, the act of laying it on with a trowel.

> They say that flattery is not
> A good way to improve your lot;

But surely you'll advance your station
If you're adept at *trullization.*
                              —MILES BLANDISH

ultracrepidarian: going beyond one's sphere of knowledge or influence in offering an opinion.

The word comes to us from a Latin maxim popularized by Pliny the Elder (A.D. 23–79), which alludes to a story about the Greek painter Apelles (c. 360–315 B.C.) and a not-so-humble cobbler. As Eugene Ehrlich tells it in *Amo, Amas, Amat and More*, "the cobbler correctly criticized the representation of a sandal in a painting Apelles was working on. Unfortunately, he went on to criticize the way in which the subject's legs were being painted. This was too much for Apelles, who responded with his memorable rebuke: *ne supra crepidam sutor iudicaret*"—"Cobbler, stick to your last," or more literally, "The cobbler should not judge above the sandal."

Ultracrepidarian may also be used as a noun for people who talk through their hats. *Ultracrepidarianism* is the act or habit of flappin' your gums about something you don't know nuthin' about.

verbigerate: (vur-BIJ-ur-ayt) to continually repeat certain words or phrases, usually unconsciously.

Teenagers are inveterate verbigerators, and the adolescent verbal tic of inserting "like" and "y'know" into every sentence is a classic example of verbigeration.

witzelsucht: (VITS-ul-suukt or VIT-sel-zuukht) a feeble attempt at humor; specifically, says *Stedman's Medical Dictionary*, "a morbid tendency to pun, make poor jokes, and tell pointless stories, while being oneself inordinately entertained thereby." The word comes from the German *witzeln*, to affect wit, and *sucht*, mania.

I leave you with a final, solitary word that applies to us all:
solivagant (sah-LIV-uh-gint), wandering alone.

❖

DOODADS, RIGAMAJIGS, AND WHATNOTS

Uncommon Words for Everyday Things

> "The time has come," the Walrus said,
> "To talk of many things:
> "Of *pintles*, *sprags*, and *bandoleers*—
> "Of *pillions* and *feazings*—
> "And where a *moonglade* can be found—
> "And why *pilcrows* have no wings."
> —ALISON WONDERWORD*

Whenever I get to talking with someone about little-known words for well-known things, nine times out of ten the person says, "I know there's a word for that plastic or metal tip on your shoelace, but I can't remember it. Do you know what it is?"

I haven't a clue why ninety percent of the people I meet associate oddball words for everyday things with shoelace tips, but I certainly do know the word that's eluding them. The sheath on each end of your shoelace is called an **aglet** (or more prosaically, a *tag*). Without aglets, I hasten to point out, shoelaces wouldn't last long because their feazings would be exposed. When that remark generates a slack-jawed stare, I explain that **feazings** are the frayed or unraveled ends of a rope.

---

*Have patience, dear reader, and read on, and the italicized words in this parodic verse will be defined herein.

At that point, unless my interlocutor is a dyed-in-the-wool wordhound, he or she abruptly thanks me for the edifying information about aglets and feazings and then scurries off—probably in search of the nearest telephone to alert the mental health department that there's a dwaling logomaniac at large.

There probably are thousands of ordinary things most of us don't know the words for. Adam and Eve had the rare privilege of naming the things around them in the Garden of Eden. We postlapsarian (after the Fall) folks are not so lucky; we have to learn what things are called. But don't despair; there's more delight than drudgery in the endeavor. Think of each thing-word you acquire as a **timmynoggy,** a device that saves time and labor, or as an **objet trouvé** (awb-ZHAY-troo-VAY), literally a "found object," something singular, aesthetically pleasing, and worthy of collection and display.

Few of life's pleasures can match the enjoyment obtained from discovering the precise word for a particular doohickey. It won't win you any prizes, and your benighted relatives and friends may think you eccentric or a trifle daft, but that shouldn't stop you from basking in the warm, wordy glow of satisfaction that comes from leading an anonymous object out of lonely darkness into purest light.

Because the vocabulary of uncommon words for common things is so vast—and in fact beyond the scope of most dictionaries—I cannot presume to cover more than a **scintilla** (sin-TIL-uh, the merest speck) of it. Instead, to preserve our common sanity and conserve a significant number of trees, I have carefully sifted through the swarf and dunnage of language and selected a smattering of uncommon terms for ordinary things that I imagine you've come across and wondered, "Is there a word for that?"

By now I suppose you're familiar enough with my verbal tricks to realize that I slipped *swarf* and *dunnage* into that last sentence because they are fine examples of offbeat words for familiar things.

Swarf (from the Old Norse *sverfa,* to file) refers to the fine metallic particles that accumulate from using a machine tool to grind, sharpen, or cut metal.

Dunnage (of uncertain origin) is a versatile word with three useful senses: (a) loose stuffing or packing material used to keep the cargo of a ship dry and to prevent it from shifting or chafing; (b) any packing material—such as excelsior (slender wood shavings), Styrofoam pellets, or bubble wrap—used to cushion or stabilize freight shipped by land or air; and finally (c) baggage, luggage, personal effects.

And with that said and dunnage, I shall now offer you a grab bag full of terms for various doodads, rigamajigs, and whatnots—along with an occasional **quoz,** something strange or absurd.

Some Well-Clothed Words

Shall we talk through our hats? Let's begin with some familiar military headpieces.

The **Pickelhaube** (**PIK**-ul-**HOW**-buh) is the spiked helmet worn by Prussian and German soldiers before World War I. The **bicorne** is that bulbous hat tapering to two points that Napoleon wore. The **tricorne** (also called a *cocked hat*) is the three-pointed hat worn by Paul Revere and the other American revolutionary warriors.

Members of the French Foreign Legion wear a cap called a **kepi.** (Soldiers on both sides of the American Civil War also wore a version of it.) The cloth covering for the neck attached to the back of the kepi is called a **havelock** (like *have lock*), after the nineteenth-century English general Sir Henry Havelock.

Do you know the word for the big, bushy hats worn by the guards at Buckingham Palace? **Bearskins.** How about the floppy beret with the pompom worn by Highland bagpipers? **Tam-o'-shanter.**

Now, what about the name of the tweed cap we associate with Sherlock Holmes—the one with earflaps and visors in the front and back? It's a **deerstalker.** The long overcoat that Holmes wears, with the short detachable cape, is called an **inverness.**

If you've been to a parade lately, then you probably saw a lot of **shakos** (SHAK-ohz), the hats typically worn by members of a marching band. The shako is tall, cylindrical, with a flat top, a short visor, and a feather cockade in front.

Going on safari? Don't forget to bring along that stiff, round, wide-brimmed hat called a **pith helmet** or **topee** (toh-PEE).

When Yasir Arafat and Yitzhak Rabin shook hands on the south lawn of the White House on September 13, 1993, it inspired the world's hope for peace in the Middle East. It also made a lot of reporters scurry to the library to find out the word for Arafat's Arab headdress: **kaffiyeh** (kah-FEE-uh).

Here's one from the neckwear department: Renaissance men and women (e.g., Sir Walter Raleigh, Queen Elizabeth I, Shakespeare) often wore a wide, circular, starched, pleated collar called a **ruff.** To the modern observer, people wearing ruffs look as if they have the air filter of a car stuck on their necks.

Moving right along to the other end of the body, allow me to share some interesting words about shoes.

Do you ever wear **zori** (ZOR-ee)? They're the rubber or leather sandals with straps passing over the instep that connect with a thong that fits between the hallux (big toe) and second toe. Zori are colloquially called "flip-flops" or "thongs."

Have you ever noticed those overlong, pointy-toed shoes that harlequins and jesters wear and wondered what they were called? For eons that word eluded me, but one day, after many a futile search, I finally found not one but two terms in the wondrous *Century Dictionary:* **poulaine** (poo-LAYN), by derivation "shoes after the Polish fashion," and **cracow** (or **crakow**), after the city in Poland.

You've probably seen lots of poulaines and cracows in paintings and woodcuts depicting scenes from the Middle Ages. They were popular all over medieval Europe among various classes, and were introduced to England in the fourteenth century during the reign of Edward II. The *Century* shows that they came in several styles: slippers with pencil-pointed or upturned toes, sometimes adorned with a ball at the tip—the courtier and jester variety; floppy-toed, ankle- or calf-length leather shoes, worn by rustics and woodsmen like Robin Hood and his merry band; and for the knight, a sharp-toed embellishment to the **solleret** (SAHL-ur-et), the flexible steel shoe in a suit of armor.

Now let's test your powers of habilamental deduction with a few more unusual words for apparel. Match each word from the following list with the appropriate definition below. Answers appear at the end of the chapter.

toque blanche	frog	jodhpurs	shapka
gi	lorgnette	yashmak	sporran
baldric	bandoleer	dandy	keeper
fez	farthingale	calypso	hoxter

1. Riding pants flared at the thighs and tight below the knees are called _____.
2. The giant hoop skirt suspended on a framework of whalebone, popular from the sixteenth to the eighteenth century, is called a _____.
3. A _____ is a belt worn over one shoulder and across the chest to hold a sword.
4. When a woman ties the tails of her shirt into a knot in front, displaying her (usually bare) waist, the style is called _____.
5. The loop behind a belt buckle through which you slip the last few unbuckled inches of the belt is called a _____.
6. A _____ is a fur-covered pouch or purse attached to a kilt.
7. The round, close-fitting, tapered, brimless fur cap worn by many Russians in the wintertime is called a _____.
8. A _____ is a pair of eyeglasses mounted on a handle.
9. An inside pocket in a coat or suit is called a _____.
10. A _____ is a man's shirt with ruffles down the front, baggy sleeves, and ruffled cuffs, popular among the gentry

from the seventeenth to nineteenth century. (You've seen guys wearing it in depictions of pistol duels and sword-fights.)

11. A _____ is a wide ammunition belt, with slots for rifle cartridges, worn across the chest by certain soldiers (for example, Emiliano Zapata).

12. An ornamental clasp on the front of a coat, an ornamental (often looped) braid on a military uniform, and a loop attached to a belt to hold a scabbard are all called a _____.

13. A chef's white, fluffy hat is called a _____.

14. A _____ is a conical, flat-topped, tasselled red cap traditionally worn by Turks.

15. The outfit worn by practitioners of judo, karate, and other martial arts is called a _____.

16. The _____ is the veil worn by Muslim women in public.

WORDS AROUND THE HOME AND WORKPLACE

How well do you know your typewriter (that is, assuming you still use one of those obsolescent beasts)? The **bail rolls** are the rubber rollers affixed to the bail arm. What's the **bail arm?** Also called a *paper bail,* it's the movable bar on the typewriter that holds the paper against the **platen** (rhymes with *flatten*), which is the proper term for what we informally call the roller.

Would you like to know some fiberoptically fascinating facts about your telephone? The handset of your phone rests in a **cradle,** and the **cradle switch** is the dingus the handset depresses to cut off the connection when you hang up. When you pick up the handset, the cradle switch pops up and you hear the caller or a dial tone.

Here are two bits of verbal trivia about rotary phones: These outmoded devices have two buttons in the cradle, which are called **plungers.** The curved metal clip attached to the dial just above the zero or operator hole is called the **finger stop.**

With nearly everyone now using a touch-tone phone to reach out and clutch someone on the infobahn, we are doing a lot of "pressing" instead of "dialing," and quite often what we press is not a number but a key with a symbol on it. The typical touch-tone phone has two symbol keys, one with an asterisk [*] and the other with a cross-hatch or pound sign [#]. Most folks call the key with * the "star key" or "star button," but in the jargon of phonespeak it's called the "memory button." What we informally refer to as the "pound key" is technically called an **octothorpe**. (In his *Word Treasury*, Paul Dickson notes that *octothorpe* was coined in 1967 by the wire-brained wonks at big Ma Bell.)

Here are some more uncommon words for ordinary things around your home and workplace that you may have wondered about:

agitator: the thing in the middle of your washing machine tub that sloshes the clothes around.

agraffe: (uh-GRAF) the wire cage that holds down the cork in a bottle of champagne. Also called a *coiffe* (KWAHF).

averruncator: a long pole with a shearing mechanism or saw at one end used for pruning trees.

colorburst (or **color bars**): the multicolored stripes displayed on your TV screen when a station goes off the air.

crawl: typed information that rolls across a TV screen, often inside a black bar at the bottom of the screen. *Crawl* may also refer to rolling credits at the end of a film or TV show.

escutcheon: (e-SKUHCH-in) a decorative metal plate around a keyhole, door lock, doorknob, or the handle on a drawer.

faxraff: 1. miscellaneous unsolicited material and junk mail transmitted by fax. 2. people who are so infatuated with their fax machines that they are compelled to fax everything. (Coined by humorist Tom Bodett.)

ferrule: (FER-ul) the metal sheath on the end of an umbrella.

   Ferrule also denotes the threaded knob or nut that holds a lampshade in place, and the protective metal ring or cap on a cane or tool handle.

harp: a metal frame around a light bulb for attaching a lamp-shade, or a metal frame inside a lampshade designed to fit over the bulb.

kerf: the initial groove made in a piece of wood to guide a handsaw, or a notch in a tree indicating where it should be chopped or sawed.

loupe: (like *loop*) the small magnifying glass used by jewelers and watchmakers.

newel: the principal post at the bottom of a banister or handrail for a flight of stairs.

pintle: the pin that holds the two pieces of a metal hinge together so the hinge can pivot on its *gudgeons,* the slots for the pintle.

punt: the indentation in the bottom of a wine bottle.

    The function of the punt is to strengthen the glass and not, as is commonly surmised, to create the impression that the bottle contains more liquid than it does.

reamer: the twirling part of a citrus juicing machine that removes the pulp and juice.

rosette: (roh-ZET) a dent or impression in a piece of wood or lumber created when the hammerer misses the nail, also called a *chatter mark.*

snath: the long, bent handle of a scythe, also called a *snead.*

    The two short handles or grips on the snath are called *doles.*

splat: a single piece of wood, usually broad and flat, in the middle of the back of a wooden chair.

    Depending on the style of the chair, splats may be plain or ornamental. If a chair has several pieces across the back, running from the seat or cross rail to the top rail, they are called *spindles,* a term that may also apply to the cross supports between the chair legs below the seat.

televelocoraptor: a VCR that eats your favorite videos.

    In a letter to me proposing this word, writer-editor Michael Bay notes that he "recently consigned a particularly tape-thirsty specimen to the electronic graveyard of the jammed."

topic box: on a TV screen, a picture or graphic inserted in a window or "box" to one side of a newscaster's head to visually identify the topic of the report.

zarf: a sleeve for a coffee cup or beer can.

Moving Right Along

Now let's look at some words for various things associated with moving vehicles, which you may take along and use when you're out and about:

bitt: a short thick post on the deck of a ship for securing ropes or cables. Such a post on a dock or wharf is called a *bollard.*

contrail: a visible trail of condensed water vapor or ice crystals coming from an airplane, rocket, or missile.

crossbuck: an X-shaped warning symbol attached to a railroad crossing sign.

flukes: the claws on the arms of an anchor.

hawsehole: the hole through which a ship's anchor is passed.

howdah: a riding seat, usually covered, on the back of an elephant.

joola: (JOO-lah) a suspension bridge made of ropes.

Mars light: the flashing light on an ambulance, fire truck, or police cruiser.

Drivers who have had too many Bud Lights wind up in vehicles with Mars lights.

pillion: (rhymes with *million*) a seat or cushion for a second person on a motorcycle or behind the saddle of a horse.

plimsoll: the line painted on cargo ships to avoid overloading.

podoscaph: a boat propelled by bicycle treadles.

ratlines: the rope ladders or steps on which sailors (or buccaneers) can scramble aloft and adjust the sails.

sprag: a block of wood or a brick wedged behind a wheel to stop a vehicle from rolling. Also called a *scotch.*

Richard Nixon's and Tom Clancy's books make excellent sprags.

thole or **tholepin:** a pin inserted in the gunwhale of a boat to hold an oar.

Uncommon Words About Animals and Nature

"When you were a kid," writes Richard Lederer in *The Play of Words*, "you probably played with those small winged thingamabobs that grow on—and contain the seeds of—maple trees. You may have glued them to your nose or watched them spin like pinwheels when you tossed them into the wind. Believe it or not, these organic whatchamacallits do have a name—*schizocarps*."

Here are some more unusual words for natural phenomena that have caught my curious, childlike eye over the years:

anthropoglot: (an-THROH-puh-glaht) an animal, such as a parrot, capable of mimicking human speech.

carapace: (KAR-uh-pays) the shell of an animal, such as a turtle, armadillo, crustacean, etc.

comb: the fleshy outgrowth or crest on the heads of roosters and various other fowl.

crepuscle: (kre-PUHS'l) the fading light at the end of the day, twilight; also called *crepuscule.*

dewclaw: the extra claw behind the paw of certain dogs; also, a false hoof on a deer or hog.

dewlap: the flap or fold of skin hanging from the throat of a cow or an ox.

Caricatures of Ronald Reagan often depicted him with a dewlap.

flews: the fleshy flaps on the sides of a dog's mouth.

heliotropism: (HEE-lee-**AH**-truh-piz'm) in plants, the phenomenon of turning or bending toward the sun or a source of light.

izles: (EYE-zuls) sparks, embers, or particles of soot rising from a fire or coming out of a chimney.

kibble: dead leaves and other organic material swept or raked up from gardens and courtyards.

moonglade: the reflection of moonlight on water, usually in a long, bright path.

plenilune: the time of the full moon.

    The crescent-shaped moon is called *falcate* (FAL-kayt); a *gibbous* (GIB-us) moon is between half and full.

scintillation: (SIN-ti-LAY-shin) the twinkling of the stars.

    Scintillate means to flash, twinkle, emit sparks.

snood: the fleshy appendage hanging from the beak of a male turkey.

spindrift: ocean spray blown by the wind.

vibrissae: (vy-BRIS-ee) the sensitive whiskers of a cat.

wattle: the fleshy appendage or growth hanging from the neck or chin of certain fowl, such as the chicken or turkey.

    A synonym is *caruncle* (kuh-RUHNG-kul), which may also apply to a bird's *comb* (see above).

DIACRITICAL REMARKS

Now let us proceed from the world of nature to the world of signs and symbols.

    Are you one of the many folks who have trouble deciphering the obscure symbols dictionaries use to indicate pronunciation? If so, then the first thing that will help you feel less befuddled is knowing that these enigmatic phonetic indicators are called **diacritics** or **diacritical marks** (*diacritical* means "serving to distinguish"). Let's take a brief trip down pronunciation lane.

    Two of the most common diacritics are the **macron** (MAY-krahn) and the **breve** (rhymes with *leave*). The macron is a horizontal line or dash placed over a vowel to represent the "long" sound of the vowel: *dāte, ēven, nīght, tōtal, mūsic*. The breve is a small curved mark, like a tiny smile, placed over a vowel to represent the "short" sound of the vowel: *căt; pĕt; sĭt; hŏt, ŭp.*

The diacritical mark people seem to have the most trouble interpreting is the **schwa.** The schwa looks like a small *e* turned on its head or printed upside-down and backward: ə. This versatile symbol indicates an unstressed vowel sound, neither long nor short but lightened, variable, or obscure: e.g., *a* in *ago, e* in *item, i* in *sanity, o* in *comply,* and *u* in *focus.*

A **dieresis** (dy-ER-i-sis) is two dots printed over a vowel. (The more familiar word *umlaut,* from German, is a synonym.) In dictionaries, the dieresis sometimes is used over an *a* to indicate an open or broad vowel sound, as in *car;* it may also appear over a *u* to represent an OO sound: *flute* (flüt), *roof* (rüf). In printing, the dieresis used to appear in words with separately pronounced adjacent vowels: *coöperate, preëminent, naïve, zoölogy.* This practice is now old-fashioned.

Finally, we have the **circumflex.** This diacritic looks like the tip of a tiny arrow, or like an equilateral triangle with the bottom line removed; it sits on top of a vowel like a little hood. Some dictionaries use a circumflex over a vowel when it is followed by *r* to indicate that the sound of the vowel blends into the *r:* e.g., *care* (kâr); *dear* (dîr); *store* (stôr); *fur* (fûr).

GETTING INTO PRINT

A few pages back you learned that *octothorpe* is the technical name for the symbol #. Did you know that # is also a printer's mark meaning "insert space here"?

Let's find out how much you know about the nonverbal aspect of writing, printing, and copyediting. Can you identify the following marks and symbols?

&   @   ?   ç   ~   « »

•   ^   /   ¶   §   ☞

Some may seem obvious—but beware. In discussing them, let's proceed from left to right.

As many folks know, the symbol & (meaning "and") is called an **ampersand,** and @ is the symbol for "at." That was easy, right? Not so fast, my friend. Did you also know that both & and @ are **grammalogues?** A *grammalogue* is a symbol used to indicate a word; other common examples include $ for "dollars" and % for "percent."

If you've shrewdly surmised that I have another trick up my sleeve regarding ?, you're right. Can you think of a single word for what we commonly call the question mark? From the Greek *erotema*, a question, comes the rare answer: **eroteme** (ER-uh-teem).

Now we have some symbols with a foreign flair. The squiggle under the letter *c* (making it *ç*) is called a **cedilla** (suh-DIL-uh). The cedilla occurs in certain foreign languages, such as French and Portuguese, to indicate a soft *s* (rather than a hard *k*) sound, as in the French *garçon*. The cedilla is uncommon in English typography, but occasionally you will see it in a word adopted from French, such as *façade* or *soupçon*.

Next we have a squiggly horizontal line ~, which appears in the Spanish letter *ñ* and sometimes above vowels in Portuguese. If you've ever studied those languages, you know that the word for that squiggly symbol is **tilde** (TIL-duh).

Have you ever heard of **guillemets?** That's the term for our next set of marks, which resemble small less-than and greater-than symbols: « ». You won't find *guillemet* (gil-uh-MET or GIL-uh-met) in *Random House II* (1987), *American Heritage,* third edition (1992), or even in the voluminous second edition of the *OED* (1989). I dug it out of the awesome *Webster 2* (1934), then found more information in *The Chicago Manual of Style,* which notes that guillemets are used as quotation marks in French, Italian, Spanish, Russian, and occasionally in German.

Moving right along to the second line of symbols, we have the **bullet,** a bold black mark, usually a dot •, that sets off items in a list. If your words are listing, loading your prose with bullets can give you a shot in the arm.

Our next symbol ∧ is called a **caret** (pronounced like *carrot*). The caret is an inedible editorial mark used to indicate the insertion of a letter, word, phrase, etc.

The familiar symbol / is probably most often associated with the locution "and/or," which appears with mindnumbing frequency in brainless bureaucratic and corporate communications. It is commonly called a slash or diagonal, but the technical term in printing for / is **virgule** (VUR-gyool), from the Latin *virgula*, a little twig or bough.

The symbol ¶, used by copy editors to mean "start a new paragraph here," is called a **pilcrow**. Why? *Random House II* and the *OED* suggest that the word's Middle English ancestor, *pylcraft(e)*, may be a corruption of *paragraph*, which comes from Old French, but "evidence is wanting," says the *OED*. All I know is that a flock of pilcrows looks fine on a page, but you will never persuade them to fly.

The symbol § has a more practical name: **section mark.** The section mark is used to indicate divisions in a book or document, or to indicate a footnote.

I'm sure you've seen our final handy symbol ☞ on many occasions, but do you know the word for it? This icon, used to draw attention to something in the text, is called a **fistnote.**

If you ∧ all for these words about writing & printing, perhaps you will find amusing ways to • your prose with some of them. @ any rate, I'm out of #, so I shall end this § not with a **bang** (editor's jargon for an !) but with an **end slug** (also called a *ballot box*), a black square or other distinguishing symbol printed @ the end of an article/item in a magazine or journal like this: ∎

A RECREATIONAL RIGAMAJIG POP QUIZ

Because your grandiloquent guide is such a good sport, I'm going to give you one more chance to get your mental muscles in shape. If you know the correct answer to at least five of the following questions, consider yourself **pancratic,** accomplished in all forms of sports and games (or, more generally, having mastery of all subjects, universally accomplished). Answers appear at the end of the chapter.

1. What's the word for the tiny indentations or concavities in the surface of a golf ball?
2. What's the word for a fencer's padded jacket?
3. What's the name of that old-fashioned bicycle with the big wheel in front and the tiny wheel in the rear?
4. Do you know the word for the wooden barrier or shelter along the side of a bullring that bullfighters can duck behind to protect themselves from a bull that's out of control?
5. What's the word for a matador's red cape?
6. In baseball, the catcher and the home-plate umpire both wear face masks that have a small flap hanging down over the neck. What's the word for this protective flap?
7. What are the pegs used in cribbage called?
8. Most athletic stadiums have large openings that serve as passageways for people entering or leaving the stands. What's the word for one of these stadium entrance/exit holes?
9. What's the word for the groove in the feathered end of an arrow where an archer inserts the bowstring?
10. The tops of billiard tables and gaming tables typically are covered with a slightly nappy green cloth. Do you know the word for this material?

WHATCHAMACALLIT HELL

We shall end this disquisition on doodads, rigamajigs, and whatnots with a brief trip to Whatchamacallit Hell, otherwise known as the Department of Dull Words for Interesting Things.

Some things that you think would have a special name just don't, and finding that out is always a major disappointment—especially to an inveterate word nerd like me who will go to a lot of trouble tracking down an elusive specimen.

Case in point: the hole in the lapel of a man's suit, where you affix a boutonniere. I was willing to bet a bundle that this inconspicuous sartorial feature would have a nifty name, maybe even something suavely Frenchified to complement *boutonniere*. But alas, knowledgeable sources I checked with in the men's clothing industry informed me that it is called simply a "lapel buttonhole." *Très* dull.

Here's another depressing example: For the longest time, every time I'd park my car in a parking lot I'd wonder what to call that narrow wedge of concrete, three to six feet long, placed at or bolted to the front end of the parking space to prevent vehicles from overrunning the space. When I finally solved this parking puzzler it was such a letdown I wanted to drive my car over the nearest cliff.

According to the people who manufacture and sell these concrete parking space wedges, the term most often used for them is *wheel stop*, but they also go by other hopelessly prosaic names, including *bumper stop, car stop, curb bumper,* and *tire stop.* An ad for the Isuzu Trooper I bumped into in *The Atlantic Monthly* (April 1995) contained this headline, which proves that copywriters can be just as uncreative as the rest of us: "The 60th Unwritten Law of Driving: *Concrete Parking Barriers Were Invented to Take Out Oil Pans*" (my italics). One source I consulted (a glib salesperson for concrete products) offered a variation that struck me as having some potential: *idiot bump.*

Come to think of it, *idiot bump* would be a good term for the lumps I get on my forehead from slapping it after I've racked my benighted brain trying to find a word for something, only to discover that it's duller than a doorknob.

Here are a few more of my dissatisfying "discoveries":

The pointy piece of rubber on the bottom of a toothbrush that you use to dig around in your gums and between your teeth is called a *stimulator tip*. Decidedly unstimulating.

On an electrical plug, the rounded third prong that grounds the connection is called a *grounding prong*. Hardly electrifying.

The small drain or receptacle for spillage under the spigot of a bottled-water cooler, the spout of an espresso machine, or a similar device is called a *drip grid*. When I discovered that term, I was positively dripping with disappointment.

The button you push on a camera to take a picture is called the *shutter release*. Another unmemorable locution of your life.

The striped bar that goes up and down at a railroad grade crossing, or at the ingress or egress of a parking lot, is called a *crossing arm* or *(barrier) gate arm*, and the name of the device at the entrance to a parking lot that spits out your ticket is called a *ticket spitter*. Ho-hum.

On a stepladder, the little platform that flips out so you can set tools and paint cans on it (and that usually has "Not a Step!" stenciled on it) is called a *tool tray*. Yawn.

The knobs on your kitchen stove that you use to control the flame or heat are called (you guessed it) *control knobs*. Snore.

Finally, the abrasive black stripe on a book or box of matches on which you strike the match to ignite it is called a *friction strip*. Zippitty-do-dah.

Finding a prosaic factlet like *friction strip* doesn't exactly light a fire in the imagination. But you never know—as dull as all these words are, you still may need them someday (if only to put yourself or someone else to sleep).

Answers to the Clothing Quiz

1. *jodhpurs* (JAHD-purz)
2. *farthingale*
3. *baldric* (BAWL-drik)
4. *calypso*
5. *keeper*
6. *sporran* (SPOR-un)
7. *shapka* (SHAHP-kuh)
8. *lorgnette* (lorn-YET)
9. *hoxter*

10. *dandy*
11. *bandoleer* (ban-duh-LEER)
12. *frog*
13. *toque blanche* (TOHK BLAW(N)SH)
14. *fez*
15. *gi* (GEE)
16. *yashmak* (yahsh-MAHK)

Answers to the Recreational Rigamajig Pop Quiz

1. *dimples*
2. *plastron* (PLAS-trun)
3. *penny-farthing*
4. *burladero*
5. *muleta* (myoo-LET-uh)
6. *goat's beard*
7. *spilikins*
8. *vomitory* or *vomitorium* (plural, *vomitories* or *vomitoria*)
9. *nock*
10. If you thought I was being devious and you guessed *felt*, tough luck. The material in question, though it resembles felt, is a woolen or cotton fabric called *baize* (rhymes with *haze*).

❖

EPILOGUE

Some Words That Make Life Worth Living

Life is just one damned word after another.
—DAN BLATHER,
news anchor and host
of *48 Hours of Words*
(The Dictionary Channel)

For those who worship words (verbolaters), coin words (neologists or verbiculturists), and who are wise to words (verbum sapientists, my coinage), life truly is one damned delightful word after another. And since this book is also a grandiloquent guide to life, it seems fitting to wrap up our long-winded lexical expedition with a last, loving look—a **belgard** (bel-GAHRD, see chapter 3)—at some words that make life worth living.

Of course, every oddball word in this book has an inimitable place in the grandiloquent scheme of things, and all of them are dear to my heart. In this epilogue, however, I would like to share with you a few "afterwords" that didn't fit neatly anywhere else but that occupy a special cubbyhole in my psyche labeled "Words That Fill Me with Wonder and Joy and Renew My Faith in the Limitless Possibility of Language to Express Everything Anyone Can Imagine—and More."

As you probably surmised, I can't fit too many nifty words in that cubbyhole because the label's so doggone long. But I suppose that's good, because at this point your brain is probably brimming with enough high-calorie language to bring on a bad case of **surfeitigo.** Coined by writer Joyce Carol Oates from *surfeit* and *vertigo, surfeitigo* appears in Jack Hitt's *In a Word* defined as "a sudden sense of being stuffed to the gills by food, drink, friends, parties, invitations," and so on, etc., ad nauseam.

Therefore, in proffering these afterwords I will keep your verbally surfeited condition in mind and proceed with gentle **jocoseriosity** (a combination of humor and seriousness) and **sophrosyne** (suh-FRAHS-uh-nee), a sound-minded word that the *Century* defines as "the quality of wise moderation, discreet good sense." (Well, at least I'll try, anyway.)

Let us begin, then, with one of the top candidates for the most jocoserious word in the language: **resistentialism.** When I found this extraordinary word I had what can only be described as an epiphany. I felt that an entire category of my experience had suddenly been uplifted from the dim region of The Unnameable into the clear, comforting light of The Known.

According to *The Insomniac's Dictionary, resistentialism* is "seemingly spiteful behavior manifested by inanimate objects." You laugh, do you? Well, take my word for it: Resistentialism is real, and it is everywhere (especially when you least expect it). Consider just a few of the many manifestations of this insidious force, which every day attempts to undermine the fragile order of our lives:

- screen doors that snap back at you and smash your nose;
- rugs that quietly curl up so they can snag your toe;
- tree branches that reach out and rap you in the head;
- microwave ovens that sabotage your food so that the first bite you take is lukewarm and the next one scalds your tongue;
- shovels and rakes that entice you to step on them so they can leap up and smack you with their handles;
- elevator or train doors that try to crush you in their grip;
- drinks that walk off by themselves, and glasses that quietly sidle into just the right position so you will knock them over;
- toilets that function obediently for months and then clog on

a Sunday morning when you have overnight guests, resulting in an emergency call to a plumber and an astronomical bill;

- computers that wait with the patience of a trapper for the precise moment when they can crash and eat your most important files (which you've neglected to back up);

- VCRs that erase, ingest, or otherwise mangle your favorite tapes (the word for this resistentialist appliance is *televelociraptor*, noted in chapter 11);

- car alarms that announce their jargling indignation to the neighborhood at precisely 2:57 A.M., 3:30 A.M., and 4:22 A.M.;

- cars that serve without complaint until the one day when you're really late, and then they refuse to start;

- those "heavy-duty" garbage bags that sense when they're about to be dumped, at which moment they decide that rather than face such an ignoble doom they will instead commit hara-kiri, splitting themselves open and spilling their icky guts all over your shoes;

- and of course, plastic wrap. (Need I say more?)

"Mankind will indeed win out over inanimate objects some of the time," says Gary Havens, editor of *The Family Handyman* magazine, "but not all of the time." He might have added: *because they practice guerrilla warfare.* Resistentialists conspire on an undetectable wavelength, and there is no discernible motivation for their terrorist acts:

> Christ, the dumb insolence of inanimate objects! He could never understand what was *in it* for inanimate objects, behaving as they did. What was *in it* for the doorknob that hooked your jacket as you passed? What was *in it* for the jacket pocket?
> —MARTIN AMIS, *The Information*

Even my daughter Carmen, at the tender age of four, is well aware of the sinister power of resistentialism and quick to point it out. For example, not long ago I heard her crying from another room. I ran to her aid and found her frowning

at a chair. "That chair bumped me," she told me between snif-
fles. "Tell it not to move like that, because I will get hurt."

Speaking of my daughter, I must tell you proudly that
she's a budding neologist who has already made a lasting con-
tribution to my list of favorite words. Several months ago she
began using the term *lasterday*. At first my wife and I thought
she meant *yesterday*, but soon we realized that she had coined a
useful word that filled an empty niche in the vocabulary of
time—and what a lovely, lilting creation it is to boot!

As Carmen uses it, **lasterday** denotes any time before
yesterday. Thus, when she says, "We went to the doctor lasterday," she may be referring to a visit we made six months ago or
to one the day before yesterday. (The context usually makes it
clear whether it's a distant or recent lasterday.) The word may
also be used as a succinct substitute for "long ago" or "once
upon a time," as, "Lasterday, when the world was young and
dinosaurs roamed the earth . . ."

By the way, should you ever need an adjective that means
pertaining to the day before yesterday, the amazing English
language has one: **nudiustertian,** pronounced N(Y)OO-di-yoo-
STUR-shin (from the Latin *nudius tertius*).

While there's still time, I'd like to tell you about another
timeless word that a world-class proscrastinator like me could not
live without: **perendinate** (pur-EN-di-nayt), to delay until the day
after tomorrow or to postpone indefinitely. Instead of displaying one of those insulting "You want it when?" signs with the picture of a cachinnating clerk rolling on the floor, the verbally
shrewd businessperson could post a sign that reads, "We are here
to serve you. We stand by our word that your order will be
promptly perendinated." Now that's grandiloquent gumption!

I could go on for a **nychthemeron** (nik-THEE-mur-ahn), a
twenty-four hour period, talking about words that make life
worth living, but my time is running out. So here's a baker's
dozen of my special favorites that I hope will brighten your day
(unless, of course, you're a triskaidekaphobe, who fears the
number thirteen or collections consisting of thirteen items):

amphigory: (AM-fi-GOR-ee) a poem that on first reading appears to be profound but that on further inspection turns out to be complete nonsense.

I wish I had known this word in college so I could have applied it to one of those immeasurably dense and immensely dull poets that professors love and students loathe (e.g., John Milton, Alexander Pope, T. S. Eliot, Wallace Stevens, Ezra Pound). Oh, wouldn't the memories of those bright college years be even brighter had I had the chance to see the consternation on a professor's face upon hearing me say, "Pound's *Cantos* are one of the grandest examples of *amphigory* in all of English poetry."

chryselephantine: (KRIS-el-i-FAN -tin) made of or adorned with gold and ivory.

demitoilet: fairly elaborate but not entirely formal dress.

The next time you have a soiree, tell your guests to come in their demitoilet.

demiurge: the creator of a world, either real or imaginary.

Jonathan Swift was the demiurge of Lilliput and Brobdingnag, J. R. R. Tolkien the demiurge of Middle Earth, C. S. Lewis the demiurge of Narnia. There are two adjectives that mean "world-creating": **demiurgic** and **cosmopoietic** (KAHZ-moh-poy-ET-ik).

dystopia: the opposite of *utopia*—a society or situation in which conditions are dreadful, people are miserable, and everything has gone awry.

esprit de l'escalier: (es-PREE duh les-kal-YAY) the perfect riposte that comes to mind later, and far too late to do you any good.

This term comes from French and means literally the "spirit of the staircase"—in other words, inspiration gained upon ascending the stairs to retire to bed, long after the opportunity for a retort has passed. The English equivalent (coined by Kirkpatrick Sale) is *stairwit*. The word for any clever remark that comes to mind after the fact is *retrotort* (coined by Bernard Cooper).

floccinaucinihilipilification: the categorization of something as trivial or worthless.

Mastering the pronunciation of this impossibly pompous twenty-nine-letter word is no trivial matter, but it's well worth the work. Here, give it a go: FLAHK-si-NAW-si-NY-hil-i-PIL-i-fi-KAY-shin. Once you've got it down, you can put it to good use the next time you're buttonholed by an obnoxious blowhard or macrologist (see chapter 5). I guarantee it will burst his bombastic balloon and give you a thrill that will last for weeks.

gigantomachy: (JY-gan-TAHM-uh-kee) a battle between giants.

This word could apply to many gargantuan grapplings: for example, a boxing match between a pair of oversized palookas, one of those monster movies that come on TV at 3:00 A.M., hostile takeover battles between huge corporations, the ratings war between the major networks, or the stormy relationship of Liz Taylor and Richard Burton.

griffonage: (GREE-fuh-NAZH) sloppy or illegible handwriting (from the French *griffonner,* to scrawl, write badly).

incunabula: (IN-kyoo-NAB-yuh-luh) books produced before A.D. 1500, in the infancy of the art of printing.

metutials: (me-T(Y)OO-shee-ulz) In his *Word Treasury,* Paul Dickson defines this delightful neologism as "small, irksome chores that must be done before anything else can be done."

nikhedonia: (NYK-hee-DOH-nee-uh) the pleasure of anticipating victory or success (from the Greek *Nike,* the goddess of victory, and *hedoné,* pleasure).

Strikhedonia (my coinage) is the pleasure that comes from being able to say the hell with it. To Nike's slogan, "Just do it," the *strikhedoniac* replies, "Just screw it."

And now, dear reader, we have reached the end of our jocoserious journey through the depths of the dictionary. Yet one question remains: Is it possible to select a single favorite word in an entire language? Of the gazillion glorious words in the English vocabulary, is there one that stands out from all the rest, that somehow "says it all"? No, not really. Sorry. For me, however, one wonderfully unusual, unusually useful, and hilarious word does come darn close to being tops: **jowfair** (rhymes with *cow pair*).

Before you make elaborate arrangements for your next vacation or social event, you must know this marvelous, merry-go-sorry word, which Joseph Wright's *English Dialect Dictionary* defines as "a term applied to anything that does not come off after everything has been prepared"—for example, "a wedding when one of the parties fails to put in an appearance at church."

NEED A WORD DETECTIVE?

A few final words for the wordstruck—or *wordstuck*, as the case may be.

Have you ever been caught off guard wondering if there's an antonym for *avant garde*? Relax, it's **arrière garde.**

Have you been yearning to know if *serenade*, a love song sung at night, has a heartfelt companion that means a love song sung at dawn? Be still, because it does: **aubade,** pronounced oh-BAHD.

Has trying to find the word for the finger cymbals worn by belly dancers given you a bellyache? Have an Alka-Seltzer. They're called **zills.**

Has time run out in your search for a word for an hourglass whose trickling flow of sand measures a minute, several minutes, or any amount of time other than an hour? Take five. It's a **clepsammia.**

If you've spent the last few months—or years—hunting for an obscure word to no avail, if you haven't found what you're looking for in this book (heaven forfend) and your dictionary fails you and your prayers to Lexaphasia (the muse of missing and misunderstood words) go unanswered, and if you're at your wit's end because the word you seek is a **crazzler** (something that tests all your capacities or powers of endurance), then before you go bonkers and become **biblio-phagic** (book-devouring), or a despondent **dysteleologist** (someone who believes in the utter purposelessness of nature), why not give the Grandiloquent Gumshoe a try? As long as the elusive beast you seek isn't **nullibiquitous,** not in existence anywhere, I may be able to track it down for you.

Lost souls in dire need of linguistic intervention from a long-suffering **lexicomane** (dictionary-lover) are welcome to write to me at this address:

> Grandiloquent Gumshoe
> c/o Gelfman Schneider Literary Agents, Inc.
> 250 W. 57th Street, Suite 2515
> New York, NY 10107

Or visit my Website and email me: http://members.authorsguild.net/chelster.

If you're not telephonophobic, include your phone number. As they say on those grocery rebate coupons, allow six to eight weeks for delivery. Inquiries accompanied by generous checks or a sales receipt for the purchase of at least five copies of this book will be given priority. All other inquiries will be perendinated. (Just kidding—sort of.)

And now, dear reader, it's time for this bodacious book to go to the Great Grandiloquent Proofreader in the Sky. I hope the highfalutin words you have discovered here have given you a few glisks, an occasional cachinnation, and some measure of relief from the chronic omnistrain and cerebropathy of modern life.*

May you forever be the wiser, and not just a wiseacre, for knowing them.

---

*If you can't remember what *omnistrain* and *cerebropathy* mean, then you may be suffering from these disorders. Before you also contract *loganamnosis* (LAHG-an-<u>um</u>-NOH-sis), an obsession with trying to recall a forgotten word, reread the introduction and chapter 1 and heal thyself.

SELECTED BIBLIOGRAPHY

The American Heritage Dictionary of the English Language, third ed. Boston: Houghton Mifflin, 1992.

Barnett, Lincoln. *The Treasure of Our Tongue.* New York: Alfred A. Knopf, 1964.

Berent, Irwin M., and Rod L. Evans. *Weird Words.* New York: Berkley Books, 1995.

Bowler, Peter. *The Superior Person's Book of Words.* New York: Dell Laurel, 1982.

———. *The Superior Person's Second Book of Weird and Wondrous Words.* New York: Dell Laurel, 1992.

Brewer, E. Cobham. *The Dictionary of Phrase and Fable.* New York: Avenel Books, 1978.

Burchfield, Robert. *Unlocking the English Language.* New York: Hill and Wang, 1991.

Byrne, Josefa Heifetz. *Mrs. Byrne's Dictionary of Unusual, Obscure, and Preposterous Words,* new and exp. ed. New York: Birch Lane Press, 1994.

The Century Dictionary. 10 vols. New York: The Century Company, 1889–1914. (Often referred to in the text as the *Century.*)

Chapman, Robert L. *Thesaurus of American Slang.* New York: Harper & Row, 1989.

The Chicago Manual of Style, thirteenth ed. Chicago and London: University of Chicago Press, 1982.

The Columbia Encyclopedia, third ed. New York and London: Columbia University Press, 1963.

The Compact Oxford English Dictionary, second ed. Oxford: Oxford University Press, 1991. (Often referred to in the text as the *OED.*)

Corbeil, Jean-Claude. *The Facts on File Visual Dictionary.* New York: Facts on File, 1986.

Dickson, Paul. *Dickson's Word Treasury.* New York: John Wiley & Sons, 1992.

Doctor, Ronald M., and Ada P. Kahn. *Encyclopedia of Phobias, Fears, and Anxieties.* New York: Facts on File, 1989.

Dossey, Donald E. *Holiday Folklore, Phobias, and Fun.* Los Angeles: Outcomes Unlimited Press, 1992.

duGran, Claurène. *Wordsmanship.* Essex, Conn.: Verbatim, 1981.

Ehrlich, Eugene. *Amo, Amas, Amat and More.* New York: Harper & Row, 1985.

————. *The Highly Selective Thesaurus for the Extraordinarily Literate.* New York: HarperCollins, 1994.

————. *SuperWordPower.* New York: A Hudson Group Book, Perennial Library, Harper & Row, 1989.

1811 Dictionary of the Vulgar Tongue. Northfield, Illinois: Digest Books, 1971.

Espy, Willard R. *Say It My Way.* New York: Doubleday, 1980.

Franck, Irene M. *On the Tip of Your Tongue.* New York: Signet Books, 1990.

Glazier, Stephen. *Random House Word Menu.* New York: Random House, 1992.

Grambs, David. *The Endangered English Dictionary.* New York: W. W. Norton, 1994.

Hellweg, Paul. *The Insomniac's Dictionary.* New York: Ivy Books, 1986.

Hendrikson, Robert. *The Dictionary of Eponyms.* New York: Dorset Press, 1972.

Hill, Robert H. *Dictionary of Difficult Words.* New York: Gramercy Publishing Company, 1990.

Hitt, Jack. *In a Word: A Dictionary of Words That Don't Exist, But Ought To.* New York: Dell Laurel, 1992.

Hook, J. N. *The Grand Panjandrum,* rev. ed. New York: Macmillan, 1991.

Johnson, Samuel. *A Dictionary of the English Language,* facsimile ed. London: Times Books, 1979.

Kacirk, Jeffrey. *Forgotten English.* New York: Quill/William Morrow, 1997.

————. *The Word Museum.* New York: Touchstone/Simon & Schuster, 2000.

Lederer, Richard. *Adventures of a Verbivore.* New York: Pocket Books, 1994.

————. *Crazy English.* New York: Pocket Books, 1989.

————. *The Play of Words.* New York: Pocket Books, 1990.

Lemay, Harold, Sid Lerner, and Marian Taylor. *The New New Words Dictionary.* New York: Ballantine Books, 1985, 1988.

Lipton, James. *An Exaltation of Larks,* second ed. New York and London: Penguin Books, 1977.

McCutcheon, Marc. *Descriptionary: A Thematic Dictionary.* New York: Facts on File, 1992.

McKean, Erin. *Weird and Wonderful Words.* Oxford, New York: Oxford University Press, 2002.

————. *More Weird and Wonderful Words.* Oxford, New York: Oxford University Press, 2003.

Mosby's Medical, Nursing, and Allied Health Dictionary, third ed. St. Louis: The C. V. Mosby Company, 1990.

Partridge, Eric. *A Dictionary of Slang and Unconventional English,* eighth ed. New York: Macmillan, 1984.

Raabe, Tom. *Biblioholism: The Literary Addition.* Golden, Colo.: Fulcrum Publishing, 1991.

The Random House Dictionary of the English Language, second ed.— unabridged. New York: Random House, 1987. (Often referred to in the text as *Random House II.*)

Reader's Digest Illustrated Reverse Dictionary. Pleasantville, N.Y.: Reader's Digest Association, Inc., 1990.

Rheingold, Howard. *They Have a Word for It.* Los Angeles: Jeremy P. Tarcher, 1988.

Rocke, Russell. *The Grandiloquent Dictionary.* Englewood Cliffs, NJ: Prentice-Hall, Inc., 1972.

Rosten, Leo. *The Joys of Yinglish.* New York: Plume Books, 1989.

Saussy, George Stone III. *The Oxter English Dictionary.* New York: Facts on File, 1984.

Schmidt, J. E. *Lecher's Lexicon.* New York: Bell Publishing Company, 1984.

Schur, Norman W. *1000 Most Obscure Words.* New York: Facts on File, 1990.

———. *British English, A to Zed.* New York: HarperPerennial, 1991.

Sisson, A. F. *Sisson's Word and Expression Locater.* West Nyack, N.Y.: Parker Publishing Company, 1966.

Spears, Richard A. *Slang and Euphemism.* New York: Jonathan David Publishers, 1981.

Sperling, Susan Kelz. *Poplollies and Bellibones: A Celebration of Lost Words.* New York: Clarkson N. Potter, 1977.

A Standard Dictionary of the English Language. New York: Funk & Wagnalls, 1897.

Stedman's Medical Dictionary, twenty-second ed. Baltimore: The Williams & Wilkins Company, 1972.

Webster's New International Dictionary, second ed. Springfield, Mass.: G. & C. Merriam Company, 1941. (Often referred to in the text as *Webster 2.*)

Webster's Third New International Dictionary. Springfield, Mass.: G. & C. Merriam Company, 1963.

Weiner, Richard. *Webster's New World Dictionary of Media and Communications.* New York: Prentice-Hall, 1990.

Worcester, Joseph Emerson. *Dictionary of the English Language.* Philadelphia: J. B. Lippincott & Company, 1884.

Wright, Joseph. *English Dialect Dictionary.* 6 vols. Oxford and New York: Henry Frowde, G. P. Putnam's Sons, 1898–1905.

INDEX